Musical Instruments
An Illustrated History
from Antiquity to the Present

Musical Instruments
An Illustrated History

from Antiquity to the Present

Mary Remnant

Amadeus Press
Reinhard G. Pauly, General Editor
Portland, Oregon

A.M.D.G.
In grateful memory of
Frank and Sibyl Merrick

Frontispiece: David plays chimebells in the initial E(xultate Deo), while other musicians play two trumpets, timbrel, clappers, portative organ, psaltery and fiddle; from the Peterborough Psalter, *c.* 1300–18. Brussels, *Bibliothèque Royale Albert I, MS 9961-2, f. 74.*

© Mary Remnant 1989
First published 1989

Printed in Great Britain

Published by B. T. Batsford Ltd
4 Fitzhardinge Street, London W1H 0AH

First published in North America in 1989 by
Amadeus Press (an imprint of Timber Press, Inc.)
9999 S.W. Wilshire
Portland, Oregon 97225, U.S.A.

ISBN 0-931340-23-3

Contents

Illustrations and Acknowledgements

34. Orpharion, 1596. *British Library Board.*
35. English guitar, *c.* 1770. *Royal College of Music.*
36. Lyre guitar, harp-guitar and dital harp, 19th century. *Royal College of Music.*
37. Rebec, 12th century. *British Library Board.*
38. Rebecs of the *rabāb* type, 1404. *Private Collection, Italy, from Thomas Agnew & Sons.*
39. Rebec with frets, *c.* 1500. *Copyright A.C.L. - Bruxelles.*
40. Two crowds, *c.* 1447. *Mary Remnant, by permission of The Vicar and Churchwardens of the Collegiate Church of St Mary, Warwick.*
41. Crwth, 1742. *Welsh Folk Museum.*
42. Medieval viol, 12th century. *H. Wehmeyer.*
43. Fiddle, 1188. *Mary Remnant.*
44. Fiddle, *c.* 1280. *Royal Commission on the Historical Monuments of England.*
45. Fiddle, 14th century. *Capitolo della Cattedrale di Pienza. Victoria and Albert Museum. Crown Copyright.*
46. Fiddle, 15th century. *München, Alte Pinakothek.*
47. Lira da braccio, *Osvaldo Böhm, Venice.*
48. Lira da gamba, 17th century. *Deutsche Fotothek Dresden.*
49. Two bass viols, viola da braccio and rebec, *c.* 1510. *Direzione dei Musei di Ferrara – Ministero della Pubblica Istruzione.*
50. Consort of viols. *Bibliothèque Nationale, Paris.*
51. Division viol, 1692. *Royal College of Music, London.*
52. Violin, 1505–8. *Commune di Ferrara: Direzione Civici d'Arte Antica.*
53. Early members of the violin family, 1535–6. *Mansell-Anderson.*
54. Violin, 1574. *Carlisle Museum and Art Gallery.*
55. Viola, late 16th century. *Ashmolean Museum, Oxford.*
56. Bass violin, *c.* 1675. *Victoria and Albert Museum. Crown Copyright.*
57. Cello, 1733. *The Trustees of the National Portrait Gallery.*
58. Double bass, 17th century. *Victoria and Albert Museum. Crown Copyright.*
59. The New Violin Family. *Carleen Hutchins. Photo: Arthur Montzka.*
60. Baryton, 1647. *Royal College of Music, London.*
61. Viola d'amore, 1719. *Victoria and Albert Museum. Crown Copyright.*
62. Kit, 17th century. *Musée Instrumental du Conservatoire National Supérieur de Musique, Paris.*
63. Kit, 17th century. *Royal College of Music, London.*
64. Kit, 1717. *Musèe Instrumental du Conservatoire National Supérieur de Musique. Photo Publimages.*
65. Trumpet marine, 15th century. *Historisches Museum, Basel.*
66. Trumpet marine, 18th century. *Royal College of Music, London.*
67. Nail violin, 19th century. *Royal College of Music, London.*
68. Organistrum, 1188. *Tino Martinez.*
69. Symphony, *c.* 1494. *British Library Board.*
70. Symphony, 1501/2. *Royal Commission on the Historical Monuments of England.*
71. Hurdy-gurdy, 18th century. *Musée Instrumental du Conservatoire National Supérieur de Musique, Paris.*
72. Clavichord, 15th century. *The Rector and Church Wardens, Loughborough Parish Church of All Saints.*
73. Clavichord, 1648. *Escher Foundation – Haags Gemeentemuseum – The Hague.*
74. Pedal clavichord, 1760. *Musikinstrumenten-Museum der Karl-Marz Universität Leipzig.*
75. Harpsichord, *c.* 1447. *Royal Commission on the Historical Monuments of England.*
76. Virginals, 16th century. *Archivio Fotografico dei Musei Vaticani.*
77. Virginals, 1675. *Somerset County Museums.*
78. Spinet, 1708. *Royal College of Music, London.*
79. Clavicytherium, 15th century. *Royal College of Music, London.*
80. Harpsichord, 1638. *University of Edinburgh.*
81. Harpsichord, 1793. *University of Edinburgh.*
82. Geigenwerk, 1620. *Bärenreiter Verlag.*
83. Piano, 1720. *The Metropolitan Museum of Art, The Crosby Brown Collection of Musical Instruments.*
84. Square piano, 1767. *Victoria and Albert Museum, Crown Copyright.*
85. Square piano, *c.* 1825. *Royal College of Music, London.*
86. Grand piano, 1788. *Musée Instrumental du Conservatoire National Supérieur de Musique. Photo Publimages.*
87. Upright piano, *c.* 1865. *Victoria and Albert Museum. Crown Copyright.*
88. Grand piano, 1963. *Royal College of Music, London.*
89. Hydraulis, 2nd or 3rd century AD. *The Trustees of the British Museum.*
90. Organ, *c.* 830. *Bildarchiv Foto Marburg.*
91. Organ, *c.* 1300. *British Library Board.*
92. Two portative organs, 14th century. *The Governing Body of Christ Church, Oxford.*
93. Portative organ, 15th century. *The Commission of Public Assistance, Bruges; Copyright A.C.L. – Bruxelles.*
94. Positive organ, 16th century. *Courtauld Institute of Art.*

95. Organ, 15th century. *Museo del Prado, Madrid.*

96. Organ, 1474–83. *Direzione dei Musei di Ferrara – Ministero della Pubblica Istruzione. Fotofast, Bologna.*

97. Regal, 17th century. *Royal College of Music, London.*

98. Organ, 1620. *Bärenreiter Verlag.*

99. Organ, 1710–14. *Stadt-und-Bergbaumuseum, Freiberg, DDR.*

100. Organ, 1597–8. *Mansell-Anderson.*

101. Organ, 1859. *Photos F. Berdoll.*

102. Organ, 1954. *South Bank Centre.*

103. Claviorganum, 1579. *Victoria and Albert Museum. Crown Copyright.*

104. Lira organizzata, 18th century. *Victoria and Albert Museum. Crown Copyright.*

105. Piano-organ, 1798. *Merseyside County Museums.*

106. Phrygian pipes and panpipes, Gallo-Roman. *Avignon – Musée Calvet.*

107. Bird whistle, *c.* 500 BC. *Mary Remnant.*

108. Pipe-and-tabor, *c.* 1325–30. *British Library Board.*

109. Gemshorn, *c.* 1488. *Universitätsbibliothek, Heidelberg.*

110. Two flageolets, 1682. *William Andrews Clark Memorial Library, University of California, Los Angeles.*

111. Recorders, *c.* 1485. *National Gallery of Art, Washington, Samuel H. Kress Collection.*

112. Recorders, *c.* 1720. *Grosvenor Museum, Chester.*

113. Flute, 1066. *British Library Board.*

114. Flutes and piccolo, 18th and 19th centuries. *Royal College of Music, London.*

115. Shawm and bagpipes, 14th century. *Bibliothèque Nationale, Paris.*

116. Shawm, *c.* 1485. *National Gallery of Art, Washington, Samuel H. Kress Collection.*

117. Oboe, 17th century. *Victoria and Albert Museum. Crown Copyright.*

118. Oboes, 18th and 19th centuries. *Royal College of Music, London.*

119. Oboe, 1951. *Mary Remnant, by permission of Tess Miller.*

120. Cor anglais, *c.* 1845. *Royal College of Music, London.*

121. Sordun, curtalls and racketts, 1620. *Bärenreiter Verlag.*

122. Bassoon, 17th century. *Suermondt-Ludwig Museum, Aachen.*

123. Bassoons, 18th and 19th centuries. *Royal College of Music, London.*

124. Bassoon, 19th century. *Royal College of Music, London.*

125. Contrebasse-à-anche, 19th century. *Horniman Museum, London.*

126. Bladder-pipe, late 14th century. *Reproduced by courtesy of the Trustees, The National Gallery, London.*

127. Crumhorns, 1513–21. *Archivio Fotografico dei Musei Vaticani.*

128. Rauchpfeifen and shawms, 1526. *Dover Publications Inc.*

129. Clarinets, 18th and 19th centuries. *Royal College of Music, London.*

130. Bass clarinet, *c.* 1815. *Courtesy Museum of Fine Arts, Boston. Leslie Lindsey Mason Collection of Musical Instruments (formerly the Galpin Collection).*

131. Basset horn, *c.* 1780. *Ruck Collection of Historic Musical Instruments in the Germanisches Nationalmuseum, Nürnberg.*

132. Saxophone, 1976. *Norlin Music (UK) Ltd.*

133. Bagpipes and pipe-and-tabor, *c.* 1300. *British Library Board.*

134. Musette, 18th century. *Royal College of Music, London.*

135. Bagpipes, 1890. *Mansell Collection.*

136. Horn with fingerholes, *c.* 1494. *British Library Board.*

137. Cornetts, trumpets and trombones, 1620. *Bärenreiter Verlag.*

138. Serpent, after 1838. *Royal College of Music, London.*

139. Bass horn, 19th century. *Horniman Museum, London.*

140. Russian bassoon, *c.* 1825. *Horniman Museum, London.*

141. Keyed bugle, 1824–9. *Royal College of Music, London.*

142. Bass ophicleide, *c.* 1840. *British Library Board.*

143. Lurs, Bronze Age. *Danish National Museum, Copenhagen.*

144. Horn, *c.* 1325–35. *British Library Board.*

145. French horns with handhorn technique, 1801. *British Library Board.*

146. Inventionshorn, *c.* 1840. *Musikhistorisk Museum, Copenhagen.*

147. Valve horn, 19th century. *Horniman Museum, London.*

148. Cornet-à-pistons, before 1845. *Horniman Museum, London.*

149. Orchestral tuba, 1955. *Annetta Hoffnung.*

150. Long trumpets, *c.* 1325–30. *British Library Board.*

151. 'Clareta' and 'Thurner Horn', 1511. *Bärenreiter Verlag.*

152. Trumpet, 17th century. *Museum of London.*

153. Trumpet with crooks, 1827–35. *Royal College of Music, London.*

154. Trumpets, 19th and 20th centuries. *Gerald Style.*

155. Trombone and cornett, 16th or 17th century.

Mansell-Alinari.

156. Harmonium, 1878. *Portsmouth City Museum and Art Gallery.*

157. Harmonica, 1880–85. *M. Hohner Ltd.*

158. Accordion, 20th century. *M. Hohner Ltd.*

159. Concertinas, *c.* 1854. *Royal College of Music, London.*

160. Kettle-drums, 6th century. *Österreichische National-albibliothek.*

161. Nakers, 1338–44. *The Bodleian Library, Oxford.*

162. Kettle-drums, *c.* 1494. *British Library Board.*

163. Timpani, before 1740. *Bärenreiter Verlag.*

164. Tympanum and cymbals, *c.* 440–430 BC. *Hirmer Fotoarchiv München.*

165. Tabor and nakers, *c.* 1450–57. *Mansell-Anderson.*

166. Military drum, 1849. *The Trustees of the Wallace Collection.*

167. Bass drum, side drum, cymbals and pedal timpani, 20th century. *Mary Remnant. Royal College of Music, London.*

168. Timbrel, *c.* 1450–57. *Mansell-Anderson.*

169. Cymbals, *c.* 1450–57. *Mansell-Anderson.*

170. Clappers, 12th century. *Ampliaciones y Reproducciones Mas.*

171. Triangle, 14th century. *The Master and Fellows of Trinity College, Cambridge.*

172. Sistrum, Roman. *Mansell-Anderson.*

173. Jingling Johnny. *Mary Remnant, by permission of the Royal Military School of Music, Kneller Hall.*

174. Chimebells, *c.* 1130–40. *The Board of Trinity College, Dublin.*

175. Chimebells, *c.* 1310–20. *The Bodleian Library, Oxford.*

176. Carillon, 1636. *Royal College of Music, London.*

177. Glockenspiel, 1609. *Lauros-Giraudon.*

178. Tuned percussion instruments, 20th century. *Mary Remnant. Percussion Services Ltd.*

179. Glass harmonica, *c.* 1780. *Horniman Museum, London.*

180. Pipe and string drum, *c.* 1494. *British Library Board.*

181. Dulcimer, 15th century. *Mansell-Alinari.*

182. Cimbalom, 1887. *Mary Remnant, by permission of John Leach.*

183. Mechanical water organ, 1650. *Royal College of Music, London.*

184. Combined harpsichord and bagpipes, 17th century. *The Metropolitan Museum of Art. The Crosby Brown Collection of Musical Instruments.*

185. Bird organ, 1742. *Reproduced by courtesy of the Trustees, The National Gallery, London.*

186. Flute clock, *c.* 1790. *National Museum van Speelklok*

tot Pierement, Utrecht.

187. Barrel organ, *c.* 1805. *Royal College of Music, London.*

188. Musical box, *c.* 1885–90. *Merseyside County Museums.*

189. Harmonichord, Chordaulodion, Orchestrion, Automaton trumpeter and Symphonion, 1851. *The Illustrated London News.*

190. The Melos Ensemble, 20th century. *Erich Auerbach, F.R.P.S.*

191. The London Serpent Trio, 20th century. *Ian Cook.*

192. Piano played with drumsticks, 20th century. *Mary Remnant.*

193. The Logical Contrabassoon, 20th century. *Barr Photographer Ltd.*

194. Ondes Martenot, 20th century. *John Morton.*

195. Telharmonium, 1907. *The Illustrated London News.*

196. Hammond Organ, 20th century. *Hammond Organ (UK) Ltd.*

197. Synthesizer, 20th century. *Electronic Music Studios.*

198. Tuba, cornua and hydraulis, Roman. *Deutsche Archaeologischen Institut.*

199. Organistrum or symphony, organ and chimebells, 13th century. *British Library Board.*

200. Singers and trumpets, etc., after 1453. *The Bodleian Library, Oxford.*

201. Choir with cornett and trombone, 1526. *Dover Publications, Inc.*

202. David and his minstrels, *c.* 1070–1100. *The Master and Fellows of Trinity College, Cambridge.*

203. David and his minstrels, *c.* 1100. *Ampliaciones y Reproducciones Mas.*

204. David and his minstrels, early 12th century. *Bibiothèque Nationale, Paris.*

205. David and his minstrels, *c.* 1190–1200. *The Master and Fellows of St John's College, Cambridge.*

206. Fiddle and gittern (citole) played for dancing, *c.* 1260–90. *British Library Board.*

207. Fiddle, symphony, harp and psaltery at a feast, *c.* 1250–75. *British Library Board.*

208. Harp and fiddle, 13th century. *Photo Ellebé, Rouen.*

209. Alfonso X of Castile and minstrels, late 13th century. *Escorial, Monastery of San Lorenzo.*

210. Minstrels who should entertain a king, 1326–7. *The Governing Body of Christ Church, Oxford.*

211. Singers and gitterns (citoles), 14th century. *British Library Board.*

212. Singers with psaltery and mandora (gittern), 14th century. *British Library Board.*

213. Singer with portative organ, and instruments on

a wall. *Ampliaciones y Reproducciones Mas.*

214. Harp and recorder, 15th century. *British Library Board.*

215. Portative organ and harp, 15th century. *Mary Remnant.*

216. Instruments at a wedding, 15th century. *Mansell-Anderson.*

217. Trumpets and shawms in a procession. *Lauros-Giraudon.*

218. Lute-playing singer from a Mystery Play, early 16th century. *Royal Commission on the Historical Monuments of England.*

219. String and wind groups, 1575. *Bayerische Staatsbibliothek, München.*

220. Singers with organ and trumpet, 1582. *British Library Board.*

221. Three choirs of instrumentalists, 17th century. *Bärenreiter Verlag.*

222. Singers and wind instruments, 17th century. *Ampliaciones y Reproducciones Mas.*

223. Cornett, violin and organ, 17th century. *Direzione dei Musei di Ferrara. Ministero della Pubblica Istruzione.*

224. Whole and broken consorts, *c.* 1596. *The Trustees of the National Portrait Gallery.*

225. Singers and instrumentalists, 17th century. *Royal Museum of Fine Arts, Copenhagen.*

226. String orchestra at a coronation banquet, 1665. *British Library Board.*

227. Wind quartet, 17th century. *Victoria and Albert Museum. Crown Copyright.*

228. A Concerto, 1744. *British Library Board.*

229. A choral work, with strings and organ. *British Library Board.*

230. Flute, recorder and cello, 1751. *Courtesy of the National Gallery of Ireland.*

231. A military band, 1759. *British Library Board.*

232. Haydn's opera orchestra, 1775. *Theater-Museum, München.*

233. A theatre band, 1843. *British Library Board.*

234. Double bass, serpent and organ. *Editions Gaud.*

235. A village choir, 19th century. *Victoria and Albert Museum. Crown Copyright.*

236. An orchestra in Covent Garden, 1846. *The Illustrated London News.*

237. The Queen's Hall Orchestra with Duo-Art Pianola, 1922. *The Illustrated London News.*

238. A symphony orchestra. *Chris Christodoulou.*

239. Romberg's Toy Symphony, 1880. *The Illustrated London News.*

240. The Hoffnung Symphony Orchestra, 1954. *Souvenir Press Ltd.*

The photograph of the author on the jacket flap is by R.W. Skinner of J.S. Photographic, Leconfield, Beverley

Preface

Thirty years ago there were comparatively few books in print on the history of musical instruments. Since that time, however, so much research has taken place, not only into the development of instruments themselves, but also into their representation in art and literature, that the number of published works on the subject has increased beyond all expectation.

Most of the recent books in English about instruments in general have tended to devote different chapters to particular periods of musical history, thus showing which instruments should be used in performing the music of those periods. This is an excellent idea in itself, but it does mean that the history of each instrument cannot be followed through continuously from the beginning to the end, or until the twentieth century. In the present work, therefore, each of the first nine chapters treats a basic instrumental family and outlines the known history of its most important members. The final chapter follows the history of instrumental groupings from Antiquity onwards, and shows the development of the modern orchestra from its beginnings in the seventeenth century until the present day. A particular feature concerns music as played by amateur musicians, as it is important to remember that musical history does not consist only of performances by the greatest virtuosi.

In *Musical Instruments of the West* (1978) I made a point of including as many pictures as possible which had not been published before in books of a musical nature, if, indeed, they had been published at all. This new edition, which also contains many new pictures, has been able to profit by the appearance of *The New Grove Dictionary of Music and Musicians* (1980) and its offshoot *The New Grove Dictionary of Musical Instruments* (1984), both of which cite in their bibiographies far more books and articles than can be mentioned here, besides those written in foreign languages. The reader is therefore referred to these works for more detail than can be found in this short outline. Acknowledgment should also be made to various exhibition catalogues, especially those of the London exhibitions *English Romanesque Art 1066–1200* (1984) and *Age of Chivalry* (1987), which have supplied the latest datings for many relevant works of art of the Middle Ages.

A book such as this owes much to so many people who have helped over the years that only a few can be mentioned by name. Prominent are those at the Royal College of Music, where I originally studied for four years and now teach. Firstly there is Mrs Elizabeth Wells, Curator of the Museum of Instruments, which under her supervision has been built up from assorted showcases around the building into a museum of international repute. To her, to Mr Oliver Davies,

Keeper of the Department of Portraits, to the Librarians Mrs Pamela Thomson and Mr Christopher Bornet, and to the staff of all those departments, particularly to Miss Celia Clarke, my debt is considerable.

So it is to the following who have all contributed in one way or another over the years: Miss Elizabeth Agate, Mr Anthony Baines, Dr Anthea Baird, Mr James Blades, Mme Chantal de Tourtier Bonazzi, Mr David Boston, Mme Josiane Bran-Ricci, Professor Giles Brindley, the staff of the British Library, Mr Samuel Carr, Mme la Comtesse Geneviève de Chambure, the staff of the Courtauld Institute, Mr Alan Crumpler, Mr Ralph Downes, Mrs Valerie Elliott-Leach, Sir Keith Falkner, Professor Carolyn Gianturco, Mr Gerald Gifford, Mr Michael Graham-Dixon, Professor Sumi Gungi, Mr Eric Halfpenny, Professor John Hancock, Mrs Peggy Hand, Dr W. O. Hassall and his assistants at the Bodleian Library, Frau Uta Henning, Mr David Higham, Mrs Annetta Hoffnung, M. Hohner Ltd, Mrs Cynthia Hollis, Mr R.P. Howgrove-Graham, Miss Anna Hulbert, Mrs Carleen Hutchins, Dr Doris Jones-Baker, Mrs Beryl Kenyon de Pascual, Miss Joy Kilkenny, Mrs Sylvia Latham, Miss Sheila Lawrence, Mr John Leach, the Rev. Professor José Lopez-Calo, S.J., Mr George Menhinnick, Mr Frank Merrick, Miss Tess Miller, Mr Christopher Monk, Mr John Morton, the Staff of the National Monuments Record, Mr Leslie Orrey, Dr Frances Palmer, Percussion Services Ltd, the Staff of Photo Graphics (formerly Chelsea Colour Laboratories), Dr Isabel Pope, Dr Richard Rastall, Professor Gilbert Reaney, Mr E.A.K. Ridley, Mr Ronald Roberts, the Staff of the Royal Military School of Music, Mr Miguel Sabater, Dr Stanley Sadie, Mr D. Roy Saer, Dr Silio Italico Sarpi, Dr Howard Schott, Dr Robert Sherlaw Johnson, Mr Robert Spencer, Dr Frederick Sternfeld, Professor James Stubblebine, Colonel Gerald Style, Professor Luigi Ferdinando Tagliavini, Dr and Mrs Lawrence Tanner, Miss Marylin Wailes, Dr H. Watkins Shaw, Sir David Willcocks and Signora Livia Zanini Barilli, and in the last stages of the book Dr Margaret Gibson, Abbé Denis Grivot, Mme Cathérine Homo-Lechner, Mme Caroline Joubert, and Mr Robert Spencer. Their contributions to the book have been invaluable, and all its deficiencies are my own.

A special mention should be made of the Winston Churchill Memorial Trust, which, under the Directorship of Major-General Anthony Lascelles, gave me a Travelling Fellowship in 1967 which produced a vast amount of information, including some of the photographs used here.

The actual production of the book is due chiefly to Mr Timothy Auger and Mrs Rosemary Dooley of B.T. Batsford Ltd, together with Mr Bruce Hunter of David Higham Associates, to all of whom I owe very particular thanks.

It is impossible to say enough for my parents, who between them provided the stimulus for my interest in musical instruments. My father left me his books, photographic equipment and much good advice, and my mother, with her musical knowledge and generosity, has been a constant support through the years. Successive cats have supervised my work, and the present book has been watched over by Marmaduke, Tinkerbell and their mother Matilda, who has an unerring knack of sitting on the most important piece of paper . . . A happy home is a good place in which to write a book.

Note on Sources

This book contains no footnotes. For certain quotations the source is given in the text, while others, e.g. Tinctoris, Burney, etc., can be traced through the General section of the Bibliography. The following list gives the less obvious published sources.

Quotation on page

132	Baines, Anthony: 'Two Cassel Inventories', *GSJ*, iv (1951), pp. 30–7.
92	Blom, Eric, ed., *Mozart's Letters*, transl. Emily Anderson, Harmondsworth, 1951, pp. 54–5.
91	Gai, Vinicio: *Gli Strumenti Musicali della Corte Medicea e il Museo del Conservatorio 'Luigi Cherubini' di Firenze*, Florence, 1969, p. 11 (translation).
40, 58 105, 116 119, 175	Galpin, Francis W.: *Old English Instruments of Music*, 4th edn., rev. Thurston Dart, London, 1965. Appendix 4, 'The Musical Instruments of King Henry VIII', pp. 217–20.
209	Ecorcheville, J.: 'Quelques Documents sur la Musique de la Grande Ecurie du Roi', *Sammelbände der Internationalen Musikgesellschaft*, pp. 608ff.
93	Kelly, Michael: *Solo Recital*, ed. Herbert van Thal, introd. J.C. Trewin, London, 1972, p. 227.
126	Marcuse, Sibyl: 'The Instruments of the King's Library at Versailles', *GSJ* xiv (1961), 34–6.
182	Ord-Hume, Arthur W.J.G.: *Clockwork Music*, London, 1973, p. 298.
121, 191 198	Perrot, Jean: *The Organ . . . to the end of the Thirteenth Century*, transl. Norma Deane, London, 1971, pp. 127, 129, 224.
116, 168	Rickert, Edith: *Chaucer's World*, ed. Clair C. Olson, Martin M. Crow and Margaret Rickert, London, 1948, pp. 75, 342.
81	Russell, Raymond: *The Harpsichord and Clavichord*, 2nd edn., rev. Howard Schott, London, 1973, p. 25.
20	M. C. Seymour, ed.: *On the Properties of Things. John Trevisa's translation of Bartholomaeus Anglicus' De Proprietatibus Rerum*, 2 vols., Oxford, 1975, i. p. 606.

* * *

The terminology of certain stringed instruments has recently been called into question, so in this period of transition I am referring to 'gittern (citole)' and 'mandora (gittern)' as indicated on pp. 39, 36.

Introduction

'An excellent band of music' was how Dr Charles Burney described a serenading party one night on the Grand Canal in Venice during his visit there in 1770. The musicians on the barge played 'violins, flutes, horns, bases, and a kettle-drum, with a pretty good tenor voice', little knowing that they would be immortalized in the diary of that Oxford Doctor of Music who in 1770 and 1772 undertook great journeys in Europe to prepare his *General History of Music* which was published in 1776 and 1789. His diaries provide a magnificent source, not only of our knowledge of musical performance in the late eighteenth century, but also of the instruments themselves, so it is appropriate that he should be quoted frequently in this short account of their history from Antiquity to the present day.

It is easy to become absorbed by the subject of musical instruments, whether we are performers, teachers, students, or those most important people, the members of the audience. Some are interested in old instruments, some in new, others in folk instruments, and many, the author included, have an obsession for finding instruments in the visual arts, as well as for playing them. The result of all this is that today more instruments are being made, more information is coming to light about their past, and more useful pictures are being discovered than at any previous period in history.

The subject, however, is so vast that only a small part of it can be written in any one book. It has been decided, therefore, to restrict this short account mainly to those instruments which were, and are, involved in the art music of the West. Certain folk instruments of today are referred to in passing, but however important they may be, they are not normally treated as separate items. Classification has been kept to a minimum, each chapter being built round instruments with similar methods of playing or construction, and where possible following the families of the orchestra. It has not been possible to include the numerous hybrids, particularly if no repertoire exists for them. Nor has it been possible to describe or to illustrate the limitless varieties and different tunings among instruments which were never standardized, particularly those from before 1500.

In spite of some notable recent discoveries, such as that of the instruments on Henry VIII's sunken flagship the *Mary Rose* which was raised to the surface in 1982, very few actual instruments survive from this early period; hence we have to rely for evidence on the visual arts, on various forms of literature, and on expense accounts. The matter of artistic licence or error is of great concern, the final test being whether or not the instrument portrayed could work. If it could not, the reason is either that the artist did not know enough, or that he never intended to be scrupulously accurate, as is indicated clearly by the more fanciful designs. Sometimes a correct instrument is held in an unplayable position for the sake of pictorial symmetry, or else purely for convenience. An angel in a church roof, for instance, may have to point his instrument downwards for it to be seen at all clearly from below, while a carved instrument close to the ground, as on a misericord, may be held in an adapted position to avoid being broken. If, however, artistic licence or error are plain in one or two details, this does not necessarily mean that the whole instrument is wrong. On a wider scale the same principle can be applied to instrumental ensembles. The pictorial grouping together of certain instruments need not be dismissed as unlikely just because one of them has an inconsistent number of strings or fingerholes. Over all these problems we have to use our discretion, as also on the subject of musicians who are shown, not as human beings, but as angels, animals, devils or grotesques. In the Middle Ages particularly, minstrels often dressed up to perform, whether for religious drama, for a village fair, or for the jollifications of a noble court, and the visual artist often portrayed what he had seen in real life. Even when a picture of angel musicians represents nothing more than a picture of angel musicians, the playing together of their particular instruments may still give valuable evidence of performance practice.

Terminology must also be treated with care. While one instrument can be known by several different names, the converse is also true, with one word being applied to several instruments. Certain words, such as *lute*, *fiddle* and *horn*, are used generically to cover a whole class of instruments, but they can also mean one type in particular. As with artistic licence, so is poetic licence a hazard, a striking example being the medieval word *rote* which seems to have been used by some poets with no particular image in mind except that it rhymed with *note*. On the whole, medieval authors referred to instruments of their own time when writing about a past age.

Robert Manning of Brunne, for instance, in *The Story of England*, described the celebrations at the court of King Arthur as being enlivened by the fourteenth-century instruments which he himself knew. More recently, writers of historical novels have tended to refer to medieval instruments by Renaissance names, while the ways in which Biblical instruments have been translated through the ages is the subject for a book in itself. Suffice it to say that only recently have real attempts been made to use words which are really representative of the instruments played by the Hebrews.

Surviving instruments themselves can be misleading, as over the years many have been altered. Lutes have been made into hurdy-gurdies, harpsichords have been enlarged and had their original pitch changed by as much as a fourth, and the celebrated gittern (or citole) now in the British Museum was several hundred years ago turned into a 'violin', and given a false back inside. Already in the Baroque era certain instruments were faked to look older, and given the name of a famous maker together with a fictitious date - only foreshadowing the numerous school violins which today bear the inscription *Antonio Stradivari*.

Related to this is the 'restoration' of art works, a notable example being in the thirteenth-century painted roof at Peterborough Cathedral, where nineteenth-century activities blatantly turned a medieval fiddle into a violin, complete with a Tourte-style bow. Repainted carvings fare better if they retain their original shape, and the making of plaster casts, such as was done many years ago for the roof bosses in Tewkesbury Abbey and the *Pórtico de la Gloria* in the Cathedral of Santiago de Compostela (this latter can be seen in the Victoria and Albert Museum, together with many other casts of musical sculpture) can add considerably to the knowledge of musicians and art historians alike. Fortunately there are now a good many restorers of art works and instruments who go to great trouble to return an object to its original appearance, while placing on record just what their work has involved.

Finally, a word about performance, without which no instruments would have been made. The great interest today in history of all kinds has brought about a desire to hear music played as nearly possible to its original sounds. Surviving instruments which are still in good playing condition can give us these at once, while others can provide the basis for reconstructions. When there are few or no instruments available, as from the medieval period, we must rely more than ever on the visual arts and on literature, which tell us, not only about the instruments themselves, but also about their groupings and the social conditions in which they were played. The angels, devils, animals and grotesques must help us to re-create the music of their own time.

Matters of Pitch

Throughout the text, specific notes will be written in italics, while keys in general, and notes at no specific octave, will be in plain capital letters.

Ex. 1 shows
a) the pitch name for each octave, written below the bass clef and above the treble clef;
b) the length in feet of an open diapason organ pipe at each C, written between the staves.

(When the C pipe is 8' long, the keyboard produces the same pitch as that of the piano. When it is 4' long the sound is an octave higher, and when 16' long, an octave lower.)

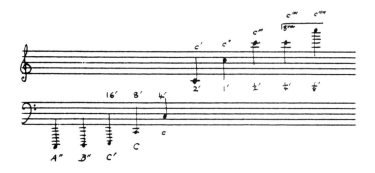

Ex. 2. The *Harmonic Series*, showing the fundamental note (in the key of C) and its overtones.

The 11th harmonic is slightly sharp, and the 13th slightly flat.

1 Kithara, played in a song contest depicted on an Attic vase, *c.* 500 BC. *Kassel, Staatliche Kunstsammlungen.*

I
Stringed Instruments
–Plucked

Several thousand years ago, Man discovered that if he plucked a taut string it would give forth a musical note. Then he found that strings of varying material, thickness and length would give different notes, and that if they were connected to a resonator the sound would be enhanced. The resulting musical instruments, which are described today as *chordophones*, are classified according to their shape as lyres, harps, zithers and lutes, and their different sounds can be obtained by plucking, striking, rubbing or bowing. Because of their greater antiquity, the plucked instruments will be treated first.

The generic family of **lyres** is characterized by a yoke, to which are attached two arms rising from the soundbox below. The strings, which are of more or less equal length, are fixed to the lower part of the instrument and continue up to the yoke, where they are adjusted. Some of the earliest surviving types, such as those excavated at the 'Royal Cemetery' of Ur in Mesopotamia (*c.* 2500 BC), had inlaid patterns or were covered with gold or silver, suggesting that they were already well established. They belong to the category of 'box-lyres', which were built up mostly or entirely of wood, and included also the Hebrew **kinnor** and the **kithara** of classical Greece and Rome, which were among the most important instruments of Antiquity.

In a more particular sense, the word **lyre** or **lyra** applies to a different form of the instrument, which was much used by the Greeks and the Etruscans, and has its origin steeped in legend. One story is that the infant god Hermes, on an expedition to steal 50 of Apollo's heifers, picked up a tortoise shell, stretched ox hide over it, and attached to it seven gut strings. When the enraged Apollo traced the thief he was calmed by the sound of the new instrument, and, after being presented with it by Hermes, became known as the god of Music. Whatever the truth of the matter, this lyre often had a resonator of tortoise shell covered with a skin belly, and instruments of this type are described as 'bowl lyres'. Its arms were sometimes of antelope horns, but they were often of wood, as was the yoke, and a type with extremely long arms was called the **barbiton**, and associated with Dionysus. Like the kithara, the Greek lyre was plucked with a plectrum, in contrast to the more ancient types and the medieval lyres, which were more often plucked by the fingers.

The **cruit**, **chrotta** or **rotta** which emerged from the Dark Ages was basically of the kithara type, varying in shape as did its forbears, and in its simplest form being almost rectangular; such was the instrument of which the remains were discovered in the seventh-century ship burial at Sutton Hoo near Woodbridge in Suffolk (fig. 3). The ninth-century Bible of Charles the Bald

2 Lyre (or lyra), played by Nike. Detail from a red-figured oil-flask by the Pan Painter, *c.* 490 BC. *Oxford, Ashmolean Museum.*

however, the lyre can still be found in many parts of the world today, notably in Scandinavia among European countries.

The Romanesque harp was generally of the type known as the 'frame harp', in which the string arm and soundchest, holding respectively the upper and lower ends of the strings, are joined by a front pillar which was, and still is, often absent from non-European harps. The medieval frame was frequently made of willow, and its strings were normally of gut, although metal and twisted hair were also sometimes used. However, the thirteenth-century Franciscan Bartholomaeus Anglicus, in his *De Proprietatibus Rerum* of *c.* 1250, warned against mixing the gut of sheep and wolves:

strengis imade of guttes of wolues destroyeþ and
fretiþ and corrumpiþ strengis imade of guttis
of schiepe 3if hit so be þat þey beþ so isette among
them as in fethele or in harpe ...

(Translation by John of Trevisa, 1398/9. British Library MS Add. 27944, f.142v).

Metal strings were often used in Ireland, according to the Norman Welsh chronicler Giraldus Cambrensis (Gerald de Barri, Archdeacon of Wales, *c.* 1146–*c.* 1220), who, in his *Topographia Hibernica* tells us that the Irish had 'strings made of brass instead of skin' ('Aeneis quoque utuntur chordis, non de corio factis'). The thirteenth-century romance *King Horn* describes a harp being played with 'nayles scharpe', a method which continued for several hundred years in Ireland, where harpists traditionally grew long fingernails.

The best known surviving medieval harp is the so-called Harp of Brian Boru, now believed to date from the fourteenth century, which is kept at Trinity College, Dublin. It is typical of the massively built instruments with a wide sound chest, distinctive curved front pillar and metal strings which became traditional in Ireland. This contrasted strongly with the more slender 'Gothic' harp of the Continent, such as would have been played by the Dukes of Burgundy Philip the Good and his son Charles the Bold in the fifteenth century, and is exemplified in the paintings of Hans Memling (fig. 7). Here the frame and sound

however, shows a three-stringed lyre with a central neck, enabling the performer to obtain more notes by stopping the strings against it with his fingers (fig. 4).

In the **harp** family the basic outline is triangular, and the strings are set at an angle perpendicular to the soundboard. Again the earliest examples include surviving instruments from the 'Royal Cemetery' at Ur, and carvings from the Aegean Islands, also dating from the third millennium BC (fig. 5). While the later pre-Christian Greeks certainly knew the harp, they and the Romans preferred the lyre types, as did the minstrels of the early Middle Ages. It was only from the Romanesque period onwards that the harp gained permanent precedence over the lyre in Europe, presumably due to the greater number of strings allowed by its shape; as a folk instrument, chest were much narrower and were pointed at the corners, and the strings were normally of gut. Many harps at that time had 'brays', L-shaped metal pins which held the strings to the sound chest, strengthening the sound and producing a somewhat buzzing effect. (An ivory harp of this type in the Louvre, which was thought to be medieval, is now believed to date from the nineteenth century.)

Although the harp is generally regarded as a 'soft' instrument (see p. 198), its versatility is acknowledged by Paulus Paulirinus of Prague, in his *Liber viginti artium*, written between 1459 and 1463:

It projects sound to a great distance, indeed farther than any other instrument aside from the trumpet, organ and portative. It may be combined with any musical instrument by plucking it louder or softer.

Around this time, however, the harp entered a period of crisis. Because it was tuned in advance to suit the key of each composition, it could not cope adequately with the increasing chromaticism in music. While it was possible to raise a string by a semitone by pressing it at the top towards the string arm, this temporarily restricted the performance to one hand instead of two. For a time, therefore, the harp gave way in importance to the fretted lute, on which all semitones could easily be played. While diatonic harps were still made, they became used more for simple and traditional music in which the instrument did not need to modulate during performance.

To retain its place in the history of art music, the harp therefore had to become chromatic, and in the sixteenth century a solution was produced, based on some earlier harps which had had two rows of strings, possibly used for elementary part music within one basic key, although they may also have allowed for an occasional chromatic note. The new **double harp** or **arpa doppia** had a row of chromatic strings alongside the diatonic ones, as can be seen in the beautiful French example now kept at the Galleria Estense at Modena (fig. 9). (For many years this figured on the 1000 lira bank note.) The **triple harp**, which according to Marin Mersenne's *Harmonie*

3 Reconstruction of an early medieval lyre (chrotta), based on the 7th century fragments excavated at Sutton Hoo. *London, British Museum.*

4 David plays a triangular harp (centre), while his minstrels, clockwise from bottom left, play a lyre (chrotta) with fingerboard, horn, crotales and a long wind instrument; from the Carolingian Bible of Charles the Bald, *c*. 846. *Paris, Bibliothèque Nationale, MS Lat. I, f.215v.*

5 Harp-player, sculpted in the Aegean Islands in the 3rd millennium BC. *New York, Metropolitan Museum, Rogers Fund.*

6 Harp with shoulder strap, held by David in the Great Canterbury Psalter; English, *c.* 1180–90. *Paris, Bibliothèque Nationale, MS Lat. 8846, f.75.*

Universelle (1636) was invented around 1600 by the Neapolitan 'Sieur Luc Anthoine Eustache', had three rows of strings, the outer ones being diatonic and played by one hand to each, while the inner one contained the chromatic notes and was plucked by either hand. This instrument features prominently in Italian paintings of the seventeenth century, but it survived longest in Wales, where one of its most distinguished performers was the blind John Parry of Ruabon (1710–82).

Meanwhile, seventeenth-century experiments in Bavaria and the Tyrol resulted in a single-strung harp in which certain strings were equipped with a hook at the top end. Each hook when twisted would tighten a string to raise it by a semitone, but here again this could only be done by a hand which was not playing, so chromatic changes were impossible during fast passages involving both hands. This problem was

7 Late medieval harp with brays; detail from *The Madonna and Child with Angels* by Hans Memling, after 1479. *Washington, National Gallery of Art, Andrew W. Mellon Collection.*

8 Angels with double harp and psaltery; detail of a Spanish reliquary (*c.* 1390) from the monastery of Piedra. *Madrid, Academia de la Historia.*

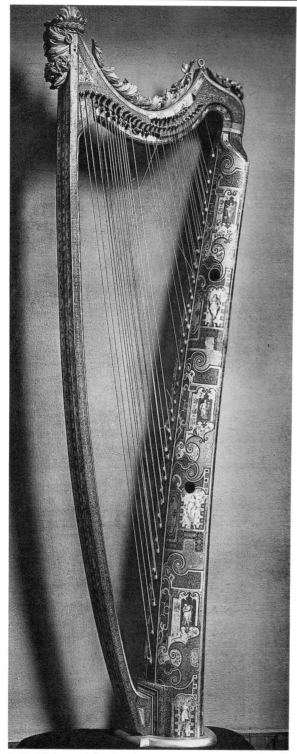

9 Double harp of the Este family; made in the 16th century by Jean le Pot of Amiens and decorated by Giulio Marescotti in the style of Ferrara, *c.* 1587. *Modena, Galleria Estense.*

solved in the **pedal harp**, which is often said to date from *c.* 1720 and has been attributed to both Jacob Hochbrucker of Donauworth in Bavaria and J.P. Vetter of Nuremberg, although Hochbrucker's son Simon claimed that his father had invented it in 1697. By means of wires or rods inside the front pillar, the hooks were connected to pedals at the bottom of the instrument. By pressing one pedal down a notch all the Cs were raised, by pressing the next pedal all the Ds were, and so on, although at first this applied only to certain notes. After a time seven pedals were used, so that all the notes could be changed, and to accommodate the connecting links inside, the front pillar was now regularly straightened. The Parisian makers Nadermann, Cousineau and Erard then tried new types of hook, known as *crochets*, *béquilles* and *fourchettes* (describing their respective shapes of hooks, crutches and forks), to ease the manner of tightening the strings.

10 Welsh triple harp of the 19th century, played by Nansi Richards Jones. *Cardiff, Welsh Folk Museum, St Fagan's Castle.*

11 An anachronistic single action pedal harp played in a
Scene from the Life of Henry VIII by Eugène Deveria (1805–
65). However, the painting is probably based on a performance
of Shakespeare's *Henry VIII*, where such a harp would have
been used in the 19th century. Caen, *Musée des Beaux-Arts*.

Nevertheless it was still impossible to play in all keys, so experiments continued, one of them being a harp with two rows of pedals, made by the Cousineau family in 1782. Sébastien Erard, who had invented the *fourchettes*, later devised a second row of them, together with an extra notch for each pedal, thus raising the pitch of a string by another semitone and enabling the performer to play in every key. (All the flats, naturals and sharps were now available, being operated respectively by the upper, middle and lower positions of the foot.) Having left France during the Revolution, Erard patented this double action in London in 1810. He also made the strings tighter and thicker, strengthened the soundchest, and decorated the head and base of the pillar with Greek maidens and lyre players, causing the instrument to be called the 'Grecian harp'. In 1835 his nephew Pierre Erard produced his own 'Gothic Harp', identified by its angels and Gothic arches. This had three extra strings, one in the treble and two in the bass, but they did not have pedals until those were added by Wilfrid Smith of London in 1958. The range of the concert harp is now from C' to g'''', allowing for the chromatic extension at each end.

The improvements made by Sébastien Erard greatly changed the position of the harp in society. The single action instruments made by him and the Nadermann and Cousineau families had been played, not only by professionals, but also by numerous amateurs including Queen Marie Antoinette of France, and many harps from this period remain to decorate the stately homes of Europe. The new instrument, being larger, heavier, and more complicated to play, was too difficult for many harpists, who, recognizing its superior qualities, gave up the harp altogether and played the piano instead. Such a musician was Dorette, wife of the violinist and composer Louis Spohr, who wrote many compositions for the harp and violin. Berlioz, who made much use of the improved instrument in his compositions, was often frustrated by the lack of performers, but he was nevertheless able to muster 25 harpists to play together the 'Prayer' from *Moses* by Rossini, at a concert involving 1022 musicians as

12 Double action pedal harp by S. & P. Erard, London, 1858. *London, Victoria and Albert Museum.*

13 Monochord played by Boethius, in a 12th-century English MS of his *De Musica. Cambridge University Library, MS Ii.3.12, f.61v.*

European pedal harp had reached Ireland. Amateurs wishing to play on a more simple instrument than that were rewarded by the small 'Royal Portable Irish Harp' produced by John Egan of Dublin *c.* 1819, in which the work of pedals was achieved by single action ditals set into the front pillar.

In contrast to that of the harp, the **zither** family consists of instruments in which the strings run parallel to the soundboard. One of the earliest examples was the **monochord**, which is said to have been invented by Pythagoras in the sixth century BC, and was much used by medieval mathematicians. Its single plucked string changed in pitch as a bridge was moved beneath it from one marked point to another on the long and narrow soundboard. Its part in music must have been very limited, but one good use could have been to give notes to singers who were about to perform unaccompanied.

A more musical form of zither was the **psaltery**, which is of obscure origin and cannot with any certainty be identified with the 'psalterium' of the Vulgate. Triangular and quadrangular instruments were described by that name in a much reproduced letter said to be from St Jerome to a certain Dardanus, but this is now believed to have been forged in the ninth century. From that time onwards, however, these shapes are increasingly seen in other contexts, the triangular ones sometimes being described as 'rota' or 'rote', as can be seen on an eleventh-century capital in the cloister of the abbey of Moissac, where one of David's minstrels is accompanied by the inscription

NAMƏ CVꟿ ROTA

part of a festival for the Exhibition of Industrial Products at Paris in 1844. Since 1889 the American firm of Lyon and Healy, and since 1909 that of Wurlitzer have further strengthened the instrument and made the mechanism smoother. Meanwhile there have been various attempts to produce a cross-strung chromatic harp without pedals, notably that by Pleyel, Wolff & Co. (patented in 1897) for which Debussy wrote his *Danse sacrée et danse profane* in 1904. Such instruments, however, could not replace the Erard harp, which is the type most used today.

Irish harping continued in the traditional manner until about 1800, by which time the

[Eman]. This example, like many similar illustrations of the period, is shaped like a straight-sided harp, but it has no front pillar and there is clearly a soundboard behind the strings, even if it is not an actual sound*box*. Nowadays the instrument is

14 Portative organ and psaltery-harp played by angels in
The Coronation of the Virgin by an anonymous German
painter, *c.* 1350. *Frankfurt am Main, Städelsches Kunstinstitut
& Städtische Galerie, Inv. nr. SG 443.*

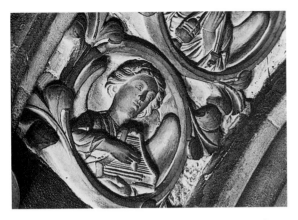

15 Psaltery with nine pairs of strings and two separate drone strings, from a mid-13th century window soffit in the north transept of *Westminster Abbey*.

described as a **harp-psaltery** or **psaltery-harp**, and Howard Mayer Brown (in 'The Trecento Harp') has pointed out that in Italy it was used in preference to the real harp until the fourteenth century (fig. 204). Another variant, which appears mainly from the Romanesque period, is a double psaltery with two sets of strings, one on each side of the instrument, which is played in an upright position.

Psalteries with soundboxes and soundholes appear with increasing frequency from the twelfth century onwards, perhaps due to the Arabic **qānūn** which was already well known in Spain. Trapezoidal in shape, and with strings tuned three or four to a note, its characteristics were soon to be seen in other psalteries, particularly those of southern Europe. (Its name was also adopted, becoming *canon* in French and *canone* in Italian, with *micanon* and *mezzo canone* being used for instruments of half the normal shape.) In the North an instrument with incurved sides and one or two strings to a note was preferred, one of its early depictions being in the Bodleian Library's MS Auct. D.2.8., f.88, dating from twelfth-century England. In eastern Europe wing-shaped psalteries were given the name **ala** (the Latin word for a wing), leading to the modern name **Bohemian wing**, and in the same area a psaltery-harp with double soundbox flourished to the end of the Middle Ages.

Psaltery strings were best made from brass or silver, according to *De Proprietatibus Rerum* by Bartholomaeus Anglicus, written *c.* 1250 and copied *c.* 1300 in the *Ars Musica* of the Spanish monk Johannes Aegidius Zamorensis. They were plucked either by the fingers or by quill plectra, as the two methods were suitable for different moods, although some psalteries sound generally better when played with a quill. Sometimes one hand used a plectrum and the other plucked with the fingers, an excellent method of playing a melody with accompaniment. While any psaltery can have a drone accompaniment plucked on its lower strings, a thirteenth century carving in the north transept of Westminster Abbey shows two strings which are apparently designed especially for playing drones, as they are a good deal thicker than the others and set apart from them (fig. 15).

Like the harp, the psaltery was frequently played to accompany singing, and their use together on an occasion of celebration is described in the fifteenth-century romance *The Squire of Low Degree*:

Ye shall have harpe, sautry, and songe,
And other mirthes you amonge;
Ye shall have rumney and malmesine,
Both ypocrasse and vernage wine...

Also like the harp, the psaltery was adversely affected by Renaissance chromaticism, and it gradually passed from the mainstream of art music, although it continued for some time to be used in Italy and Spain; in the latter country its pitch descended to *C*, and in the eighteenth century it was sometimes used as a continuo instrument. Its late variants included (a) an upright double psaltery called **arpanetta** in Italy and **Spitzharfe** in Germany, in which the right hand played the melody and the left hand the accompaniment on the other side, (b) the **Bell Harp**, which was apparently invented by John Simcock of Bath, *c.* 1700, and has struck strings, and (c) the **bowed psaltery**, which was not a medieval instrument at all but a Tyrolean folk-instrument of no great antiquity. Since the 1930s it has been used a great deal in education, particularly in Germany, where it was promoted by Edgar Stahmer. The more important descendants of the medieval psaltery were the plucked zither and harpsichord (p. 82ff.), and the struck dulcimer (p. 172ff.), which itself led eventually to the piano.

When the word **zither** is used in the particular as opposed to the generic sense, it denotes an instrument which is little used in art music but nevertheless deserves a mention. In its earliest form, the **Scheitholt**, it was long and narrow like the monochord, but had frets for diatonic notes on its soundboard. According to Praetorius (1619), its three or four brass strings could be tuned to the unison, fifth or octave, although the exact arrangement was variable. To play a tune, the performer pressed the strings against the frets by means of a small stick in his left hand, while his right thumb strummed on them near the bridge. As the frets stretched across the whole soundboard, the effect would have been somewhat reminiscent of parallel organum. Later forms of the instrument, however, had extra strings which were not stopped by the fingers, and were used for giving a droning chordal accompaniment to the melody. The Scheitholt led to many different types of zither, its approximate shape being retained in the Hungarian **cithera** and the French **épinette des Vosges**. In Ger-

manic countries, however, the soundbox was gradually extended to allow for a greater number of strings, and during the nineteenth century the instrument acquired its present forms. It now has chromatic frets, and about five melody strings which are plucked by a metal plectrum attached to the performer's right thumb. The unstopped strings have increased in number to over 30, and are tuned in such a way that, by plucking with separate fingers of his right hand, the player can obtain different chords as required. Throughout its history the zither has been used mainly for domestic and folk music, but in the twentieth century it has found a prominent place in films, a notable example being *The Third Man* starring Orson Welles.

The generic family of **lutes** consists of those instruments in which a neck proceeds from a body, and the performer presses the strings against the neck or touches them above it with his fingers to obtain the notes required. Normally, those with vaulted backs are classified as lutes and those with flat backs as guitars, but this is not an inflexible rule and there are many hybrids. While their history in Asia, northern Africa, Greece and

16 Zither by Franz Nowy, Vienna, *c.* 1950. *London, Collection of John Leach.*

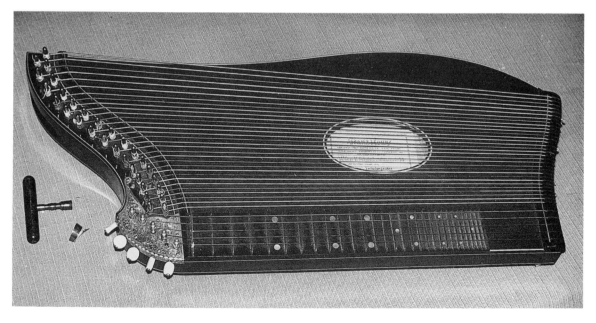

Rome can be traced back to Antiquity, there is little evidence of these instruments in northern Europe before the early Middle Ages. Some of them, however, may have come northwards through Byzantine influence, which was already strong before the Moors invaded Spain in 711, bringing their own instruments with them.

In the specific sense, the vaulted **lute** (the name comes from the Arabic *al-úd*, meaning 'the wood') was certainly established in Spain by the tenth century, but our knowledge of it in England only dates from the late thirteenth, so it is reasonable to suppose that it was brought here by minstrels in the entourage of Eleanor of Castile when she married Edward I. Its curved back may originally have been made from one piece of wood (particularly in the long-necked lutes played in southern Europe in the earlier part of the Middle Ages), but as the instrument grew larger this was replaced by ribs of hard wood such as maple or sycamore, and some late examples are of ivory and ebony. The soundboard or belly was of a softer wood, and it contained either open soundholes or, as in most cases, a carved rose. The gut strings passed from a frontal stringholder to a pegbox bent back at a right angle to the neck; this was short, and from the fourteenth century onwards was increasingly fitted with gut

17 Lute with four strings played by one of two musical angels; detail from *The Coronation of the Virgin* by Agnolo Gaddi (*fl.* 1369–96). *Washington, National Gallery of Art, Samuel H. Kress Collection.*

frets. Early European lutes often had four single strings or 'courses', apparently tuned to pitches relative to *c f a d'*, and these were plucked with a plectrum. Then the courses became double (with the exception of the top string which normally remained single), and the pitch was extended, first upwards to *g'*, and then downwards to *G*, resulting in the late fifteenth-century six-course lute which was attributed to the Germans by the Flemish writer Johannes Tinctoris in his *De inventione et usu musicae* of *c.* 1487. He added that they sometimes reinforced the sound by making one string of each pair in brass, tuned an octave below the other. Also during this period there evolved the technique of plucking with the fingers, thus giving greater musical scope to the performer, and leading to an idiomatic lute style. According to Tinctoris

...some teams will take the treble part of any piece you care to give them and improvize marvellously upon it with such taste that the performance cannot be rivalled. Among such, Pietro Bono (Avogari), lutenist to Ercole, Duke of Ferrara, is in my opinion pre-eminent.

Furthermore, others will do what is much more difficult; namely to play a composition alone, and most skilfully, in not only two parts, but even in three or four. For example, Orbus the German, or Henri who was recently in the service of Charles, Duke of Burgundy: the German was super-eminent in playing in this way.

Soon afterwards there was established in Bologna a celebrated school of German lute-makers. Laux (Luca) Maler, who was living there from 1518, was the son of Conrad (Corrado) Maler, a lute-maker of 'Alemania alta'. When Laux died in 1552 he owned three shops, left 998 new lutes besides 127 incomplete ones, and his will referred to over 1000 soundboards. The Bologna school eventually passed to native Italian makers such as Girolamo Brensi, and was followed by similar centres at Padua, Venice and Rome.

As the pitch of individual instruments varied, lutenists played not from normal notation but from tablature, in which the stave represented the strings, and letters or numbers (according to the type of tablature in use) indicated the required frets. Different tablatures were used in France, Germany and Italy, and an early one was known in the district of Naples. It is thought that tablatures may have developed from the time that the lute regularly had frets, and at this time they were written in manuscript. The earliest lute music to appear in print was a collection of *ricercari* and song arrangements by Francesco Spinaccino, published by Ottaviano dei Petrucci at Venice in 1507.

With the increasing need for lower notes during the Renaissance period the lute acquired more bass strings, and in the late sixteenth century Antonio Naldi ('Il Bardella') invented a new form of the instrument to provide continuo accompaniment for the 'New Music' of that group

18 Six-course Renaissance lute; detail from wall paintings by Garofalo, 1505–08. *Ferrara, Palazzo di Ludovico il Moro, Sala del Tesoro.*

19 Chitarrone accompanying a singer in a 17th-century wall
painting by Clemente Maioli. *Ferrara, Church of Santa Maria
dei Teatini.*

of Florentine musicians and writers known as the *Camerata*. This **tiorba** or **theorbo**, which also became known as the **chitarrone**, had a large body and a set of very long unstopped bass strings with their own pegbox at the end of the extended neck. Because of their length the top two courses could not stand the tension required for the tuning of the normal lute pitch, so they were tuned down an octave and the third course was used for the main melodic parts. The stopped courses could be either single or double, and of gut or metal. A related form of instrument was the **arciliuto** or **archlute** (also known as **liuto attiorbato** or **theorboed lute**), which Alessandro Piccinini claimed to have invented in Padua in 1594. Although it had unstopped bass strings with their own pegbox beyond that of the stopped strings, its body was that of a normal lute, so its upper courses did not have to be lowered an octave. This characteristic made it more suitable for solo music than the former instrument, and was the main distinguishing feature between the two. There were, however, many differences within the general meaning of the word 'theorbo', which varied according to time and place, and

20 Archlute by Michael Rauche, London, 1762. *London, Victoria and Albert Museum.*

21 Baroque lute, in *A Man with an Arch-lute*, attributed to Isaack Luttichuijs (1616–73). *Glasgow Art Gallery.*

some of these have been quoted by Robert Spencer in his article 'Chitarrone, theorbo and archlute'. One of them must have been the type of 'theorbo' which Samuel Pepys took to be converted from single to double courses in London in 1661. A further member of the family was the **angelica** or **angel lute**, which had about 16 strings tuned diatonically and therefore did not need to be stopped by the fingers. The Baroque lute of the seventeenth and eighteenth centuries was double strung like the Renaissance instrument, but had some unstopped bass strings which were fixed to a separate pegholder. Its tunings varied, to suit the demands of such composers as Denis and Ennemond Gautier in France, and Esaias Reusner and Silvius Weiss in Germany. Although the lute was on the wane in the eighteenth century, it was called for in suites by Bach, concertos by Vivaldi, and chamber music by Haydn, while Dr Charles Burney, on a visit to Paris in 1770, heard 'M Kohaut, who played very well, on the Arch Lute'. Meanwhile, a long-necked lute of Asiatic style had appeared in Italy under the name **colascione**, but its use was restricted mainly to amateur music-making.

One of the smallest and narrowest forms of lute was known in Antiquity as the **pandoura**. Occasional variants of it are seen in early medieval art, but it was not until *c.* 1300 and the period of the *Ars Nova* that its descendants were frequently portrayed throughout Europe. At that time the body was probably carved from one piece of wood, and its pegbox was either sickle-shaped, often ending in a carved animal head, or turned back at a right angle like that of the larger lute. Its gut strings (which were in single or double courses) could be attached to a frontal string holder or to end pins, and they were plucked with a plectrum. Frets were normal by the late Middle Ages. The terminology of this instrument has undergone a great deal of thought. It has long been called 'mandora' or 'mandore' in view of the instrument of that shape and name which was popular from the sixteenth century onwards. However, the word is seldom seen in literature between 1300 and 1500, when representations of the instrument were most frequent, and Laurence Wright, in 'The Medieval Gittern and Citole: A Case of Mistaken Identity', has suggested that it should be called 'gittern'. The present writer, however, has been hoping for more time to consider the matter, so for the present will refer to it as **mandora (gittern)**.

Many true **mandoras** have survived from the Renaissance and Baroque periods, when they were tuned in fifths and fourths, e.g. *c g c′ g′ c″*. Since then the chief developments have been in Italy, where the instrument varied according to the district, under the general name **mandolino** or, in English, **mandolin**. The Milanese type (which was not restricted to Italy) represented the culmination of the mandora, keeping its pairs of gut strings and frontal string holder, while the Neapolitans preferred metal strings tuned to *g d′ a′ e″* as on the violin, with the strings passing over a low bridge to be attached to pins on the back. The bass mandolin was often known as *mandola* or *mandolone*. While it did not become a regular member of the orchestra, the mandolin has from

22 Pandoura, in a statuette from Tanagra, 3rd century BC. *Paris, Musée du Louvre.*

23 Mandora (gittern) played by one of two musical angels; detail from *The Coronation of the Virgin* by Agnolo Gaddi (*fl.* 1369–96). *Washington, National Gallery of Art, Samuel H. Cress Collection.*

time to time appeared with it for special effects. Vivaldi wrote concertos for it, Mozart gave it an obbligato part in a serenade in *Don Giovanni*, and Beethoven wrote pieces for it with the pianoforte or fortepiano of his day. Burney, in an eye-witness account of the welcome given in Brescia to the native singer Luini Bonetto, on his return from Russia in 1770, wrote that he

was welcomed home by a band of music ... consisting of two violins, a mandoline, french horn, trumpet, and violoncello; and, though in the dark, they played long concertos, with solo parts for the mandoline.

Instruments of the **guitar** family, with parallel or incurved sides and generally with a flat back,

are often seen in European art from the thirteenth century onwards. Before that time they are less frequent, passing back through Romanesque examples of Spain and Italy (e.g. in the *Pórtico de la Gloria* of the Cathedral at Santiago de Compostela and in the Baptistery at Parma) to the Stuttgart Psalter of *c.* 830 (fig. 90) and clearly foreshadowed in a carving of the first century AD from the Russian Buddhist monastery at Airtam near Termez. This is now in the Hermitage Museum, Leningrad.

Jean Ruiz (*c.* 1280–*c.* 1350), Archpriest of Hita, spoke in his *Libro de Buen Amor* of the 'guitarra morisca' and 'guitarra latina', instruments which are both known to have been played at the Court of the Duke of Normandy in 1349. The *guitarra morisca* is thought by some authorities to have been a long-necked instrument with oval-shaped body and vaulted back, while others believe that it was the mandora (gittern). The *guitarra latina*, which is generally known by the

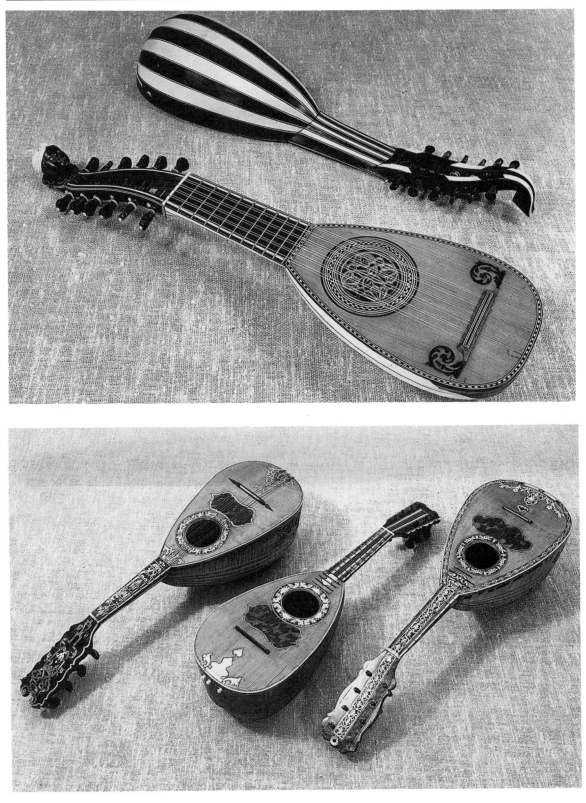

24 Mandoras by (top) Joseph Molinari, Venice, 1757, and (bottom) Jean Nicolas Lambert, Paris, 1752. *London, Victoria and Albert Museum.*

25 Mandolins by the Neapolitan makers Antonio Vinaccia, 1772, and Vincenzo Vinaccia, 1761 and 1785. *London, Victoria and Albert Museum.*

name **gittern** (or **citole**, according to Wright), resembled the Airtam carving in its approximately parallel sides, and normally had a flat back. (All three types are among the illustrations to the *Cantigas de Santa Maria* manuscript made in the late thirteenth century for King Alfonso X 'The Wise' of Castile, and now kept at the Escorial Library, MS j.b.2.) One of the most popular shapes resembled that of a holly leaf, while another was more curved at the lower end and had pointed 'wings' at the upper end of the body, causing Emanual Winternitz to include it among the instruments derived from the kithara. The neck was normally fretted, sometimes extending backwards to contain a hole for the left thumb, as can be seen in the surviving early fourteenth-century gittern (citole) which was formerly in Warwick Castle and is now in the British Museum. (Unfortunately only the back and sides of this instrument are in their original condition, as in the sixteenth century there was an attempt to turn it into a violin, and since that time other alterations to it have taken place.) The gut strings were plucked with a plectrum, but their medieval tuning is not known to have been recorded; it is possible that they were tuned in the same way as the early lutes, i.e. *c f a d'*, and this certainly works well on the reconstructed instrument in the author's possession. It is based to a great extent on the gittern (citole) from the Ormesby Psalter, as can be seen in fig. 27, and here the presence of a tailpiece and absence of a separate bridge indicate that the tailpiece would have had feet or a bridge below (see p. 47). This device on the reconstruction creates a perfect sounding length for the tuning given above, with all strings

being made of gut. The gittern (citole) was frequently used for singing and dancing, and in pictures can often be found in duet with a fiddle (fig. 206). During the fourteenth century it gradually gave way to the lute, being out of fashion, although just still extant, after 1400.

By the mid-fifteenth century there had emerged in Spain a new form of guitar covered by the term **vihuela de mano**, and soon afterwards it arrived in Italy and there became the **viola da mano**. With six courses of strings like those of the lute, it was plucked in the new manner, with the fingers. (A guitar still plucked with a plectrum was described in Spain as a **vihuela de peñola**.) Tinctoris, who worked in Naples, said that 'while some play every sort of composition most delightfully on the lute, in Italy and

26 Spade-shaped instrument of the guitar family (plucked here, but often bowed), played by Ethan in a 12th-century Italian Bible. *Rome, Biblioteca Apostolica Vaticana, MS Barb. Lat. 587, f.194.*

tradition of the medieval gittern (citole), its use as an instrument to provide rhythmical drones is brought to life by the character Dobinet Doughtie in Nicholas Udall's play *Royster Doyster* written before 1553:

Anon to our gitterne, thrumpledum, thrumpledum, thrumpledum thrum,
Thrumpledum, thrumpledum, thrumpledum, thrumpledum thrum.

By the late sixteenth century the guitar had acquired a fifth course below the others and become known as the **Spanish Guitar**, being described in this form in Juan Carlos Amat's book *Guitarra Española de Cinco Ordenes* which was published for the first of several editions in 1596. His tuning is *Aa dd' gg bb e'e'*, being very close to that of the modern guitar. Much music was

27 Gittern (citole) played by an angel in the Ormesby Psalter, English, *c.* 1310–25. *Oxford, Bodleian Library, MS Douce 366, f.9v.*

Spain the viola without a bow is more often used'. For such an instrument Luis de Milán published his instruction book *El Maestro* at Valencia in 1535/6, and a surviving example from this period can be seen in the Musée Jacquemart-André, Paris.

After Henry VIII died in 1547 an inventory of his instruments included

Foure Gitterons with iiii cases to them: they are caulled Spanishe Vialles.

These would seem to be the vihuela type mentioned above, but about that time there was also a new 'Gyttern' which, according to the Autobiography of Thomas Whythorne (1528–96) was 'stranȝ in England, and þerfor þe more dezired and esteemed' when he stayed in London at the age of 17. According to Alonso Mudarra's *Tres libros de Musica* (1546) there were two tunings for its four double courses, the 'old' of *ff c'c' e'e' a'a'* and the 'new' of *gg' c'c' e'e' a'a'*. Following the

28. Medieval guitar (vihuela) from a Spanish Book of Hours, *c.* 1480. *London, British Library, MS Add. 50,004, f.70v.*

29 Viola da mano with double pipe, lira da braccio, carnival whistle and two incomplete woodwind instruments, from an early 16th-century intarsia panel in the *studiolo* of Isabella d'Este. *Mantua, Palazzo Ducale*.

30 *The Guitar Player* by Jacob van Schuppen (1670–1751). *Liverpool, Walker Art Gallery.*

written for the instrument in Italy, where, according to Praetorius, 'the *Ziarlatini* and *Salt' in banco* use them for simple strummed accompaniments to their *villanelle* and other vulgar, clownish songs'. The Italian actor Francesco Corbetta was largely responsible for its popularity at the French Court of Louis XIV after *c.* 1655, and from there it spread to the England of Charles II who, according to Pepys's diary of 8 June 1660, brought a 'gittar' with him at the time of the Restoration. From this period there survive many guitars of fine workmanship by the best instrument makers of the day, leading to those of Antonio Stradivari

of Cremona and Joachim Tielke of Hamburg. Some of these instruments had slightly vaulted backs, but in the **chitarra battente**, an Italian variant, this characteristic was normal; its chief difference from the regular instrument was in having metal strings plucked with a plectrum.

Shortly before and after 1800, several changes occurred. The shape of the guitar, which had been narrow and deep, became wider and shallower, and with greater incurving of the sides. The belly, which had been supported below by parallel bars, was now given fan-shaped barring, with considerable benefit to the sound, and its carved rose was omitted from the soundhole. The string courses became single and a sixth one was added, while the tuning was established at its present *E A d g b e'*. The fingerboard was lengthened to enable the performance of higher notes (although frets had previously been set into the belly above the fingerboard of some earlier instruments), and the pegs, which had been inserted from behind the pegbox, were replaced by machine pegs fitted at the side.

A Spanish guitar revival was brought about by the Cistercian Don Basilio (Miguel García) in the late eighteenth century, resulting in a flood of compositions by such composers as Fernando Sor (1778–1839) and Mauro Giuliani (1781–1829) who recognized the need for a more powerful and sonorous instrument. This became established in the mid-nineteenth century, largely due to Antonio Torres (1817–92), who built the larger instrument which is still in use today. He also deepened the finger-board, and widened it to cope more easily with the six strings, providing the model on which modern technique was founded by Francisco Tárrega (1852–1909). The great interest in the guitar today, together with numerous solo pieces and concertos which continually enlarge its repertoire, is largely due to the self-taught Andrés Segovia, whose musicianship and virtuosity have inspired his disciples around the world.

The family of the **cittern** resembled that of the guitar in having a flat back, but it differed in the tapering outline of its body, and in its metal strings. The medieval **citole** may have been one of its forerunners, but convincing illustrations of such an instrument are hard to find, as medieval illustrations do not often show the necessary shape of the back view. Canon Galpin said that 'on the front of the Minstrels' Gallery in Exeter Cathedral we have one of the best examples of the instrument', and from the front view it could certainly be an ancestor of the cittern, as the strings, which are in four double courses, pass over a bridge and are attached to pins on the base of the instrument. The snag concerns the shape of the back, which should be flat, but when the present writer examined the carving from scaffolding in 1976, the back was clearly vaulted. It is certainly not a conventional lute, and the body is too wide to be a normal mandora (gittern), so if it is not just a hybrid (which is possible), then perhaps we can allow for the artist to have made a mistake over the shape of the back, which is also possible. Such things are very tantalizing.

An early example of the Renaissance **cittern** seems to have been the 'cetula' described by Tinctoris (*c.* 1487) as having four brass or steel strings and being 'only used in Italy by rustics to accompany light songs and lead dance music'. From the next two centuries many citterns survive. Praetorius enumerated several different types, from that with four courses 'fit for cobblers and tailors' ('Italian' if tuned to *b g d′ e′* and 'French' if tuned to *a g d′ e′*), to the cittern with 12 courses, which was 'almost as long as a bass violin' and which 'gives a rich, powerful sound, of the same quality as that of a clavicymbal or symphony'; this was the archcittern, tuned to

31 Chitarra battente by Giorgio Sellas, Venice, 1627. *Oxford, Ashmolean Museum.*

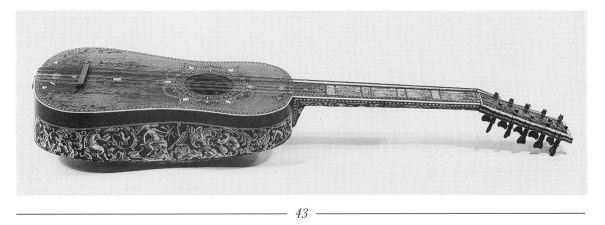

32 *The Guitar Player* by Pierre-Auguste Renoir, 1897. *Lyon, Musée des Beaux-Arts.*

e^b B^b f c g d a e b g d' e'. Mersenne said that the Italian citterns had fixed frets crossing the complete width of the finger-board, while on French ones certain frets were set only below the top string. This, however, was not a fixed rule.

Larger instruments of the cittern family included the **bandore**, which was apparently invented by John Rose of London in 1562, and the **orpharion**, which was tuned like a lute but had metal strings. Its stringholder was fixed onto the belly at a slanted angle, in order to give the lowest strings the longest possible sounding length. Further types included the **penorcon**, the **polyphant**, the bell-shaped cittern known as **Hamburger Cithrinchen** which is particularly associated with Joachim Tielke, and the eighteenth-century **English guitar**, a large cittern with deep sides and six double courses tuned to

33 Cittern with the 'French' arrangement of frets; detail from the German MS *Splendor Solis*, 1582. *London, British Library, MS Harl. 3469, f.2.*

34 Orpharion from the title page of William Barley's *A nevv Booke of Tabliture for the Orpharion, 1596. London, British Library, K.i.c.18.*

35 English guitar by John Preston, London, *c.* 1770. *London, Royal College of Music.*

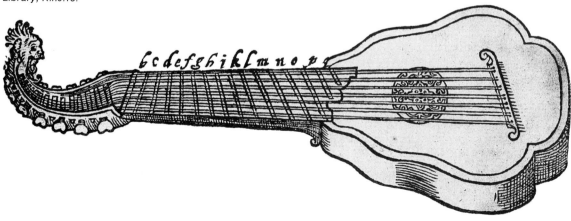

36 Lyre-guitar by F. Roudhloff Mauchand, Paris, early 19th century; Harp-guitar, English, early 19th century; Dital harp by Edward Light, London, *c.* 1816. *London, Royal College of Music.*

c e g c′ e′ g′. In 1783 Christian Claus produced citterns and guitars played by means of a small keyboard, but this turned out to be a passing whim.

Around 1800 there appeared various hybrid types which combined characteristics of the lyre, harp, lute and guitar. Being decorous in appearance and easily portable, they were popular for amateur music-making and for decorating the studios of artists, but in spite of the virtuosity of occasional musicians such as Schubert's friend Johann Michael Vogl, they did not find a place in the permanent musical repertoire.

II

Stringed Instruments
‒Bowed

W hile the plucking of strings fades into the mists of Antiquity, bowing is a comparatively recent invention. Werner Bachmann has suggested that it originated in Central Asia, around the River Oxus, not later than the ninth century AD. This part of the world produced very fine hunting bows, and it may be that one of these was eventually brushed against the strings of a hitherto plucked instrument, thus creating a new sound. The discovery spread in all directions, being well documented soon after 900 in the lands of the Islamic and Byzantine empires, where bowed instruments known respectively as *rabāb* and *lūrā* have been played ever since. (The Moroccan rabāb of today is often narrow in shape, with a right-angled pegbox and two strings, while the modern piriform Greek lyra is wider, with a pegbox extending from the neck in the same plane, and three strings. Both instruments have a vaulted back.) Pictorial sources show that the bow had arrived in Spain and southern Italy in the tenth century, and by the early eleventh it had reached northern Europe.

Bowed instruments of medieval Europe were of many shapes and sizes, and their tuning was not standardized. They can, however, be divided broadly into the types of the rebec, crowd, medieval viol, medieval fiddle and trumpet marine, although generically the word 'fiddle' covers them all. (In this book the word is used in its particular sense,

for the medieval fiddle.) Among these different categories could be found bridges which were either flat or curved; most of the former allowed a melody and drone accompaniment to be sounded together, while the latter enabled each string to be sounded separately. Sometimes the bridge and tailpiece were combined, or else the tailpiece rested on the bridge, which would be nearer to the lower end of the sound board than if it were separate. This would allow a longer sounding length for the strings, thus enabling them to produce a deeper pitch. It must be remembered that covered strings did not exist during the Middle Ages, and that a single low-pitched gut string is sometimes insufficient for melodic use, although it can be played for droning. However, there are many pictures and carvings which show that two strings are very close together, and even attached to one peg. While it would be easy to dismiss this as artistic inaccuracy, Alan Crumpler has experimented with the idea, and has found that when two such strings rub against each other they do not produce a discord, but a single note which is greatly reinforced; this should solve the problem of fiddlers who wish to play melodies in the lower register of their instrument. He has also found that if studs of different heights are fixed to the bridge or its equivalent (as in fig. 37), they can enable the strings to be sounded separately. (The author has discussed the matter of medieval bridges in

37 Rebec with tailpiece studs at different heights, to enable the strings to be played separately. From an English Bible, *c.* 1130. *London, British Library MS Roy. I.C.vii, f.92.*

greater detail in *English Bowed Instruments from Anglo-Saxon to Tudor Times*, pp. 24–6.) The chief unifying factor was the bow, which varied in shape from being very arched to quite straight, and which, from early in its history, was strung with horsehair. It should be added here that there is a great deal of pictorial evidence for the bowing of instruments which were normally plucked, and vice versa, when certain sound effects were required.

The **rebec** family, which had reached England by *c.* 1050, had a vaulted back carved from one piece of wood, and its neck was formed by the gradual tapering of the body. It included both the rabāb and lūrā types, accounting for the Latin names *rubeba* and *lira* which were often used for it during the Middle Ages, as were variants of *fithele*, and possibly of *gigue*. The actual word '*rebec*' appears mainly from *c.* 1300, coinciding with the development of a sickle-shaped pegbox which eventually led to the scroll of the violin. The Dominican friar Jerome of Moravia (*d.* 1304), in his *Tractatus de Musica* written in Paris after 1272, said that the 'rubeba' was tuned to *c* and *g*; here not only the name but also the tuning suggest the rabāb, which has traditionally been tuned in fifths. In general, however, the number of strings varied from one to about five, and sometimes they were tuned in pairs. When, as often happened, there was a flat bridge or its equivalent allowing for drones around a melody, the strings would have been tuned in a mixture of fifths and fourths, as were those of certain fiddles (p. 53). There seem to be no known medieval pictures of consorts of rebecs in different sizes, but they had appeared by the time that Martin Agricola wrote his *Musica Instrumentalis Deudsch*. In the edition of 1545 (it was originally published in a shorter version in 1528), he gave the following tunings: treble *g d′ a′*; alto and tenor *c g d′*; bass *F G d a*. Although he said that these 'kleine Geigen one bünde' generally had no frets, he was only describing the average rebec of his time, and there are in fact a good many pictures of fretted rebecs from the late thirteenth century onwards. In northern Europe the usual playing position was up at the shoulder (even if pointing downwards), but in the South it was often down in the lap, particularly when the instrument

38 Two rebecs of the rabāb type, from an altarpiece of *The Madonna and Child with Saints Francis and James the Great* by Nanni di Jacopo, 1404. *Italy, Private Collection.*

39 Rebec with frets, played with a lute in *The Virgin and Child with Musical Angels, c.* 1500, by the anonymous Flemish artist, the Master of the Morrisson Triptych, *Brussels, Musées Royaux des Beaux-Arts*.

resembled the rabāb.

The sound of the rebec has been described as coarse and as resembling the voice of an old woman (see Mary Remnant, *English Bowed Instruments . . .*, pp. 38–9), but Johannes Tinctoris, in his *De Inventione et Usu Musicae* of *c.* 1487, said that it and the fiddle were his favourite instruments, which 'stir my heart most ardently to the contemplation of heavenly joys'. However, he does admit that they were sometimes used for the 'profane occasions and public festivities' of which there is so much evidence in art and literature, and particularly from the court of Henry VIII, by which time the rebec was beginning to develop into the dancing master's kit (p. 71 ff.).

When the bow arrived in northern Europe it was very soon applied to different forms of lyre, and particularly to that which had a central neck running from the yoke to the sound board (p. 20). The resulting instrument is seen in the visual arts of many parts of Europe during the Romanesque period, but after that time it became restricted to the North, and particularly to Scandinavia and the British Isles, in the latter area becoming known as the **crowde** or **crouthe**. A typical example can be seen in the Seal of Roger Wade the Crowder (British Library, Seal no. lxxxvii), where an almost rectangular instrument with four strings is accompanied by a short and pointed bow (see Mary Remnant, *English Bowed Instruments . . .*, plate 62). Sometimes there were also two lateral drone strings and, as the Welch **crwth**, this type was played as accompaniment to the voice in ceremonies of the Bards. Although it was still being played traditionally in Wales in the twentieth century, known instances of it within living memory are rare, so the following incident is worth recording. When the present writer played a medieval piece on it to a London school *c.* 1961, the Welsh headmaster exclaimed to his pupils afterwards 'How glad I was to see the crwth again – they played it in my home when I was a small boy!'

No medieval tunings for the crwth family are known, but in the eighteenth century both Daines Barrington in *Archaeologia* (1775) and Edward Jones in *Musical and Poetical Relicks of the Welsh Bards* (1794) gave *gg'* / *c'' c' d' d''*, to be followed

40 Two crowds played by angels in feathered costumes such as were worn in dramatic performances. Detail from stained glass windows made by John Prudde in *c.* 1447. *Warwick, St Mary's Church, Beauchamp Chapel.*

41 Crwth by Richard Evans of Llanfihangel Bachellaeth, 1742. *Cardiff, Welsh Folk Museum, St Fagan's Castle.*

soon afterwards by *a a' | e' e'' b' b''* recorded by William Bingley in *North Wales* (1804). (However, J. Marshall Bevil has pointed out that Jones's pitches were relative to each other and not necessarily at a fixed pitch, as he recommends tuning the top string as high as possible without breaking it. Canon Galpin has suggested that Bingley's tuning should be an octave lower.) Each upper pair of strings was to be bowed together, one string in each case droning an accompaniment to the melody, while the two lateral drones (the first two notes listed for each tuning) could be plucked by the left thumb. That the crowder played at least two notes at once during the Middle Ages is evident from the commentary on Psalm 150 by Richard Rolle of Hampole (*c.* 1340), who renders 'in choro' as 'in croude, that is, in pesful felagheship and concord of voicys...'. The Latin word *chorus* was often used for the bowed lyre in England at this time, and is listed in the *Promptorium Parvulorum* by Frater Galfridus, OP (*c.* 1440) as 'Crowde, instrument of musyke. *Chorus.*'

The **medieval viol**, which flourished during the Romanesque and early Gothic periods, answered the need for a large bowed instrument which could produce lower notes than the rebec, although it did itself exist in smaller versions. The performer was usually seated, holding the viol down on his lap and gripping the bow from below. The shape of the instrument varied from being almost oval to like a figure-of-eight, and there was nearly always some indentation of the sides. The pegbox was flat, the strings generally numbered from three to five, and the bow sometimes had a carefully-shaped handle. The author has found no evidence of frets, nor of the instrument being played in consorts of different sizes as were viols of the Renaissance and Baroque times. No special name seems to have been used for this type of instrument, so it must have been covered by the Latin *viella* and *viola*, and the various forms of the word 'fiddle' which appear in different languages of the period. European art shows it most often from the twelfth and thirteenth centuries, but it is traceable back to the tenth century in Spain; by soon after 1300 it had gradually disappeared.

Medieval minstrels often walked as they played,

42 Medieval viol played by David in the St Albans Psalter; English, *c.* 1120–30. *Hildesheim, Church of St Godehard.*

wood. The best kind of fiddle combined these ingredients, some of them having all the strings over the neck (with or without a fingerboard), and others having a lateral drone string. This type can be seen in the Angel Choir of Lincoln Cathedral (fig. 44), which also shows the prevalent flat-topped pegbox. It is almost contemporary with Jerome of Moravia's three tunings for the 'viella', the first of which had just such a string formation: $d/Ggd'd'; dGgd'd'; GGdc'c'$. (Christopher Page, in 'Jerome of Moravia on the *Rubeba* and *Viella*', has suggested that these tunings are only relative, and do not mean that the medieval fiddler played as low as the modern *G*.) Unfortunately he does not give tunings for the many fiddles with three, four and six strings, but the existence of three separate tunings for that with five, does mean

43 Fiddles played by Elders of the Apocalypse in the *Pórtico de la Gloria*, 1188, at *Santiago de Compostela Cathedral.*

for instance in processions and dances, and for this the medieval viol was unsuitable. The answer to the problem came with the instrument which has become known in the particular sense as the **medieval fiddle**, having been called *fedyll, fiedel, fithele, fyþele, viella, vielle, viola, viheula de arco*, etc., **during the Middle Ages. It had already been** depicted in Byzantine manuscripts of the eleventh century, such as the Theodore Psalter of 1066 (British Library MS Add. 19352, f.191), and then came gradually up through Italy, Spain (with superb examples in the *Pórtico de la Gloria* of the Cathedral of Santiago de Compostela (fig. 43) where at least one fiddle has a soundpost) and France, finally arriving in English art, in its fully developed shapes, after 1200. This fiddle, which was generally held in the same positions as the rebec, could be found in numerous shapes and sizes, but its chief characteristics were either (a) a flat back, or (b) a neck which was distinct from the body even if carved from the same piece of

44 Fiddle with five strings, including a lateral drone, in the Angel Choir built before 1280 at *Lincoln Cathedral*.

45 Fiddle with curved bridge, from the Pienza Cope, made in England *c*. 1315–35. *Pienza, Museo della Cattedrale*.

that there was a great deal of choice left to the performer, according to what kind of music he wished to play. Tinctoris, writing in the 1480s, also described a tuning of fifths and unisons for a fiddle ('viola') with five strings, but said that one with three strings was tuned in fifths. He pointed out that at that time the bridge was generally curved, so that the bow could touch one string alone, a necessity for the polyphonic instrumental music of the age. Pictures of fiddles from that time are often shown with frets, such as those in the paintings of Hans Memling. However, contrary to some previous opinions, frets on them can be traced back at least to *c*. 1300, if not before.

The great versatility of the fiddle was indicated by Johannes de Grocheo in his treatise *De Musica* (*c*. 1300), where he said:

thus does the fiddle ['viella'] include within itself all other instruments.... A good artist plays on the fiddle every *cantus* and *cantilena* and every musical form in general.

This implies that the fiddler could play in many different styles and must therefore have known about slurred bowing, a point which for some time was disputed. Grocheo's remark that at feasts it was used for the performance of songs and dances is corroborated by many pictures and references from literature. Tinctoris, besides saying that the fiddle ('viola cum arculo') was used in the recitation of epics, describes

a recent event, the performance of two Flemings, the brothers Charles and Jean Orbus, who are no less learned in letters than skilled in music. At Bruges, I heard Charles take the treble and Jean the tenor in many songs, playing this kind of fiddle so expertly and with such charm that the fiddle has never pleased me so well.

The medieval fiddle continued to be used into the sixteenth century, and two examples were found on Henry VIII's ship the *Mary Rose* (see *English Bowed Instruments*, plates 150, 151), which sank outside Portsmouth in 1545 and was brought to the surface in 1982.

Meanwhile, Renaissance Italy had produced two developments from the fiddle. These were the **lira da braccio** and the viola de braccio, both of which were played at the shoulder or chest. The first represents the culmination of the Lincoln-type fiddle (fig. 44), the chief differences being that (a) the lira da braccio generally had five strings over the fingerboard and *two* lateral drones, tuned, according to the relative pitch of Giovanni Maria Lanfranco (*Scintille di Musica*, Brescia, 1533) at $d\,d'$ / $g\,g'\,d'\,a'\,e''$, and according to Praetorius (1619) at $d\,d'$ / $g\,g'\,d'\,a'\,d''$; (b) the sides were often, but not invariably, more indented; (c) the back and sides of the instrument were now regularly made from separate pieces of wood, a technical advance which is shown in certain pictures of fiddles from the fourteenth century onwards, but was not present in the fiddles found on the *Mary Rose*. The bridge was either slightly curved or completely flat, allowing the performer to play on all the strings or not as he pleased. Singing to one's own accompaniment, with the instrument sounding either above or below the voice, was regarded in Renaissance

46 Fiddle showing overlapping edges and a wedge between the neck and fingerboard; both characteristics were later to be found on early violins. Detail from *The Coronation of the Virgin* by the anonymous German artist, the Master of the Life of Mary (*fl.* 1460–80). *Munich, Alte Pinakothek.*

Italy as being one of the best ways of making music, and among its known performers were not only professional musicians such as Francesco di Viola and Alfonso di Viola, but also the artist Leonardo da Vinci, who was invited to play to Ludovico Sforza at Milan. According to Vasari's *Lives of the Artists*,

Leonardo took with him a lyre [*lira*] that he had made himself, mostly of silver, in the shape of a horse's head (a very strange and novel design) so that the sound should be more sonorous and resonant. Leonardo's performance was therefore superior to that of all the other musicians who had come to Ludovico's court.

47 Lira da braccio and lute; detail from *The Virgin and Saints* by Giambattista Cima da Conegliano (c. 1459–1517/18). *Venice, Galleria dell' Accademia.*

A larger and deeper instrument of the same family, which emerged somewhat later, was the **lira da gamba** or **lirone**. This was played betweeen the knees or on the lap, and could have as many as 14 strings over the fingerboard (with different re-entrant tunings to facilitate the playing of chords) besides two lateral drones. It was particularly cultivated in Venice, Florence and Rome, and is known to have been played in Roman oratorios, such as the *Oratorio di Santa Caterina* by Luigi Rossi (*d.* 1653).

The name **viola da braccio** must have covered that other derivation from the medieval fiddle, one which was almost identical with the violin family but differed from it in perhaps one or two respects (variable in each case), such as the *c*-shaped sound holes in the church of Santa Maria della Consolazione at Ferrara (fig. 49). This type of fiddle often had deep sides, which were clearly indented resulting in pronounced bouts, and *c* or *f*-shaped soundholes. The peg box could be flat or ending in a scroll, and frets were optional. There were about four strings over the fingerboard, and no lateral drones. Pictures show this instrument being played for feasts and dances, and by characters from mythology such as Apollo and Orpheus (who also play the lira da braccio).

However, the term *viola da braccio* (or *da brazzo*) was used in Italy in a general sense to cover most bowed instruments played up at the shoulder or

across the arm (as opposed to the viol family held *a gamba* at the legs, or on the lap), so it was sometimes applied also to the lira da braccio and to members of the violin family, even those which were played on or between the knees.

While these instruments were leading to the appearance of the violin, and indeed overlapping with it, a new **viol** had emerged in Spain, and according to the researches of Ian Woodfield, this happened in the second half of the fifteenth century, in the area of Valencia in the kingdom of Aragon. It was held *a gamba* like its medieval predecessor (which was not its direct ancestor), but it greatly resembled the plucked vihuela de mano of the period, complete with frets. Like that instrument it usually had a flat bridge, so was best suited to chordal or drone accompaniment, whether the melody was played on itself or by a

48 Lira da gamba, played by the *Homer* of Pier Francesco Mola (1612–68). *Dresden, Gemäldegalerie.*

singer or other instrumentalist. By the 1490s it was in Italy (Woodfield suggests that it came by way of the Borgia connection in Rome and Ferrara and the Aragonese kingdom at Naples), and there it went through a transformation which gave it deeper sides and an arched bridge, thus making it suitable for consort playing. At first this type of instrument had no standardization of shape or tuning, but by the time that Sylvestro Ganassi's *Regola Rubertina* was published at Venice in 1542/3, certain sizes were played regularly together. Ganassi gave several tunings for them, including those for six strings which eventually became the most used: discant *d g c′ e′ a′ d″*; alto

49 Bass viol, viola da braccio, viola da mano, rebec and bass viol, played by one of four groups of musical angels from the apse wall paintings of *The Coronation of the Virgin* attributed to either Ludovico Mazzolino or Michele Coltellini, *c.* 1510. *Ferrara, Church of Santa Maria della Consolazione.*

and tenor *G c f a d′ g′;* bass *D G c e a d′.*

He also mentions viols with three or four strings. The viol was characterized by deep sides and a flat back sloping inwards at the upper end, while the belly, which was slightly curved, contained two soundholes, either *c* or *f*-shaped, and sometimes also a carved rose. The neck ended in a sickle-shaped pegbox surmounted by a scroll or carved head in most cases, although some early pictures show the pegbox to be flat or at a right angle.

While there is a good deal of evidence as to the use of viols on the Continent in the late fifteenth century, they apparently did not become established in England until the reign of Henry VIII. The earliest known viol players at his court had Flemish names, such as Matthew, Philip and Peter de Wilder, who arrived in 1515, and in 1517 'Matthew de Welder' was referred to in the royal expense accounts as being a 'player upon the lutes and veoldes'. Later they were joined by other viol players from Germany and Italy. When the King died in 1545 he owned 25 viols 'great and small', and by that time other noble families, such as those of the earls of Rutland and Exeter, also had collections. The earliest known picture of a viol in England seems to be in Holbein's sketch of Sir Thomas More's family at Chelsea in *c.* 1527, where it is shown hanging on the wall.

In the subsequent large painting based to a great extent on the sketch, its position is changed to lying on the sideboard (*English Bowed Instruments*, plates 148, 147 and pp. 74–5). The instrument which had arrived so late in England was then cultivated to such an extent that its makers there, such as John Rose, Henry Jaye and Barak Norman were among the best in Europe. The London lawyer Roger North (*c.* 1651–1734), writing about music in seventeenth-century England, said that a 'chest of viols' (consisting of two trebles, two 'meanes' and two basses) 'seldome wanted in a musicall family'. His reference to the '*Respublica* of Consort' shows how the viols of different sizes were equally important during the Golden Age of polyphony:

The viols bore all an equall share in the consort, and carrying the same aire, there was no reason to choose one part before another.

The consort of viols reached its culmination in the fantasias of Henry Purcell (1680), but it was already giving way to instruments of the violin family. The bass viol, however, stayed in use for some time as a continuo instrument, and was occasionally given a special *obbligato* part such as in 'Komm, süsses Kreuz' from Bach's *St Matthew Passion*. Yet even in the age of consorts the bass viol had been used as a virtuoso instrument, its complexity already being shown by Diego Ortiz in *Tratado de Glosas* (Rome, 1553), and later by Christopher Simpson in *The Division Viol* (London, 1667). Divisions in this case were variations on a ground bass, and to facilitate the

50 A consort of viols playing during the journey of Queen Louise of Lorraine from the Louvre to the Faubourg Saint-Marceau. From an anonymous drawing of 1584. *Paris, Bibliothèque Nationale.*

51 Division viol by Barak Norman, London, 1692. *London, Royal College of Music.*

technical problems involved, the instrument on which they were played was usually slightly smaller than a consort bass. So also was the **lyra viol**, which flourished during the seventeenth century and had many different tunings (sometimes with sympathetic strings) to suit its music, most of which was written in tablature. This instrument, of all the viols, came closest to playing complete polyphony on its own. Among its outstanding performers was the composer John Jenkins, who, according to North,

once was brought to play upon the lyra viol afore King Charles I, as one that performed somewhat extraordinary; and after he had done the King sayd he did wonders upon an inconsiderable instrument.

The double bass viol, known in Italy as the *violone* (the term also used for other large viols and for the double bass of the violin family), was already in use in the sixteenth century but continued to be played long after the smaller members of the family had gone out of fashion. With six strings tuned about a fifth below those of the consort bass, it was played when needed in viol consorts, or as a continuo instrument, eventually merging with the violin family's double bass.

The smallest viol appeared late upon the scene. Known as the *pardessus de viole*, it emerged in France around 1700, and was used mainly by ladies of the French court. It was smaller than the treble viol and tuned a fourth higher, often having only five strings, and its repertoire consisted to a great extent of variations on popular tunes.

When Jenkins played to Charles I he was using an instrument of noble traditions, for the Frenchman Philibert Jambe de Fer, in his *Epitome Musicale* (Lyon, 1556), said that the viol was played by 'gentlemen, merchants and other virtuous people'. The **violin family**, however, had, according to North, 'bin little used in England except by comon fidlers' until the reign of Charles II. That monarch, when he came to the throne in 1660 after spending part of his exile at the French Court, 'set up a band of twenty-four

52 One of the very earliest pictures of a violin, from a wall painting by Garofalo, 1505–08. *Ferrara, Palazzo di Ludovico il Moro, Sala del Tesoro.*

violins to play at his dinners, which disbanded all the old English music at once'. Being brighter in sound than the viols, the violin family was better suited to the new Italian-type music which needed instruments capable of standing out in contrast to others, and yet able to blend when necessary. In appearance the **violin** had, and still has, shallower sides than the viols, its soundboard and back are both slightly curved with overlapping edges, and its soundholes are *f*-shaped. The neck, with its unfretted fingerboard, ends in a pegbox surmounted by a scroll, while the four strings pass over a curved bridge before being attached to a tailpiece at the lower end. The usual tunings of the smaller instruments of this family are now violin – *g d′ a′ e″*; viola – *c g d′ a′*; cello – *C G d a*, but the cello in its earlier days was generally larger than now, and called the **bass violin**, sometimes being tuned to *B♭ F c g*. The intermediate **tenor violin** (fig. 155) was played from the sixteenth century to the eighteenth, and was tuned about half way between the viola and the bass violin. It may

have been the instrument to which Dr Burney referred when, writing about the Bohemian Franz Benda, he said that 'early in his life... he was remembered to play the tenor, in the concerts performed by the singing boys at Dresden'. (It should be remembered, however, that the expression 'tenor violin' had also been applied to the viola, of which some examples were larger than others – see p. 67). In the seventeenth and eighteenth centuries there existed also a **violino piccolo**, tuned higher than the normal violin; its bottom string was sometimes *c′*, but Bach set it at *b♭* in his First Brandenberg Concerto (1721). Leopold Mozart, in his *Treatise on the Fundamental Principles of Violin Playing* of 1756, said that as violinists were now playing in higher positions this smaller violin was no longer needed. Another short-lived instrument of the family was the **viola**

pomposa or **violino pomposo** which had five strings, usually those of the ordinary viola with the addition of the violin *e″*; its repertoire dates mainly from the eighteenth century. *Scordatura*, (the tuning of strings at unusual intervals to faciliate double stopping) has always been a possibility, and was used to great effect in the *Mystery Sonatas* of the German Heinrich von Biber (*c.* 1676).

The first violins were until recently thought to date from the 1520s, but now earlier sources have come to light, among them a painting dated 1505–8 by Garofalo or his assistants at the Palazzo di Ludovico il Moro at Ferrara (fig. 52). In 1535–6 Guadenzio Ferrari painted the cupola of the Santuario at Saronno (not Saronno Cathedral, as it is sometimes described), showing numerous musical angels, one of which plays a violin (this is generally assumed, although the front view of the instrument is not visible) and another, a viola; a further instrument, apparently a small bass or large tenor, is shown with frets (fig. 53). Although the earlier violins are believed to have had three strings, four had become established by 1556 when Jambe de Fer described the instruments and gave the modern tunings for the violin and viola.

One of the earliest known violin makers was Andrea Amati of Cremona, who was born not later than 1511. Two three-string violins made by him in 1542 and 1546 were said to be in existence during the nineteenth century, but both have since disappeared. A violin dated 1564 at the Ashmolean Museum in Oxford and one of 1574 at the Carlisle Museum and Art Gallery (fig. 54) are from a reputed collection of 38 violins, violas and basses which he was commissioned to make for Charles IX of France (a 1574 viola from the same set is also at Oxford). These instruments represent the fully-fledged violin with four strings, which was brought to perfection by his grandson

53 Three different sizes of the violin family, together with a lute, cymbals and hybrid fiddle (back view), painted by Gaudenzio Ferrari in 1535–6. *Saronno, Church of Santa Maria dei Miracoli (Il Santuario).*

54 Violin, made by Andrea Amati of Cremona for Charles IX of France, in 1574. Bequeathed by Miss S. Mounsey Heysham in 1949 to the *Carlisle Museum and Art Gallery*.

Nicola Amati (1596–1684) and the latter's pupil Antonio Stradivari, known as Stradivarius (1644–1737). The Amati violins were characterized by considerable arching of the soundboard, as were those of Jakob Stainer (*c.* 1617–83) of Absam near Innsbruck, for many years the chief violin maker outside Italy. In contrast to this, the town of Brescia, which had long been a centre for expert instrument-making, produced much flatter models, made at first by Gasparo da Salò (Gasparo Bertolotti, 1540–1609) and his pupil Giovanni Paolo Maggini (*c.* 1581–*c.* 1632). Stradivarius, after making his earlier instruments in the style of Amati, finally settled for a smoother shape in his 'classical' model, as exemplified by the celebrated 'Messiah' violin (1716) which is now in the Ashmolean Museum.

In the lifetime of Andrea Amati, instruments of the violin family were used mainly to double voices or other instruments, and were played particularly for dancing, with dance music surviving for them from the *Balet comique de la Royne* of 1581 (p. 207). No solo violin music has come down to us from that period. By the early seventeenth century, however, special pieces were being written with the violin in mind, although they could also be played on other instruments. Some of the works by Giovanni Battista Fontana (*d. c.* 1630) and Biagio Marini (*c.* 1587–1663), for instance, were for 'violin or cornett' and continuo. The pursuit of a violinistic idiom and the development of technique were furthered to a great extent at Modena, Bologna, Venice and Rome, coinciding with the lives of Stradivarius and his contemporary Giuseppe Guarneri 'del Gesù' (1698–1744) of the Guarnerius family.

By the late eighteenth century, conditions of performance had changed so much that the instruments needed to be altered. This was partly due to the need for a stronger and more penetrating sound, particularly when a soloist was playing a concerto in a large hall and had to hold his own against an orchestra. To contribute to this sound, the performance pitch was raised and the strings tightened. The consequent increase in tension demanded the strengthening of the bridge, together with that of the soundpost and bassbar, through which it transmitted vibrations to the back and belly respectively. Other alterations involved the neck and fingerboard. As early as 1715, Vivaldi's 'fingers almost touched the bridge, so there was hardly any room left for the bow', according to the diary of Johann Friedrich Uffenbach. It was necessary, therefore, for the neck and fingerboard to be lengthened. In its existing position the neck was built to continue in the same plane as the belly, and the fingerboard was tilted into a suitable playing position by an intermediary wedge. The wedge was now removed and the fingerboard made to rest directly on the neck, which itself was tilted at an oblique angle. The removal of the wedge enabled the performer to climb more easily into the higher positions than before. These changes were accomplished just in time for the appearance on

55 Portrait of a musician with a bass viol. The viola on the wall is typical of the wide shapes used in Venice. Late 16th century, Venetian. *Oxford, Ashmolean Museum.*

56 Bass violin played in *A Musical Party* by Pieter de Hooch, *c.* 1675. *London, Wellington Museum, Apsley House.*

the scene of the supreme Italian virtuoso Nicolò Paganini (1782–1840). Since that time no great structural changes have taken place in the violin itself, but the addition of the chin rest by Louis Spohr in *c.* 1820 gave the performer a better grip on the instrument, thereby allowing more freedom of movement to the left arm.

Although the violin, viola, tenor and bass violins and the double bass were all in existence during the sixteenth century, the treble violin had for a long time been the most important member of the family, the others being used mainly for supporting roles. The reduction in size of the bass violin was reflected in the instruments made during the long life of Stradivarius. During that time the word **violoncello** emerged, apparently at Bologna, where Giulio Cesare Arresti may have been the first to use it, in his *Sonate* op. 4 (published at Venice in 1665). Domenico Gabrielli (1651–90), also of Bologna, not only composed for the instrument but also became a virtuoso on it, thus paving the way for more refined and difficult music than before, such as the concertos of Vivaldi and the solo sonatas of Bach.

The **viola** had a small tone, due to its shallow

sides and short length in proportion to the depth of its sound, so at first it was given little consideration by composers, apart from its use as a filler in of inner parts. In seventeenth-century France the inner lines of five-part string works were often played by three violas; they were all tuned with *c* as the bottom note, but were of different sizes, each sounding best at a different register. Only from the mid eighteenth century did music for the instrument begin to acquire a real independence, with the flowering of the string quartet. Mozart's *Sinfonia Concertante* for violin and viola, one of the earliest concertos for the latter instrument, called for it to be tuned a semitone higher than usual in order to produce a brighter sound. In spite of Berlioz's *Harold in Italy*, a 'symphony with viola solo' written originally for Paganini in 1834, and the latter's own *Sonata per Gran Viola* written soon

afterwards, the viola's repertoire increased only gradually during the nineteenth century, and there were few good players. Only in the last 60 years has its recognition been consolidated, largely due to the efforts of Paul Hindemith, William Primrose and Lionel Tertis, who, together with the violin maker Arthur Richardson, produced a highly successful larger and more powerful model which was first played publicly in 1939.

The **double bass**, making a harsher sound than the violone of the viol family, was for a time used for less distinguished music, and the first works known to survive for it as a solo instrument

57 Cello, harpsichord and mandora played together in *Frederick, Prince of Wales, and his Sisters*, by Philippe Mercier, 1733. *London, National Portrait Gallery.*

58 Double bass, made in Italy in the 17th century; this extra-large specimen was once owned by Dragonetti. *London, Victoria and Albert Museum.*

are sonatas dating from *c.* 1690 by (or possibly for) Giovannino del Violone. Around 1800, however, the two instruments merged, the general shape of the violone being preserved, but with fewer strings and no frets. Even so, the result did not become standardized like the higher members of its family. Its shape can still resemble a violin or viol, and its strings have varied in number between three and five, although today the most usual number is four, tuned to *E A d g*, and sounding an octave lower.

Just as the altered violin appeared in time for Paganini, so the adapted double bass was ready for the virtuoso Domenico Dragonetti (1763–

1846), whose reputation was such that he could command the same fees as the best singers of his day. Until this time the bow had been held in the viol manner with the palm uppermost, but it was that other great Italian virtuoso, Giovanni Bottesini (1821–89), who introduced the violin way of bowing (with the palm facing downwards) to the double bass.

An extra large instrument with three strings was called an **octobass**, but in 1851 the French violin-maker Jean-Baptiste Vuillaume invented one which was so tall that, although the performer used a normal bow, he could not reach high enough to play on the strings with the fingers of his left hand. Instead his feet pressed a set of pedals which pulled down wires, and these in turn activated mechanical 'fingers' above. This gigantic instrument, which was tuned to *C' G' C*, is now in the museum of the Paris Conservatoire.

Besides the instruments themselves, the strings and bow have also undergone changes. At first gut strings were normal for all the viol and violin families, but as the thickness of the lowest one generally produced an inadequate tone, composers avoided it when they could, particularly in solo music. This problem was resolved by the lowest strings for each instrument being wound round with wire, an invention which may have taken place in Bologna in the 1660s, but was attributed in Jean Rousseau's *Traité de la Viole* (Paris, 1687) to the Sieur de Sainte-Colombe *c.* 1675. The frequent breaking of the violin gut *e″* led to its being made of wire (which had already been used on instruments with sympathetic strings) from early in the twentieth century. Nowadays strings for all modern bowed instruments can be obtained in very varying materials, ranging from nylon to wire covered by aluminium or silver.

The **bow** or **fydylstyk** of the Middle Ages varied from being quite straight to very curved, depending to a great extent on the shape of the instrument's bridge and on the type of music to be played. Its hairs were generally knotted or glued at each end. Many Renaissance pictures show at the heel a knob which might possibly represent some form of screw, but is perhaps more

59 The New Violin Family (its contrabass is 8' long) made by
Carleen Hutchins of Montclair, New Jersey.

60 Baryton by Magnus Feldlen, Vienna, 1647. *London, Royal College of Music.*

likely to have been a covering for an otherwise untidy end. Often the hairs are supported in position by a nut or frog, which could be of one piece with the bowstick, or else detachable so that the hairs could be loosened. During the seventeenth century the tension was sometimes regulated by a series of notches, but by 1700 its smooth and gradual alteration by means of a screw was well established. The Renaissance and Baroque bows were generally convex and with a carefully tapered point which was well suited to the musical style of the time. With the need for a more powerful sound, the bow gradually became longer and concave in shape and swelled out towards the point, this form being perfected *c.* 1785 by François Tourte in France and John Dodd in England, and still in use today. Viola bows are longer than those of the violin, but cello and double bass ones are shorter and heavier, the latter type varying in shape according to whether it is played with the palm of the hand facing up or down. Since 1964 a **New Violin Family** has been developed by Mrs Carleen Hutchins and others of the Catgut Acoustical Society of America. Built in the proportions of the actual violin, and with particular attention to acoustical values, there are eight different sizes, ranging from 'large bass' (bottom string E') to 'treble' (top string e'''). When played together they produce a full and homogenous sound hitherto unknown, and special works have been commissioned for them.

Two instruments of the seventeenth and eighteenth centuries combined characteristics of the viol and violin families. These were the baryton and the viola d'amore, both of which were widely played, not as regular members of consorts and orchestras but in special compositions for which they were scored.

The **baryton** somewhat resembled a bass viol in size and shape, but was distinguished by a row of wire sympathetic strings, arranged in such a way that they could be plucked from behind by the left thumb. Several different tunings were possible. The instrument was described by Mersenne in *Cogitata physico mathematica* (1644), and its earliest surviving example is that by Magnus Feldlen, dated 1647 (fig. 60); it is unusual in having frets. Although some anonymous dances and other pieces for it date from *c.* 1614, its chief extant repertoire was written by Joseph Haydn between 1765 and 1778 for his patron Prince Nicholas Esterhazy, who had bought a baryton by Johann Joseph Stadlmann in 1756. This instrument is now in the National Museum at Budapest.

The **viola d'amore** was played at the shoulder like the violin, and was also normally unfretted. The early ones, such as that described by the diarist John Evelyn on 20 November 1679, had about five metal playing strings, but those which developed from it and were played in the eighteenth century had six or seven gut and covered melody strings, doubled by sympathetic strings of steel below the fingerboard. To allow for elaborate double stopping there were numerous *scordatura* tunings. In his treatise of 1756, Leopold Mozart wrote that the viola d'amore sounded 'especially charming in the stillness of the evening', and described a form of the instrument with 14 sympathetic strings as the 'English violet'. (A related instrument which has survived until today as a folk instrument in Norway is the much decorated Hardanger fiddle.)

Although the viola d'amore was used less after the Baroque period, it never disappeared altogether, being included in a good many nineteenth-century compositions and being called for by Berlioz in his dream orchestra of 465 instrumentalists (see p. 220): 'Forty violas, divided into firsts and seconds, if necessary; at least 10 of the players able to play the viola d'amore'. Twentieth-century composers for it have included Hindemith, and a new form of the instrument has been made by Montagu Cleeve of London.

The smallest bowed instrument, and one of the most interesting on account of the diversity of its construction, is the **kit** or **pochette**. Emerging from the rebec in the sixteenth century, it soon took the shape of a narrow boat, and after 1600 began to resemble viols, then violins, and eventually viole d'amore. This last type, with its sympathetic strings, was known as the *pochette d'amour*. The kit had a long unfretted neck and was tuned about a fourth or fifth above the violin,

61 Viola d'amore by a German maker, 1719. *London, Victoria and Albert Museum.*

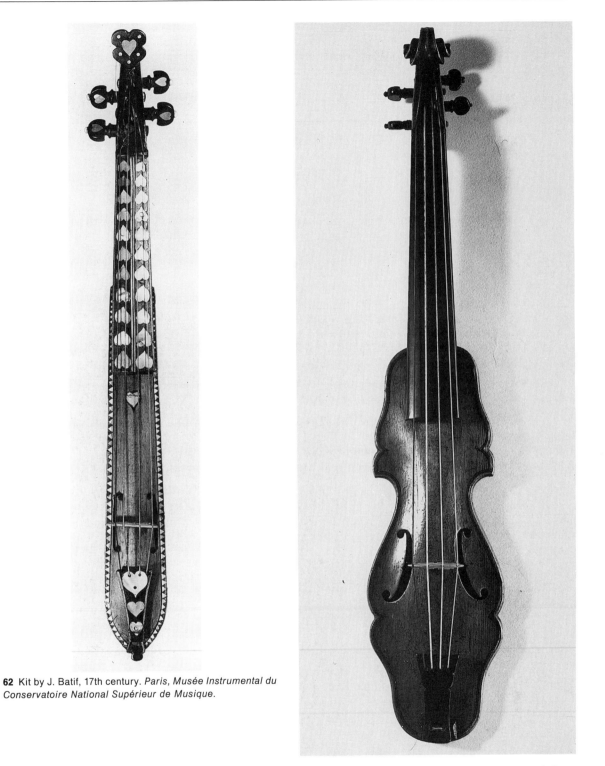

62 Kit by J. Batif, 17th century. *Paris, Musée Instrumental du Conservatoire National Supérieur de Musique.*

63 Kit by a 17th-century Italian maker. *London, Royal College of Music.*

64 Kit by Antonio Stradivari, Cremona, 1717. *Paris, Musée Instrumental du Conservatoire National Supérieur de Musique.*

65 Trumpet marine, in stained glass from the workshop of Peter Hemmel von Andlau, Strasbourg, late 15th century. *Basel, Historisches Museum.*

or even an octave higher when there were only three strings. It was used to a great extent by dancing masters and lasted into the nineteenth century, being used for a gavotte in the opera *Les trois Nicolas* (1859) by Louis Clapisson, who had recently acquired a kit by Stradivarius. This instrument is now in the museum of the Paris Conservatoire, where Clapisson was the first curator (fig. 64).

Unconnected in any great degree to the foregoing instruments was the **arpeggione**, a form of bowed guitar with metal frets, invented by Georg Staufer of Vienna in 1823. Although it was not given lasting recognition, its place in history has been assured by the sonata written for it in the following year by Schubert; nowadays this is normally played on the cello.

Of curious distinction is the **trumpet marine**

66 Trumpet marine by Sébastien Renault, Paris, late 18th century. *London, Royal College of Music.*

(**tromba marina, Trumscheit**). Descended from a plucked form of monochord carved on a Romanesque capital in the abbey church at Vézelay, it was bowed from the fifteenth century onwards, being played up at the shoulder or resting on the ground, and at that time it had from one to four strings. These were touched lightly by the fingers of the left hand, producing the notes of the harmonic series. A 'rattling, clucking sound' (Praetorius) was produced, either by one foot of the bridge being free to vibrate against the soundboard, or by an extra piece of wood suitably placed for that purpose. Praetorius, quoting from the *Dodecachordon* of Glareanus, also says 'The effect is much more pleasant at a distance than otherwise.'

The trumpet marine survived for several hundred years, acquiring a virtuoso in Jean Baptiste Prin (*c.* 1669–after 1742), who wrote a *Traité sur la Trompette Marine* (1742) on the history and construction of the instrument, as well as how to perform on it. From the seventeenth century onwards there are pictures and references, and indeed surviving instruments, which show that the trumpet marine sometimes had sympathetc strings, a device which was to arouse the great curiosity of Samuel Pepys.

In the *London Gazette* of 4–8 February 1675 there appeared the notice:

A Rare Concert for four Trumpets Marine, never heard before in *England*. If any persons desire to come and hear it, they may repair to the Fleece Tavern, near St James's, about two of the clock in the Afternoon every day in the Week (except Sundays). Every concert shall continue one hour and so to begin again; the best places are one shilling, the other [sic] six pence.

This may have been the first public performance of such instruments in England, but Pepys had already written in his Diary about a performance by (presumably) Prin's father on 14 October 1667:

...we went to see a Frenchman...one Monsieur Prin, play on the Trump. Marine, which he doth beyond belief; and the truth is, it doth so far out-do a Trumpet as nothing more, and he doth play anything very true and it is most remarkable; and at first was a mystery to me that I should hear a whole consort of chords together at the end of a pause, but he showed me that it was only when the last notes were fifths or thirds one to another, and then their sound like an Echo did last, so as they seemed to sound all together. The instrument is open at the end I discovered, but he would not let me look into

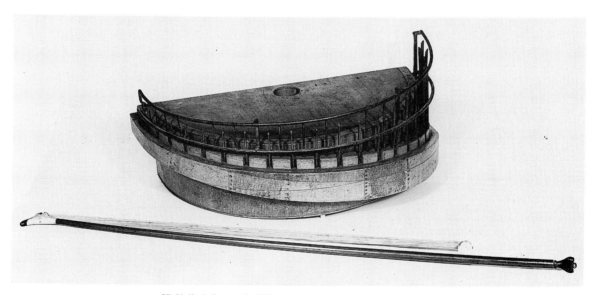

67 Nail violin, early 19th century. *London, Royal College of Music.*

it; but I was mightily pleased with it, and he did take great pains to show me all he could do on it, which was very much – and would make an excellent consort, two or three of them, better than trumpets can ever do because of their want of compass.

Perhaps the enthusiasm of Pepys led to the concerts in the Fleece Tavern nearly eight years later.

(*Postscript.* It seems that an unusual way of playing the trumpet marine was known in England in the fifteenth century. It was held up, but instead of pointing outwards from the chest, or resting on the ground, it pointed backwards over the shoulder. Having said in *English Bowed Instruments* that only two examples had come to light – in the glass of the Beauchamp Chapel at Warwick and on the screen of York Minster – the author soon afterwards found two others, both on a poppyhead at Fordham Church near Cambridge).

One of the strangest bowed instruments was the **nail violin**, which is said to have been invented by the Court violinist Johann Wilde of St Petersburg c. 1740, after noticing that a squeak occurred when he hung up his bow on a nail. He therefore devized a circular-headed soundbox on which were fixed nails of different sounding lengths and thicknesses, and these were duly bowed. The instrument was given sympathetic strings by Senal of Bohemia *c.* 1780, and crept into the realm of art music by being included in special compositions, among them the Quartet for nail violin, two violins and cello by Friedrich Wilhelm Rust, dating from 1787.

III

Stringed Instruments
with Keyboards

The first stringed instrument to receive a keyboard mechanism was the **organistrum**, which was well established in Europe by the middle of the twelfth century. Built in a shape resembling that of a medieval viol, it was laid across the laps of two performers. One of them turned a handle which rotated a rosined wheel, and this itself rubbed against the strings, taking the place of a bow in producing the sound. The other player activated the knobs which determined the pitch of each note, but the way in which they worked probably varied from one instrument to another, depending on their inner construction.

One possibility is that each knob was at the end of a revolvable rod, part of which was shaped to form a bridge-like tangent. When the rod was turned, its tangent came into contact with all the strings at once, causing them to sound together. It would be necessary for the strings to be tuned to consonant intervals such as the fourth, fifth and octave, and the musical result would be parallel organum, with the sounds moving at those intervals apart. It may even be that the instrument is called *organistrum* because it can produce that style of music. Such a mechanism can be seen in Martin Gerbert's *De Cantu et Musica Sacra*, published at the German monastery of St. Blasien in 1774. The drawing shows eight knobs on the left side of the instrument, and these,

together with the open string, are labelled to form an octave from C, including both B natural and B flat. Other letters marked on the soundboard have been interpreted in different ways. The problem here is that Gerbert's drawing was based on a thirteenth-century original which was itself later destroyed, so there is no way of checking the authenticity of the copy.

The other possibility was that the rods were pulled up from above, and that on each there was an inner tangent which touched just one string. That string would be used for the melody, while the others would play drones, and while this method was suitable for much church music, it was also better for the performance of secular tunes. Whatever the tuning, the organistrum was not a chromatic instrument, because when it flourished in the twelfth and early thirteenth centuries instruments with fixed pitches had only one written note outside our key of C major, and that was B flat, which was essential to the soft hexachord starting on F.

The organistrum continued to be used into the thirteenth century, and then gradually gave way to a smaller version which is known today as the **symphony (sinfonia)**, although at the time when they both existed the names were interchangeable. The symphony was carried and played by one person, who turned the handle with one hand and played on the keyboard with

68 Organistrum, played by two Elders of the Apocalypse in the *Pórtico de la Gloria*, completed in 1188, of *Santiago de Compostela Cathedral*.

69 Symphony, played by an angel in a Book of Hours made in Milan for the Sforza family, *c.* 1494. *London, British Library, MS Add. 34294, f.32.*

70 Symphony with chromatic keyboard in the stained glass made in 1501/2 for the north transept of *Great Malvern Priory*.

the other. Instead of being turned or pulled up from the top, each key was now pressed by one finger, either up from below or down from above, according to where the keyboard was placed. The inner tangents played on the melody string (which became known as he *chanterelle*), while the other strings gave open drones. This system allowed for much faster playing than before, and was better suited to secular songs and dances than that of the larger organistrum. In those contexts the symphony was mentioned in many poems, one example being John Lydgate's *Pilgrimage of the Life of Man* (translated from the fourteenth-century French of Guillaume de Deguileville), where Miss Idleness says:

I teche hem ek (lyk ther ententys)
To pleye on sondry Insrumentys,
On Harpe, lut & on gyterne,
And to revelle at taverne,
Wyth al merthe & melodye,
On rebube and on symphonye...

It was, however, gradually losing prestige, as this poem indicates, and although by 1500 it had acquired several new strings and sometimes a chromatic keyboard (fig. 70), it became associated chiefly with wandering minstrels and with folk music.

In the eighteenth century, when the French nobility created for themselves a genteel rusticity, the existing **vielle à roue**, as it was called, returned to court. New ones were built, often of a magnificence unknown to the peasantry, while others were made from converted lutes and guitars. A frequent tuning arrangement consisted of 2 melody strings (*chanterelles*) tuned to g' (with a compass of two octaves), plus 4 drone strings, i.e. *trompette* (copper) tuned to c' or d'; *mouche* (gut) tuned to g; 2 *bourdons* (wire-covered) tuned to G and c or G and d; and certain instruments were given sympathetic strings. In England the name of the instrument was **hurdy-gurdy**. Several hybrid types have appeared from time to time, one form using a bow instead of a wheel, as can still be seen in the Swedish *nyckelharpa*, while another version had the wheel but no keys, with the strings touched directly by the performer's fingers. In the eighteenth century the addition of pipes resulted in the **organ hurdy-gurdy or lira organizzata**, an instrument played by King Ferdinand IV of Naples for whom Haydn wrote five concertos. Today the hurdy-gurdy is a respected folk instrument in several countries, notably Hungary, the North of Spain, and the central part of France.

The next stringed keyboard instrument to appear seems to have been the **exchiquier** or **chekker**, which was already known in England in 1360, when Edward III gave one to John II of France; Guillaume de Machaut, in his poem *La Prise d'Alexandrie* (c. 1367) emphasizes the

71 Hurdy-gurdy or *viella-à-roue*, by an anonymous French maker of the 18th century. *Paris, Musée instrumental du Conservatoire National Supérieur de Musique.*

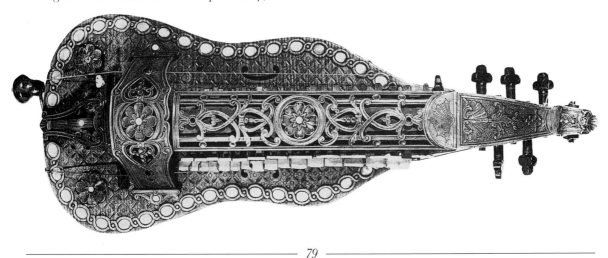

72 Clavichord, played by a mid 15th-century roof angel at *Loughborough, Church of All Saints.*

Edwin Ripin (*Galpin Society Journal*, xxviii, pp. 11–25) has argued that the 'chekker' was a clavichord, and Christopher Page (*Early Music*, VII/4, pp. 482–9) has suggested that the name was not restricted to any one kind of instrument. Unfortunately no solution has yet been forthcoming from the visual arts of the fourteenth century.

The **clavichord** was a rectangular instrument with its strings running parallel to the keyboard. When a key was depressed, it levered up a brass tangent which struck a pair of strings from below and remained there until the performer's finger left the key. Thus the sound was sustained, although it was very quiet, due to the short distance which the tangent could travel; a vibrato (*Bebung*) however, could be obtained for expressive purposes.

The strings of the clavichord sounded only between the tangents and a bridge at the right-hand end of the instrument, as their other sections were dampened by felt at the left-hand end. Just as the pitch of the monochord could be adjusted by a movable bridge, so on the clavichord (which is really a collection of monochords) it was dependent on the placing of tangents. The early clavichords were 'fretted', having more keys than strings. Most strings were therefore available to be struck by two or more tangents, so care was taken to ensure that they produced notes which were not normally sounded together. At first all the strings were of equal length and tuned to the same note, with the tangents placed so as to produce about one diatonic octave. By about 1440, however, when Henricus Arnault of Zwolle wrote a treatise on the building of certain instruments (Paris, Bibliothèque Nationale MS Lat. 7295), the range had reached three chromatic octaves (B–b''), all obtainable from nine pairs of strings. The next step was to increase the number of strings, and to make them in different lengths and pitches, an advance which had taken place before 1500 and is well represented in the excellent intarsia representation of a chromatic clavichord in the ducal palace at Urbino. The latest important development came in the eighteenth century with the appearance of unfretted cla-

English connection by his reference to 'l'eschaquier d'Engletere'. In a letter of 1387 John I of Aragon refers to 'an instrument called *exaquier*', and in another of 1388 he mentions 'an instrument seeming like organs which sounds with strings'. Although these may not be identical the possibility cannot entirely be ruled out, especially as in each case the king expressed concern lest the instrument should be damaged in a journey, implying that it was large and fragile. The description of the second instrument suggests a clavicytherium, whether or not it was the 'exaquier'.

vichords, in which each key had its own pair of strings, and the range had reached five octaves. To suit the greater number of strings, the instruments were made larger and stronger than before, a notable example being that made for C.P.E. Bach by Gottfried Silbermann. As the German composer Johann Friedrich Reichardt wrote in *Briefe eines aufmerksamen Reisenden* (Frankfurt, 1774),

Herr E. Bach plays not only a very slow and songlike Adagio with the most touching expression...he is also able to sustain in this slow *tempo* a tone of six quavers duration with all degrees of power and softness; and this he can do in the bass as well as the treble. But he can accomplish it probably only on his precious Silbermann Clavichord, for which he has also specially written some Sonatas, in which he has introduced such long sustained tones. The same remark applies to the

extraordinary power with which he renders some passages. Indeed it is the strongest *fortissimo*; and any other clavichords but Silbermann's would be knocked to pieces by it. And then again we have the most delicate *pianissimo* which it would be impossible to produce on any other clavichord.

A special type of clavichord, much used by organists, was that with pedals and two manuals. As organ practice necessitated being in a church at times when it was unheated, and paying a servant to work the bellows, the pedal clavichord (and pedal harpsichord, and later the pedal pianoforte) provided the answer. Organ music could be played on it in the warmth of a private

73 *Double Portrait at a Clavichord by Jan Barentsz Muyckens, 1648. The Hague, Gemeentemuseum.*

74 Pedal clavichord by Johann Gerstenberg, 1760. *Leipzig, Musikinstrumenten-Museum in der Karl-Marx-Universität.*

house, and needed the help of no other person. J.S. Bach's set of six Trio Sonatas for organ could be played equally well on one of these instruments.

Pictures of the **harpsichord** appear from early in the fifteenth century, when it was known by variants of the Latin name *clavicymbalum*, a word which has been traced back to 1397 in Padua. It was virtually a keyed psaltery, and three different plucking mechanisms, as well as one for striking the strings, were described for it by Arnault. The action which became traditional, however, was as follows. When a key was pressed down its inner end would push up a wooden frame known as a 'jack', which contained a pivoted wooden tongue on which was a quill plectrum; when the jack rose up the quill plucked

the string, but avoided doing so on descent through the swinging back of the tongue. In 1698 Roger North emphasized the care needed in selecting quills for such instruments, when he wrote a letter 'concerning my cosen's espinette...if ever any new pens are put in, let'em not be stiff and hard, which spoyls all'.

The earliest known shape of the harpsichord (as in fig. 75) continued to be used throughout its history, but there also existed smaller and simpler keyboard instruments which were used mainly for domestic purposes, and because the harpsichord lasted longer than either of them, they will be treated first. The terminology of these instruments can be confusing, as even in their own days the words 'virginal' and 'spinet' were interchangeable. In comparatively recent years 'virginal' applied to an outwardly rectangular instrument and 'spinet' to a polygonal one, even if the interior was almost identical. Now, however,

75 Harpsichord in the stained glass made by John Prudde *c.1447 for Warwick, St Mary's Church, Beauchamp Chapel.*

the words are given for convenience to two distinct types of instrument, both of which normally have just one 8′ string for each note, although some very small examples exist at 4′ or 2′ pitch.

The **virginal** or **virginals** could be outwardly rectangular or polygonal, but the interior was characterized by the plane of the strings being parallel to the keyboard. In the fifteenth century Paulus Paulirinus said of the 'Virginale':

The virginal has the shape of a clavichord, and metal strings which produce the sonority of a harpsichord. It has thirty-two courses of strings voiced by striking the fingers on projecting keys, sounding sweetly in both whole-tones and semi-tones. It is called a virginal because, like a virgin, it soothes with a sweet and gentle voice.

The rectangular shape was used most in northern Europe, particularly in England and the Low Countries during the period of Byrd, Bull and Sweelinck, at which time it rivalled the harpsichord in importance. Normally there was no way of changing the tone quality, but two exceptions are worthy of note. The first was the double virginal, in which a smaller instrument, tuned at a higher pitch, was placed above one of normal size, so that both could be coupled together or each played separately. This dates from the late sixteenth century onwards and was desribed by Praetorius (see below), but it was made chiefly in Flanders. So too was the second device, which appeared on certain examples of the *muselar*, a late seventeenth-century virginal with its keyboard built to the right of centre on the long side of the instrument. The innovation here was a special stop called the 'arpichordum', which created a buzzing effect for the deeper notes in contrast to the more singing tone of the higher register.

In these northern virginals the mechanism was usually built into the case (in some early examples this itself was polygonal), from which it was not removed. In Italy, however, it had a light wooden frame, often polygonal in shape, which was sometimes kept in a rectangular case but could be taken out of it at will.

The description by Praetorius gives the names

76 Polygonal virginals in an intarsia door by Giovanni Barile da Siena, 1513–21. *Rome, Vatican, Stanza della Segnatura*.

of the virginal in different countries, showing how easily ambiguities could arise. Under the title 'Spinetta', he says:

The *Spinetta* (Italian, *Spinetto*) is a small rectangular *Instrument*, tuned an octave or a 5th above the usual pitch. One of these is often built into the larger *Instrument*. In Italy, both the large rectangular and the small ones are called *Spinetta*, without distinction. All such *Instruments*, large or small, are in England called *Virginall*; in France, the name is *Espinette*; in the Netherlands, *Clavicymbel*, or *Virginall*; in Germany, *Instrument*, in the narrow sense of the word.

It may have been through experiments with the polygonal forms that there appeared the

instrument now known as the 'bent-side' **spinet**, in which the wrest-plank was parallel to the keyboard, and the strings moved away from it at an oblique angle from left to right. Its invention has been attributed to Girolamo Zenti, an Italian who made instruments for several royal courts, including that of Charles II of England, and his earliest known example is dated 1637. Like the virginal, which it eventually superseded, the spinet took up less space than the harpsichord, and, having one set of strings and less wood, was also cheaper to make.

The earliest **harpsichords** also had just one 8′ string to a note, as did the upright version called the **clavicytherium**, of which the oldest example is kept at the Royal College of Music (fig. 79). Double stringing on harpsichords was, however, already known to Arnault of Zwolle, and this necessitated a second row of jacks, sometimes controlled by a stop lever to render it playable or silent. The second string was also at 8′ pitch, although by 1600 it had been replaced by a 4′ stop on certain instruments. Much use was made of the bass 'short octave', a device which saved the instrument in size and cost. As the lowest chromatic notes were seldom needed, their keys were used to supplement the diatonic scale. A typical short octave, which can be seen in the harpsichord made by Jerome of Bologna in Rome in 1521 (now in the Victoria and Albert Museum), which renders the apparent notes *E F♯ G♯* to sound as *C D E*.

Such was the harpsichord during the first three quarters of the sixteenth century, when, judging by surviving instruments, the chief makers were Italian. Then there became established in Antwerp the dynasty of Hans Ruckers (*c.* 1550–*c.* 1620), whose virginals and harpsichords, and those of his descendents, became the most prized in Europe. Their influence passed to France, where Nicolas Blanchet started a harpsichord-making business at Paris in 1686. This remained in the family when, in 1766, the widow of François Etienne Blanchet II married his apprentice Pascal Taskin. Few good harpsichords from Germany have survived until those of the eighteenth century, notably by the families of Hass, Silbermann

77 Virginals by Charles Rewallin, Exeter, 1675. *Taunton Castle Museum.*

and Stein. England imported many from abroad, although examples by John and Charles Haward of London point to good native work in time for the compositions of Purcell. Hermann Tabel, who had studied in Antwerp, came to London *c.* 1700 and later taught some of the best makers in England. These included Jacob Kirkman of Germany and Burkat Shudi (Tschudi) of Switzerland, who, as well as Shudi's Scottish son-in-law John Broadwood, produced excellent harpsichords in their latest stages of development.

The growth of the harpsichord reflects in particular its place in the history of music. The single-manual instruments of the sixteenth century were quite adequate for the solo dances and abstract pieces of the time. As a continuo instrument, however, when the harpsichord was played more often with other instruments and with singers, a choice of pitch was sometimes needed. New instruments, the earliest ones dating from before 1600, were therefore built with two manuals set at different pitches to ease transposition, but inevitably this led to the idea that a second manual could be used to greater effect if it gave a contrasting sound to the first. From the mid-seventeenth century, therefore, the construc-

78 Anonymous English spinet, dated 1708. *London, Royal College of Music.*

79 Clavicytherium, probably made in South Germany, *c*. 1490. This is thought to be the oldest surviving stringed keyboard instrument. *London, Royal College of Music.*

tion was altered so that both manuals were tuned to the same pitch, and their respective stops could be sounded separately or coupled together for greater volume. An extra set of strings was often added to the existing two, resulting in an instrument where the upper manual controlled one 8′ stop, and the lower manual one at 8′ and one at 4′. This process of changing an existing instrument, including the extension of its compass to five octaves (often from *F′*), was largely carried out by French makers, who called it *ravalement*. It made possible such compositions as Bach's Italian Concerto, which could not be played effectively on a contemporary single-manual harpsichord because it requires one hand to be playing *forte* while the other is *piano*.

The instrument with two stops at 8′ and one at 4′ was the basic requirement of the eighteenth century. Other stops, however, were frequently added at this time to give greater variety to the sound, the rarest examples being registers at 2′ and 16′. Most usual were the harp stop, which moved pads of buff leather up to the strings to create a pizzicato effect, and the lute stop, which, by having its jacks near to the nut of the instrument, produced a sound not unlike that of the lute. Both of these stops had existed in the seventeenth century, and Thomas Mace, in *Musick's Monument* (1676), said that he had a harpsichord by John Haward which contained pedals for changing registers. Surprisingly, this was not generally adopted, and it was not until *c.* 1765 that the machine stop, another English invention, enabled the performer to change pre-arranged stops with a pedal for the left foot, so that both hands could go on playing. Pascal Taskin invented a similar device controlled by knee levers. He also used plectra of buff leather to give contrast to those of quill. Another difference to the usual timbres was produced by Johann Christoph Fleischer's **Lautenclavecin** of 1718, in which the strings of its two registers were of gut. Fleischer also made a **Theorbenflügel** with two registers of gut and one of metal.

With the appearance of the pianoforte, in which *crescendi* and *diminuendi* were no problem, efforts were made to make the harpsichord more

80 Harpsichord by Jan Ruckers of Antwerp, 1638. Its two manuals are pitched a fourth apart for transposing purposes. *Edinburgh, The Russell Collection of Harpsichords and Clavichords, St Cecilia's Hall.*

expressive. The chief result was the swell. Already known on the organ, it appeared in the 1760s as the Nag's Head Swell, which involved part of the lid being raised by means of a pedal for the right foot. The Venetian Swell, patented by Shudi in 1769, also used such a pedal, which opened a row of shutters placed above the strings. It is significant that the machine stop and the swell were not present in the harpsichords of Bach, Handel and Domenico Scarlatti, and that these masters, while having at their disposal two manuals and several stops, could effect no crescendi (save by playing progressively more notes at once), and had to change their registration by hand.

The harpsichord disappeared from music soon

after 1800, but has been revived in the twentieth century. Some of these new instruments (particularly the most recent ones) are based as faithfully as possible on those of the past, while others have purposely been brought 'up to date'. Modern developments include regular 2′ and 16′ registers, a pedal to change each stop, and greater use of plectra of buff leather. Many instruments are made of more durable materials than before, to cope with travelling conditions and extreme changes of temperature resulting from concert tours.

Before considering the history of the pianoforte itself, we should note two instruments which foreshadowed it in their power of expression. One was the huge dulcimer made by Pantaleon Hebenstreit and known as the **Pantaleone**, which is described on page 174. The other was the **Geigenwerk**, invented *c.* 1575 by Hans Hayden of Nuremberg, who published a booklet about it in 1610; much of this is quoted by Praetorius. Of a similar shape to the harpsichord, it contained

81 Harpsichord by John Broadwood, London, 1793. This represents the latest form of the instrument before it gave way to the piano, having pedals for machine stop and swell. *Edinburgh, The Russell Collection of Harpsichords and Clavichords, St Cecilia's Hall.*

Nürmbergiſch Geigenwerck.

beneath its strings five or six rosined wheels which were set in motion by means of a pedal or bellows. According to Praetorius, 'when a key is depressed, the appropriate string moves on to one of the revolving wheels, and produces a sound such as would be given if it were actually bowed'. Varied dynamics could be produced from it, and, according to Hayden, it could be made to sound, among other things, like violins, a band of trumpets, a lute, a hurdy-gurdy, a shawm or bagpipes.... Some examples had kettledrums attached, and these were worked by their own stop.

In view of these and other developments, harpsichord makers in many parts of Europe were trying to make their instruments more expressive, and in the first two decades after 1700 various solutions were put forward involving the use of hammers instead of plectra. In 1708 the Frenchman Cuisinié made an instrument in

82 The Geigenwerk invented by Hans Hayden of Nuremberg. Praetorius, *Theatrum Instrumentorum*, Wolfenbuttel, 1620, plate III.

83 The oldest surviving piano, by Bartolomeo Cristofori, Florence, 1720. *New York, Metropolitan Museum of Art, Crosby Brown Collection.*

which the strings were pressed down by hammers onto a revolving bow, and this may have influenced the hammer action in the **clavecin à maillets** produced by Jean Marius in 1716. In 1717 Christoph Gottlieb Schröter of Dresden, who knew Hebenstreit and the Pantaleone, devised a mechanism in which the strings could be struck from above or below. In fact all these attempts had long been foreshadowed by the fifteenth-century **dulce melos** in which, according to Arnault of Zwolle, the jacks were surmounted by pieces of lead instead of plectra, and the strings were therefore struck instead of plucked. Unfortunately the dulce melos did not survive.

It now seems certain that the **pianoforte** (also called **fortepiano** in its early days, and henceforth in this book 'piano') was invented by Bartolomeo Cristofori, Keeper of Musical Instruments to Prince Ferdinand dei Medici at Florence. According to the diary of Francesco Mannucci for February 1711, Cristofori was already working on it in 1698, and an inventory of the Prince's instruments in 1700 included:

an *arpicembalo* of Bartolomeo Cristofori, a new invention, which plays *piano* and *forte* ... with some dampers of red cloth touching the strings and some hammers which make the *piano* and *forte*.

Also in 1711, the Marchese Scipione Maffei published an article in the *Giornale dei Letterati d'Italia* about Cristofori's piano which he had seen two years earlier, thus giving rise to the long-standing misconception that it was actually invented in 1709.

The *gravicembalo col piano e forte*, as it was also known, was virtually a harpsichord but with hammers instead of plectra, and at first it was equipped with 'single action'. When a key was depressed, it pushed up an intermediate lever on which was pivoted a hopper (escapement). This in turn hit the hammer which hit the string, and at the same time a damper was moved from the string, leaving it free to vibrate. (The hammer butt then rested on the edge of the pivoted hopper a short distance away, and its shank was supported by crossed silken threads.) When the

key was released, the damper, hammer and hopper returned to their original positions. After further experimentation Cristofori produced a 'double action', which survives in his piano of 1726, now in the Musical Instrument Museum of the Karl Marx University, Leipzig. On this the hopper was hinged to the key itself, with the intermediate lever between it and the hammer. When the hammer had struck the string, it fell back to a check which held it in position until the key was released. This mechanism had several advantages over the single action. Firstly the hammer had a greater chance of hitting the right pair of strings than before, due to having a shorter upward journey. Secondly, for the same reason, there was greater control over the quality of tone produced, particularly in soft passages. Thirdly, the hammer would not bounce back and accidentally hit the string again. Cristofori also made an *una corda* device, which, controlled by hand, shifted the mechanism so that only one string at a time was played upon by each hammer, thereby producing a softer sound. In 1732 there appeared in Florence the first known music to be composed especially for the piano, the *Sonate da cimbalo di piano e forte* by Lodovico Giustini of Pistoia, and dedicated to Prince Antonio of Portugal, a pupil of Domenico Scarlatti.

The first important maker of pianos in Germany was Gottfried Silbermann of Saxony, whose action was like that of Cristofori. In 1736 he showed one of his pianos to J.S. Bach for an opinion, but Bach observed that the treble was too weak. Eleven years later, however, he gave his approval to a more balanced design, although still preferring to play on the older keyboard instruments. Royal patronage came from Frederick II of Prussia (later the Emperor Frederick the Great), who bought several Silbermann pianos to install in his palaces. These included handstops, not only for the *una corda* mechanism, but also one for lifting the dampers off the strings, allowing them to sound more freely, as in the dulcimer.

The next landmark in the development of the mechanism was the 'German' or 'Viennese' action, attributed to Johann Andreas Stein of Augsburg, *c.* 1770. Here the hammer was connected to the key itself, while the escapement was on a separate frame. The resulting tone was more even than that of the Silbermann pianos, and needed a lighter touch. It was exactly right for the music of Mozart, who praised Stein's instruments in a letter written to his father on 17–18 October 1777, adding:

He himself [Stein] told me that when he has finished making one of these claviers, he sits down to it and tries all kinds of passages, runs and jumps, and he polishes and works away at it until it can do anything. For he labours solely in the interests of music and not for his own profit; otherwise he would soon finish his work.

Meanwhile a small rectangular instrument, known as the **square piano**, was designed *c.* 1740 for those people who would previously have had a spinet rather than a harpsichord. (The earliest one known to exist was made by Johan Söcher of Swabia in 1742, and is now in the Germanisches Nationalmuseum at Nuremberg.) Its greatest period of popularity seems to have been after Johannes Zumpe, a former pupil of Silbermann, settled in London *c.* 1760 to work with Shudi. His instruments were small and economical (fig. 84), and, unlike his former master, Zumpe preferred to use single action. According to Burney, writing in Rees's *Cyclopaedia*, 'he could not make them fast enough to gratify the craving of the public'. The first public solo piano recital in England was given by Johann Christian Bach on a Zumpe square piano in 1768, although the piano had been used in a concert the previous year to accompany a singer. Zumpe did not, however, bring the first piano to England, because, according to Burney in the afore-mentioned source, a certain Samuel Crisp bought one *c.* 1752 which had been made for him in Rome by an English priest, Fr Wood. The adaptability of square pianos can be seen from an anecdote, recounted in the reminiscences of the singer

84 Square piano by Johannes Zumpe, London, 1767. *London, Victoria and Albert Museum.*

Michael Kelly, about Richard Brinsley Sheridan coming to dinner to discuss plans for songs and choruses in drama:

85 Square piano by Clementi & Co., London, *c.* 1825. *London, Royal College of Music.*

After the cloth was removed, he proposed business. I had pen, ink, music-paper and a small piano-forte (which the Duke of Queensberry had given me and which he had been accustomed to take with him in his carriage when he travelled) put upon the table with our wine.

Double action for the English square piano was patented by the German-born John Geib in 1786.

While Silbermann's pupil Zumpe was largely responsible for the success of the square piano in England, another of his disciples who had gone to London, the Dutchman Americus Backers, had a considerable influence on the development of the grand piano. Together with the Englishman Robert Stodart and the Scot John Broadwood, he invented between 1772 and 1776 the 'English grand action' which was based to a great extent on that of Cristofori, and had better control than before on the descent of the hammers. The earliest use of this action seems to have been in a combined harpsichord and piano made by Stodart in 1777, when it was patented. Broadwood (who had

arrived in London in 1761 to work with Shudi, and later married his daughter Barbara) used the 'English grand action' in his own grand pianos, of which the first is dated 1781. By this time the *una corda* and sustaining effects were no longer worked by hand, and therefore did not impede performance. In pianos by Stein, Taskin and others, these devices took the form of knee levers, while instruments by Backers and Broadwood had pedals (still used today) adapted from those of the machine stop and swell of the later harpsichords. The left pedal made the music softer by moving a soft pad up to the strings, while the right one raised the dampers to sustain the sounds.

As the earliest pianos were made to the proportions of the harpsichord, they were inadequate for the tension produced by the hammer mechanism. The wooden frame therefore had to be strengthened, and by the late eighteenth century onwards it was increasingly supported by metal. Broadwood's grand pianos were among the first to be made larger and heavier than

86 Grand piano by Pascal-Joseph I Taskin, Paris, 1788; its sustaining and *una corda* effects are obtained by means of knee levers below the keyboard. *Paris, Musée Instrumental du Conservatoire National Supérieur de Musique.*

before, being extended to six octaves. They were well suited to the dramatic music of Beethoven, whose powerful playing often broke the strings of delicate instruments, and in 1818 the composer gladly accepted a piano from the firm which by then was known as John Broadwood and Sons. The first completely iron frame was made for a square piano by Alpheus Babcock of Boston, Massachussetts, in 1825. Not until 1851 did the complete iron frame appear in a Broadwood grand (built for the Great Exhibition at Crystal Palace), and four years later in one by Steinway and Sons of New York. (Heinrich Steinweg had moved from Germany to America in 1848 and had altered his name to Steinway.) By 1859 Steinway had adapted to the grand piano the technique of overstringing (apparently invented in 1833 by Bridgeland and Jardine of New York), in which the strings are not all in the same plane as before, but are arranged in two parallel rows. This not only saved the space required by the strings, but also balanced the tension.

Two important events occurred towards the end of Beethoven's lifetime. The first was the 'double escapement action' invented by Sébastien Erard in 1821. By this means the hammer did not need to fall back to its base before the note could be played again; as long as the key was depressed the hammer remained poised near the string, and was enabled by the mechanism to strike it again more rapidly than had hitherto been possible. The other event was the introduction, by Henri Pape of Paris in 1826, of felt hammers to replace the leather ones which had so often been used before.

Already in the eighteenth century certain grand pianos had been made in an upright position, with their strings rising upwards from the level of the keyboard, as in the old clavicytherium. In 1798 this idea was applied to the square piano by William Southwell of Dublin, who set its own soundboard in a vertical position. In 1800 the Englishman John Isaac Hawkins, working in Philadelphia, and the German Matthias Müller of Vienna separately invented pianos in which the strings were perpendicular to the ground, and nearly reached it. Following these came William

87 Upright piano by Collard & Collard, London, *c.* 1865. *London, Victoria and Albert Museum.*

Southwell's *Cabinet Piano* (1807), and in 1811 Robert Wornum of London produced his *Cottage Piano*. This set the basic pattern for the traditional **upright pianos** which finally superseded the square ones. These later grew larger, but a popular small model appeared in the 1930s in the form of Percy Brasted's Minipiano, based on a miniature instrument by Lundholm of Stockholm. From time to time the piano has been furnished with stops to give different effects, one of the favourites being the sound of 'Turkish' percussion instruments. The player piano, in which music is produced by means of paper rolls, is described in Chapter IX among the mechanical instruments.

Pianos of today have been considerably strengthened since those of the mid-nineteenth century, one of the most recent developments being Alfred Knight's incorporation of worthy plastic materials into the mechanism. The strings,

88 Grand piano by Steinway and Sons, New York and Hamburg, 1963, played by Frank Merrick. *London, Royal College of Music.*

which were originally in pairs and later sometimes triple, are now single and very thick in the bass, double in the middle and triple for the thin strings of the upper register. Most pianos have a compass of seven octaves from A'' to a'''', while some extend to c'''''. A third pedal, invented by C. Montal in 1862 to sustain low chords below freely-moving upper parts, is used today in Steinway pianos, but has not been universally adopted. The third quarter of the twentieth century has produced methods of playing inside the piano (see page 183), thus opening up a completely new range of sounds undreamt of by Bartolomeo Cristofori.

IV

Organs

During the Hellenistic period one of the chief centres of scientific discovery was Alexandria, and it is believed to have been there that the organ was invented, in the middle of the third century BC, by the engineer Ktesibios.

Using the syrinx as his model for arranging the pipes, Ktesibios devised the **hydraulis**, which was described in detail by Hero of Alexandria in the first century AD. Air was pumped by one man into a perforated vessel (*pnigeus*) standing in a cistern of water, and from the pnigeus it was further directed into the windchest below the pipes, with pressure from the water maintaining its steadiness. The pitch was determined by any key which, when pressed, set in motion a slider between the pipes and the windchest. When a hole in the slider came into contact with the lower end of the pipe, the air from below was released to cause a sound. The Roman Vitruvius, writing at about the same time as Hero, described a more advanced hydraulis which had two pumps working alternately and at least four ranks of flue or reed pipes which could be selected as required. The number of ranks determined the number of holes in each slider.

From the beginning, when it was played by Thaïs, the wife of Ktesibios, the hydraulis attracted considerable attention, and in 90 BC it was one of the instruments used in a musical festival at Delphi, in honour of Apollo. Evidence of it in Rome dates from the first century AD, when one of its outstanding performers was the Emperor Nero, who may himself have been responsible for its importation from Greece.

The hydraulis was a large instrument, but by the second century AD there had emerged a smaller organ into which air was pumped by bellows. It had no water to compress the air, so its pressure was at first unsteady, until an air reservoir (possibly of leather) was added. Such a **pneumatic organ** (dated AD 228) was excavated in 1931 at the Roman settlement of Aquincum near Budapest, but its perishable parts had been destroyed in a fire. Enough remained, however, to permit a partial reconstruction, showing that the instrument had four ranks of 13 flue pipes made of bronze. Three of the ranks were 'stopped' at the top, thus producing lower notes than if they were open. According to a remark by Bishop Theodoret of Cyrrhus (387–450) (quoted by Perrot, p. 63) it seems that the bellows of a pneumatic organ may sometimes have been worked by feet, although not necessarily those of the performer.

After the Barbarian invasions and the recession of the greater Roman Empire in the fifth century the organ was forgotten in most of Europe, but it remained in the Eastern Empire centred at Constantinople (Byzantium), where it was particularly associated with imperial entrances and exits even though it was not by custom played in church. However, during this period of uncertainty in the West, certain writers mentioned the organ, although there is no proof that they actually had them. St Aldhelm of Malmesbury (639–709), for instance, in his *De Virginitate*, says 'just as organs are made to breathe with the air from bellows' and 'Let him listen to the mighty organs with their thousand breaths', implying that at least he knew about the instrument.

Our next definite knowledge of organs in the West dates from 757, when, as part of a diplomatic gesture, the Byzantine Emperor Constantine Copronymus sent one to King Pepin the Short of the Franks, and this was hailed by chroniclers as being hitherto unknown in France. After 826, when the Venetian priest Georgius built an organ for Louis the Pious at Aix-la-Chapelle, the instrument gradually spread through Europe. Only from the tenth century, however, is there much evidence of its use in church, at first just for important feast-days and special celebrations. Among many known organs of this period was one given by St Dunstan (*c*. 909–88) to the abbey at Malmesbury, and on or by it there was a bronze plaque saying that 'These organs [were made] by Bishop Dunstan in honour of St Aldhelm'. (The plural 'organs' is often used, even when there is only one instrument.) The abbey of Fleury (St Benoît-sur-Loire) acquired one *c*. 1077, and Canterbury Cathedral is known to have had one in the north aisle of the nave at the time of a fire in 1114. That at St Peter's, Winchester, is the best known from this early period, due to a detailed but somewhat imaginative poem written about it by the monk Wulstan to Bishop Elphege II of Winchester in or after 984. It tells of 400 pipes, 12 bellows worked by 70 strong men, and continues to say that 'the sound clamours such . . . that one closes by hand the openings of his ears, hardly able to bear the roar in drawing near . . . and the melody of the muses is heard everywhere in the city . . .'. Modern scepticism even suggests that this organ never existed, but James McKinnon, in his very reasoned article 'The Tenth Century Organ at

89 Hydraulis, made as a clay lamp; Roman, 2nd or 3rd century AD. *London, British Museum*. (The other side of it can be seen in the author's *Musical Instruments of the West*, Plate 75.)

eu fecdm multitudine magnitudinifer ;

90 Organ with three men treading on the bellows. Above it are a horn, an instrument of the guitar family and crotales. Illustration of Psalm 150 from the Stuttgart Psalter, made in France *c*. 830. *Stuttgart, Wurttembergische Landesbibliothek, MS Bibl. fol. 23, f.163v.*

Winchester', believes that it did, although in a much less dramatic form than that mentioned by Wulstan. Perhaps it can be assumed that this organ played the single line (indicated by letter notation) which accompanies polyphony in the Winchester Troper (Cambridge, Corpus Christi College MS 473), dating from just about the same time as Wulstan's poem.

From the eleventh century there survive two important treatises giving detailed instructions for the building of church organs. One is by Theophilus, a monk who lived in Germany or eastern France, and the author of the other is known as the Anonymous of Berne, although he is thought to have been a monk at Fleury. Both writers specify pipes of copper, but those of Theophilus are conical in shape and those of the Anonymous are cylindrical. While Theophilus has slow-moving sliders which need to be pulled out to produce a note, the Anonymous has keys with a spring mechanism (similar to that of Hero) enabling them to return automatically to their

91 Organ with two apparent chromatic notes visible, and a drone pipe with its special key; an angel accompanies on a timbrel; from a Flemish Book of Hours, *c.* 1300. *London, British Library, MS Stowe 17, f.129.*

92 Two portative organs (showing front and back views) played with timbrel and fiddle in the anonymous Florentine *Musical Angels* of *c.* 1350. *Oxford, Christ Church Picture Gallery.*

93 Portative organ with chromatic keys, played by an angel in the *Triptych with St. John the Baptist and St. John the Evangelist*, 1479, by Hans Memling (*c.* 1430–94). *Bruges, St. Janshospitaal*

to provide contrasting sounds when needed. The positive, however, was not restricted to church use, and was frequently used for secular occasions. Perhaps it was the instrument played by Janin Lorganistre among the entertainments for the Feast of Westminster at Pentecost in 1306, when Edward I knighted his son, the future Edward II.

Until this time all organ pipes had to be above their own sliders or keys, so that the air could rise directly upwards. Wide pipes needed wide keys, and when these were heavy they had to be pressed down by a whole fist. The problem was solved by the fourteenth-century invention of rollers, which enabled the 'tracker' action of rods and wires to be directed sideways and the pipes placed further away from the keyboard. The number of pipes could therefore be greatly increased and the keys reduced in width, each becoming easily playable by one finger and allowing for much faster playing. Small positives with narrow pipes and keys did not always need such devices, and it may have been for such an instrument that there was written the music in the Robertsbridge Fragment, dating from *c.* 1325–50 (see pp. 196–8). This calls for a chromatic keyboard, which is rare, although not non-existent, in pictures of the period.

It was around 1300 that the smaller **portative organ** started to appear frequently in the visual arts, having been seen seldom before that time in northern Europe, but more noticeable in the Iberian peninsula. The whole instrument was played by one person, who worked the bellows with one hand and played on the keyboard with the other. The keys were either button-shaped or flat, and the technique of playing varied somewhat according to each type. At first all the keys looked the same, although they may have included a B flat, and many portatives had one or two drone pipes. Some sources of the fifteenth century show them to be completely chromatic, such as the Memling example in fig. 93, where the back row of button-shaped keys is carefully arranged in groups of two and three. The *organetto*, as it was called in Italy, usually had from one to three ranks of pipes, and certain Italian paintings show that the selection of these could be varied

94 Positive organ with pedals. Detail from *The Seven Planet Series – Mercury* by Hans Sebald Beham (1500–50).

original position. These and other sources indicate that the names of the notes were often written on or by the sliders or keys, and that B flat was the only accidental, the range being approximately from one to three octaves. The number of bellows and blowers varied according to the size of each organ.

Although Theophilus suggested placing the organ high up in an arcade, organ lofts were not frequently built until the fourteenth century, by which time some of the instruments were very large; this type eventually became known as the **great organ**. The smaller **positive organ** (which also needed separate people to work the bellows and play on the keyboard), could be moved about between performances, and was sometimes adjacent to the great organ in order

96 Organ by Lorenzo di Giacomo da Prato, made between 1474–83, and with subsequent alterations. It is the oldest surviving organ known to have had separate ranks of pipes from the beginning. *Bologna, Church of San Petronio.*

95 Church organ in a gallery, played for the Circumcision in *Scenes from the Life of Christ* by a 15th-century Hispano-Flamenco painter (possibly Louis Alimbrot). *Madrid, Museo del Prado.*

by stops. A well-known example is that played by *Musica* painted by Andrea da Firenze in the *Cappellone degli Spagnoli* at the church of Santa Maria Novella, Florence.

Although most of the large medieval organs had several ranks of pipes to each note, these could not be detached from each other. Hence the sound was a great 'mixture' of diapason unisons, fifths and octaves, which in Germany became known as the *Blockwerk*. Then other departments were added in the Netherlands and Germany, the first being the pedals and the positive. Lodewijk van Valbecke of Louvain (*d. c.* 1312) is said to have been the first to use pedals for lower notes, but at first they just pulled down the lower keys of the manual. Soon afterwards they became an independent part having their own pipes. The positive organ which had some-

times been placed behind the great was now installed behind the organist's back. He could either turn round to perform on it, or, if the action passed beneath his feet, he could play on it from a second keyboard under that of the main instrument. This department became known as the *Ruckpositiv*, one of its earliest examples being at Utrecht Cathedral *c.* 1400. Basically the great organ could sound at 8′ pitch, the positive at 4′ and the pedals at 16′, although this was not a fixed rule. Sometimes two manuals could be coupled together to sound simultaneously (this was already known at Rouen Cathedral in 1386), even though only one was being played upon.

Although drawstops seem to have been re-invented before 1400 to separate the different ranks within each department, it was a long time before they were widely used, and Arnault of Zwolle (*c.* 1440) described organs only of the Blockwerk type. In Germany and Flanders stops served to detach certain registers from the

97 Regal, possibly German; early 17th century. *London, Royal College of Music.*

98 Organ showing a *Rückpositiv* behind the organist's seat. Praetorius, *Theatrum Instrumentorum* (1620), plate II.

99 Organ by Gottfried Silbermann, 1710–14. *Freiberg Cathedral, DDR*.

Blockwerk, while in Italy they enabled each rank to be played separately. The earliest surviving organ of this latter type was built between 1474 and 1483 by Lorenzo di Giacomo da Prato for the church of San Petronio at Bologna. Some instruments, however, kept the Blockwerk system for the great organ and used a positive for the independent stops, an example being the church of St Bavo at Haarlem, where the organ remained like that until 1630.

During the fifteenth century there appeared also the **regal**, in which the pitch was determined not so much by the length of the resonators, which were very small, but by the thickness and length of the beating reeds. The name *regal* was also given to the reed stop itself, and to some organs containing both flues and reeds. One of the 'regalles' of Henry VIII had 'one Stoppe of pipes of woode a Cimbell of Tinne and a Regall'.

(The cymbel is a high-sounding mixture stop.)

Renaissance and Baroque organs developed distinct national styles, of which the most progressive were those of northern Germany and the Netherlands. Their interweaving polyphonic music demanded that each melodic line should, if needed, be distinguishable from the others, so many new stops were invented, based to a great extent on the sounds of other instruments; the first to appear was that of the flute. A typical German organ of the Renaissance was described by the Heidelberg organist and composer Arnolt Schlick in his *Spiegel der Orgelmacher und Organisten* (Speyer, 1511). Instruments imitated in its stops include the gemshorn, flageolet, Rauschpfeife, Zinck (cornett), crumhorn, trumpet or trombone, and a percussion sound which 'resembles that of a small boy hitting a pot with a spoon'. The trumpet or trombone stop was played by the pedals.

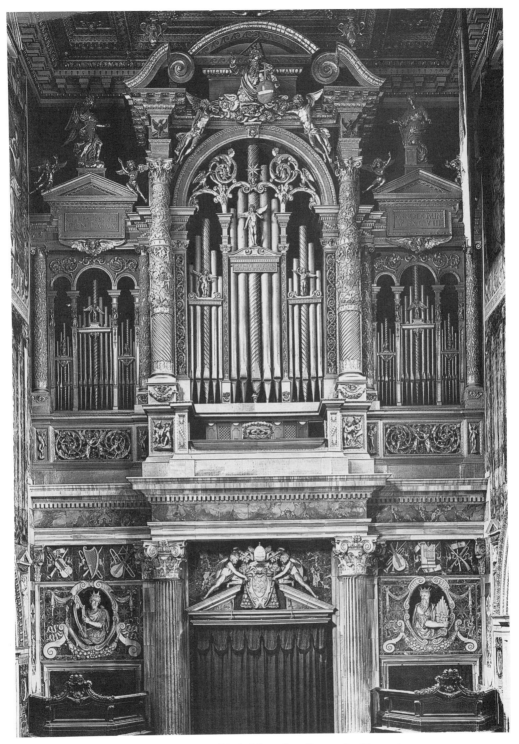

100 Organ by Luca Blasi of Perugia, with case by Giovanni Battista Montano of Milan, 1597–8. *Rome, Basilica of San Giovanni in Laterano.*

Soon further departments were added, each one containing the basic requirements of the diapason chorus (the remains of the *Blockwerk*), flutes and reeds, and having its own manual. In addition to the *Hauptwerk* (great), *Rückpositiv* and pedals, a section known as the *Brustwerk* (by its position just above the breast of the organist) was added below the great, and also one above the great, the *Oberwerk*. In certain elaborate Rococo designs, such as that by J. Gabler at Weingarten (1737–50), there is even a *Kronwerk* above that. It was not necessary, however, for each organ to have all these departments. The music of Bach, for instance, needed only two manuals and a pedalboard, such as can be found in the organ now at Capel in Jutland, rebuilt in 1695 by the celebrated Arp Schnitger, whose instruments represent the summit of excellence and versatility in North Germany. Other fine organ builders included the brothers Andreas and Gottfried Silbermann.

In contrast to the Germanic and Netherlandish organs, those of Italy remained simple, with the Renaissance instruments being best represented by those of the Antegnati family at Brescia. An average instrument would have only one manual, with a soft principal chorus, and sometimes the slightly off-pitch *fiffaro* with which this undulated. Pedals, when they existed, were pull-downs, such as can be seen in the sixteenth-century organ in the chapel of the Palazzo Pubblico at Siena. Two-manual organs were rare, one being that by D. Benvenuto and F. Palmieri (1585–7) in the church of Santa Maria in Aracoeli, Rome. Here there was a *Rückpositiv* containing a *Regale* stop (both rare in Italy), besides, on the first manual, stops for the effects of drums and birds which were becoming popular in many parts of Europe. Apart from the flute, few other instruments had been named in Italian stops before this time. Their increase during the seventeenth century was largely due to foreign craftsmen such as the Silesian organ-builder Johann or Eugen Caspar, who changed his name to Eugenio Casparini. His organ built in 1694 for the church at Maia Bassa (Merano) contained such Italianate names as *Superottava* and *Vigesimaseconda* together with the German *Nachthorn* and *Gemsflöte*.

Organs of Renaissance France varied in style, some being of the simple Italian type, and others reflecting the long-standing artistic influence of Flanders. There soon developed, however, a definite French organ which was described in detail by Dom Bédos de Celles in his *L'Art du Facteur d'Orgues* (Paris, 1766–78). It often had two manuals and pedals, and the stops, among which reeds were prominent, became so standardized that such composers as de Grigny, Clérambault and François Couperin were able to specify exactly which were to be used. (In other countries this was unusual due to the individuality of each organ, and variety of registration was expected.)

Spain was also influenced to a certain extent by its Flemish connections, producing organs with two manuals and pedals, and stops imitating other instruments, besides special effects such as 'an unusual device of bells, suitable for the Elevation of the Host' which appeared in an organ by Mathieu Telles for the Cathedral of Lérida in 1554. One of the chief characteristics of Spanish organs was the strength of their reeds, emphasized in the Baroque period by dramatic trumpet pipes projecting horizontally in front of the organ. It was in Spain that the swellbox originated. Previously the different ranks had by their very nature been contrasted, and the placing of certain pipes in a closed box had produced an echo effect. In late seventeenth-century Spain a foot lever enabled the lid of such a box to be opened and shut, thereby making the sound progressively louder and softer.

English organs were for a long time similar to those of Italy, having one manual, no pedal pipes (although pull-downs may occasionally have been used), and stops which were mainly diapasons with the addition of a flute or recorder. Thomas Dallam's organ at King's College, Cambridge (1606) may have been the first English one to have two manuals, as did his organ in Worcester Cathedral (1613), which had a 'chaire' (choir) organ, equivalent to the *Rückpositiv*. A new age of organ-building began with the Restoration in 1660, after the Commonwealth in which so many organs had been destroyed, or removed to other places. (That from Rochester Cathedral had been transferred to a tavern in Greenwich, to cite one example of such a move.) New ideas from the continent were incorporated into the designs of 'Father' Bernard Smith and his younger rival Renatus Harris. Smith introduced the echo organ to England at the Temple Church in 1683, while Harris built the first four-manual English organ at Salisbury Cathedral in 1710. Both introduced continental stops which were new to England. Although Harris included six manuals, a pedal board and a swell mechanism in a grandiose scheme for St Paul's Cathedral, this instrument was never built. It was left to Abraham Jordan to introduce a swell box (different from the Iberian type) at the church of St Magnus the Martyr, London Bridge, in 1712. Among the first authenticated pedals (even these were pull-downs) in an English church were those in the organ at St Mary Redcliffe, Bristol, built by John Harris, a son of Renatus, and his brother-in-law John Byfield I in 1726. Later in the century the best English organs were built by the Swiss settler Johann Snetzler and by George England, who, with his son George Pike England, worked in the traditions of Renatus Harris.

An interesting glimpse into society at this period can be seen in the organ by Robert and William Gray (1790) at Burghley House, Stamford. The 9th Earl of Exeter used to play it late at night with his butler pumping the bellows, but understandably the butler got tired of doing it, so he paid for a special pedal to be built into the instrument. This meant that the Earl could pump and play both at once, and the butler could go to bed. (For this information the author is most grateful to Mr Gerald Gifford.)

English organs, however, were still conservative, and when Mendelssohn visited London in 1829 he could find few instruments suitable for the organ music of Bach. It was William Hill, together with Dr Henry John Gauntlett, who made independent pedal pipes more easily accessible. Hill also improved the swell mechanism and added new stops, such as the *Grand Ophicleide* at Birmingham Town Hall in 1837, before completing his masterpiece for the George Street Chapel,

Liverpool, in 1841. While remaining in the classical tradition, Hill can be said to have brought the English organ up to date.

In the same year, however, Aristide Cavaillé-Coll, the creator of the French Romantic Organ, came to prominence when he built an instrument for the Abbey of St Denis. His aim was to produce an instrument of great expressiveness and symphonic proportions, in keeping with the taste of the day. In doing so he certainly produced an organ capable of playing French Romantic music, but incapable of playing authentically anything composed for the instrument before that time. He excluded, for instance, the mutation stops (those which give an overtone without its fundamental), which had been such a feature of classical organs and only brought them back in later years at the request of such scholarly organists as Saint-Saëns and Guilmant. He also made a feature of dramatic reed choruses, arranging his trumpets horizontally (*en chamade*) as in Spain. With a ventil system he caused great *crescendi* and *diminuendi* by bringing into action progressively more ranks while still playing, and since this involved much coupling together of manuals, he used the pneumatic action developed by Charles Spackman Barker in 1832. This caused a lighter touch on the manuals than if the whole instrument were worked by tracker action. One of the Cavaillé-Coll's best known organs was that at the church of Sainte Clothilde in Paris, where for many years the organist was César Franck (fig. 101).

In England the Romantic Organ came to prominence at the Great Exhibition of 1851, with the work of Henry Willis and the German Edmund Schulze. Willis was then commissioned to build an organ for St George's Hall, Liverpool, an instrument which, when completed, was one of the most progressive of its day, containing numerous devices for simplifying the action. These included thumb pistons, which when pressed during performance could change several pre-arranged stops at once; also pneumatic lever action, and a steam engine to help with the wind supply. The pedal board was concave and radiating, an arrangement which came into widespread but not universal use. This organ was

101 Organ by Aristide Cavaillé-Coll, 1859; for many years it
was played by César Franck. *Paris, Church of Ste Clothilde.*

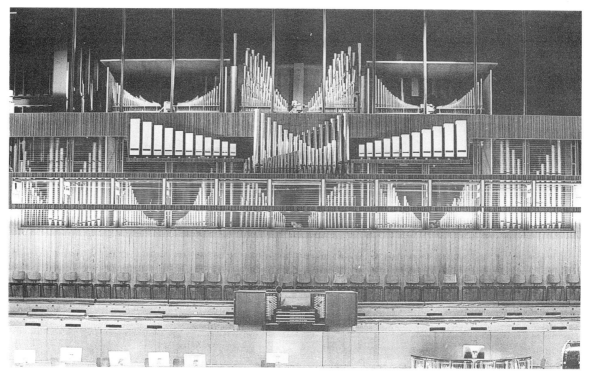

102 Organ designed by Ralph Downes and built by Harrison and Harrison of Durham, 1954. This view shows the organ as it was in 1988. *London, Royal Festival Hall.*

played upon for many years by W.T. Best, who was renowned for performing arrangements of orchestral works at a time when concerts were comparatively rare. Willis's organ at Canterbury Cathedral (1886) was one of the first to be activated on a large scale by electricity. The family firm of Willis survives to this day, as do other nineteenth-century dynasties such as those of Walker and Harrison and Harrison.

The chief developments of the present century have stemmed from the Classical Revival in Germany in the 1920s (the *Orgelbewegung*), resulting in the building of organs in the Baroque style (some with tracker action), and the restoration of countless early ones to their original condition. These organs, however, were not made for Romantic music, so the next step was to build large ones containing the ingredients necessary for music of all periods. In England the process was in reverse. No significant return to classical

principles had taken place until, in a clean break with ultraconservatism, there appeared in 1954 the organ of the Royal Festival Hall, London. Designed by Ralph Downes and voiced under his direction, it was built by the Durham firm of Harrison and Harrison. Here there are to be found the chief principles of the German *Orgelbewegung* together with the best features of English, Dutch and French organ design of the nineteenth century. Although its actions are electro-pneumatic, it has proved to be more than adequate for the stylish performance of any kind of music (fig. 102).

The economic depression of the 1970s and 1980s, coinciding with a desire for organs reproducing as faithfully as possible those of the Renaissance and Baroque periods, has resulted in a record vintage of small encased organs with light tracker actions. In spite of their size they have a strong carrying power which in large buildings reintroduces a perspective and dimension long since forgotten. The clear response of their tone and mechanism has led to a marked improvement in the standard of organ playing

103 Claviorganum by Lodewijk Theeuwes, London, 1579. *London, Victoria and Albert Museum.*

today. Inevitably, however, they are unsuitable for the performance of Romantic works, as they were not intended for such music. The solution can be found in a building which already possesses a good organ of the late nineteenth or early twentieth century. By the preservation of this and the acquisition of a new organ with tracker action, the organ repertoire can be performed as faithfully as possible.

Before leaving the organ, mention should be made of some of the ways in which it has been combined with other instruments. In the Renaissance and Baroque **claviorganum** it was coupled to a harpsichord, and as such was heard by Burney as the accompaniment to nuns' voices in Rome. As the **lira organizzata** it became one with the hurdy-gurdy, and was fashionable at the Court of Naples in Haydn's day. As the **barrel organ** it was combined with the mechanical cylinder and used in churches from about 1700

104 Lira organizzata or organ hurdy-gurdy, possibly made by a Frenchman living in London, 18th century. *London, Victoria and Albert Museum.*

onwards. Perhaps the most curious example is the **piano-organ** made by Johann Samuel Kühlewein of Eisleben in 1798 for a church in Heligoland. Combining organ pipes and the mechanism of a piano, its chief interest is in the 'pipes'. The inaccessibility of the island during the winter months would have prevented an organ builder from coming over from the mainland to do repairs, so Kühlewein substituted for the more orthodox pipes an ingenious arrangement of glass bottles, ranging in diameter from 62″ to $\frac{1}{4}$″ (152.4–6 mm), and all carefully tuned by the insertion of an appropriate amount of wax. This curious hybrid is to be seen today in the City Museum, Liverpool.

105 Piano-organ with bottles instead of pipes, by Johann Samuel Kühlewein of Eisleben, 1798. *Liverpool, City Museum.*

V

The Woodwind Families

I n *The House of Fame* Chaucer said that 'soun ys nocht but eyr ybroken' – sound is nothing but broken air. Air can be broken in countless different ways, and it is according to these that instruments are classified. Among woodwind instruments (which are made not only of wood but also of bone, metal and, more recently, of plastic), these methods can be summarized as the pressure of air against (a) a sharp edge in the instrument itself, or (b) a reed or two reeds at or near the upper end. While the word 'pipe' covers them all genericaly, 'flute' applies only to those in the first category. Wind instruments in general are classified as *aerophones*.

In early days Man discovered that he could produce a sound by blowing across one end of a tube, and then he found that pipes of different lengths became deeper in pitch as they became longer. By fixing a set of such pipes together the ancients devised the **syrinx**, which, through its association with the Greek god Pan became known as **panpipes**.

It was also found that a single pipe with finger holes could produce different notes according to the placing of the fingers, and this principle became used in various ways. One is seen in the transverse flute, where the sound is made by air blowing directly against the edge of the mouth hole. Another involves the insertion of a wooden block (sometimes, but not always, called a 'fip-

ple') into the top of an end-blown pipe, leaving only a narrow air passage. Below the block is cut a small window, with its lower edge set to break the oncoming air. Pipes in this category are known as *duct flutes*, and include flageolets, tabor pipes, recorders, gemshorns and pitch pipes, while related instruments include bird whistles and carnival whistles (fig. 29), where the duct is fashoned out of other materials such as clay.

One of the most simple duct flutes is the **pitch pipe**, which was designed to give a single note to church choirs when they were about to sing unaccompanied. A marked stopper was inserted into the bottom end of the pipe, and, when moved up or down by one hand, it altered the sounding length to give the required note. The instrument was used mainly between 1750 and 1850.

In the one-man combination of the **pipe-and-tabor** the left hand plays a pipe while the right hand accompanies on a drum which is usually suspended from the left arm. The pipe has two fingerholes in front and a thumbhole at the back, and about two octaves can be obtained from it by over-blowing. It was frequently shown in Gothic art from the first half of the thirteenth century until well into the sixteenth, and during that time it was played in all strata of society. Later, however, its use became restricted mainly to folk music and to traditional events, which so often are closely connected. One such occasion is

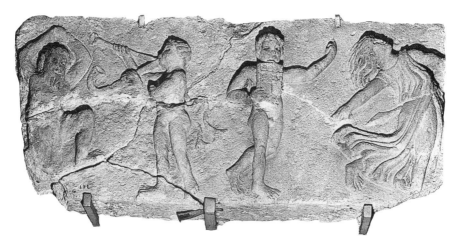

106 Phrygian pipes and panpipes, playing in a Bacchanalian scene on a Gallo-Roman relief found at Vaison. *Avignon, Musée Calvet.*

107 Bird whistle from a settlement at Spina, near Ferrara, *c.* 500 BC. The player blows through a hole in the bird's tail, and by covering the hole in each wing, can produce the sound of a cuckoo. This instrument is the direct ancestor of the cuckoo used in toy symphonies. *London, Author's Collection.*

108 Pipe-and-tabor, played by a man dressed as a devil; from a margin of the Smithfield Decretals, written in Italy but illustrated in England, *c.* 1325–30. *London, British Library, MS Roy. 10.E.iv, f.201v.*

109 Gemshorn, held by a skeleton in *The Dance of Death*, illustrated by Heinrich Knoblochtzer, Strasbourg, c. 1488. *Heidelberg University Library*.

110 Two flageolets from the frontispiece of Thomas Greeting's *Pleasant Companion*, London, 1682. The source from which this plate was taken is a profusely extra-illustrated copy of *Samuel Pepys, Diary and correspondence of...with a life and notes by Richard Ld. Bolingbroke...Notes by Mynors Bright*, London, 1879, vol. VI, between pages 2 and 3. *Los Angeles, William Andrews Clark Memorial Library*.

at the May Morning revels in Oxford, when it is played around the town by Morris dancers after the choir of Magdalen College has sung on top of the Chapel tower at 6 am.

The **gemshorn** was a late medieval and early Renaissance horn which was blown, not from the narrow end but from the wide one. This was blocked up except for a narrow air passage, and the appropriate window was cut into the horn below the block. Fingerholes enabled tunes to be played on it, and it gave a soft flute-like tone. It was particularly associated with Germanic countries, and was not representative of Europe as a whole.

From the Middle Ages onwards the word **flageolet** has been used for a **whistle pipe** (Latin, *fistula*) with an unstandardized number of holes, such as can be traced back to Antiquity. The instrument is mentioned in medieval poems as providing the music for dancing, and Pepys, who carried a 'flagelette' around with him, played it in such situations as when, on 9 February 1660,

> ...Swan and I to a drinking-house near Temple-bar, where while he writ, I played of my flagelette till a dish of poached eggs was got ready for us.

Other places where he played it included St James's Park, 'The Greene Dragon' on Lambeth Hill, a boat on the Thames, in a coach approaching The Hague, and in the cellar of Audley End in Essex, 'there being an exellent Echo'.

This may have been a pipe with four finger holes and two thumbholes which was chiefly associated with France, or a similar one used also in England for teaching birds to sing. Tunes for such a **bird pipe** were published by Richard Meares in *The Bird Fancyer's Delight* (1717), where popular songs were set for 'Ye Wood-lark, Blackbird, Throustill, House-sparrow, Canary-bird' and others, including the parrot and the East India nightingale. Later types of flageolet included the single, double and triple pipes made by William Bainbridge of London from 1803 onwards, and the tiny **Picco pipe**, first made by the Italian shepherd Picco, who could produce from it a range of three octaves. At the present time there are still memories of the 'penny whistle', although as inflation goes this simple pipe will never again cost a penny.

It is uncertain when the **recorder** developed from a more primitive pipe, such as those which have five or six fingerholes and no thumbhole and can still be found as folk instruments in many parts of the world. One of the difficulties in identifying the recorder from the visual arts is that if only the front view is visible we cannot see if there is supposed to be a thumbhole at the back, and even if there is supposed to be one and it is covered by the performer's thumb, we are none the wiser. One picture which does *not* show a recorder is that from the twelfth-century York Psalter (Glasgow University Library, MS Hunter 229 – formerly U.3.2 – f.21v.), which has led several authorities to give it that name on account of its shape. However, M.H. Armstrong-Davison, in 'A Note on the History of the Northumbrian Small Pipes' (*Galpin Society Journal* xxii, 1969, pp. 78–80), has shown without doubt that there is a small bag leading from the top end of the pipe, and tucked under the performer's arm. This is clearly seen by looking at the manuscript itself, or at a colour reproduction.

Basically the recorder should have a rear thumbhole and seven fingerholes in front. In early examples two holes were set for the little finger, depending on whether the player was right or left-handed, and the unused hole was blocked up with wax. These requisites are all present in a medieval recorder which was excavated at the *Huis te Merwede* near Dordrecht, and is now kept at the Gemeentemuseum in The Hague. One curious feature for such an early instrument is that each end is shaped to form a tenon, but the pieces which should have been attached to them have not survived. Experiments have shown that with an added foot joint the bottom note would have been about c''. It has been said that the Dordrecht recorder dated from the thirteenth century, but it is now believed to be from the late fourteenth, which conveniently coincides with the earliest known reference to the name; this appears in an account book of the house of Henry, Earl of Derby (later Henry IV), where payment is made for a 'fistula nomine Ricordo', as observed by Brian Trowell in 'King Henry IV, Recorder-player', *Galpin Society Journal*, x, 1957, pp. 83–4).

Once the true recorder had appeared there must have been considerable uncertainty about it, not only among writers but also among artists. Two cases come to mind. One is the will of Stephen Thomas of Leigh in Essex, who in 1419 left to Thomas Chesse 'my best gown of the King's livery that is at home at my house, and my gold ring, and my whistle', and the other concerns the fifteenth-century tomb of Dame Margaret Pype in St Bartholomew's Church at Tong in Shropshire. Two brass shields show pipes fashioned so carefully that it is reasonable to hope that they are supposed to be recorders. However, although there is a pair of alternate bottom holes for the little finger, the final total of fingerholes is only six, and we cannot see if there is a thumbhole...

During the fifteenth century the recorder was made increasingly in different sizes with a view to consort playing, and pictures from that time often show three being played together. After the bass of the family appeared *c.* 1500 (it was shown by Virdung in 1511) a consort could consist of descant, treble (alto), tenor and bass, although the descant was often omitted in favour of another of the more mellow instruments. In the early stages the pitch varied from one set to another, and the inventory of Henry VIII's instruments refers to a 'greate base Recorder of woode', but its pitch is not known. By the time of Praetorius the sizes ranged from a great bass in F to a sopranino ('Exilent') in g'', with alternative pitches for different sizes. Praetorius himself suggested making recorders in two sections to remedy problems of tuning, but the idea was not widely adopted at the time, and most recorders, as far as we know, remained in one piece. The tuning eventually became standardized as relative to $f\ c'\ f'\ c''$, bearing in mind that the recorder is a transposing instrument and its music is written an octave lower than it sounds.

During the middle of the seventeenth century great changes were made in the structure of woodwind instruments, largely due to the work of Jean Hotteterre the Elder, who came from the village of La Couture-Boussey near Evreux in Normandy. Together with members of the Philidor and Chedeville families, he played in the bands of Louis XIV's *Grande Ecurie*, besides making and repairing instruments for their use.

111 Recorders of three sizes, and below them, from left to right, a harp, dulcimer and lute; detail from the Flemish painting *Mary Queen of Heaven*, by the Master of the St Lucy Legend, *c.* 1485. *Washington, National Gallery of Art, Samuel H. Kress Collection.*

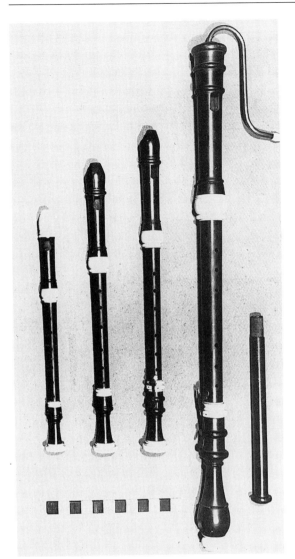

112 Treble, alto, tenor and bass recorders by Pui Bressan, *c.* 1720. *Chester, Grosvenor Museum.*

Around 1650 he started to make recorders in three sections: the head joint containing the mouthpiece and window, the tapering middle joint with six fingerholes, and the foot joint with one hole for the little finger, this hole sometimes being controlled by a key. As the foot joint could be turned round to suit the player, the old extra hole became redundant. While the Renaissance recorder with its wide cylindrical bore had a mellow tone which blended well for the consort music of its period, the new Baroque instrument gave a more penetrating sound, capable of holding its own in Bach's Second Brandenburg Concerto. The treble recorder was used for this, and for most solo work and trio sonatas, in which it was often interchangeable with other instruments. The recorder family as a whole, however, was unsuitable for the expressive music being written from *c.* 1750 onwards, as it could not grow much louder or softer without becoming out of tune. It gave way, therefore, to the transverse flute, and had to wait until the twentieth century to be revived by Arnold Dolmetsch. Since then it has had a new lease of life and has acquired many virtuoso performers, besides being used to a considerable extent in schools. One notable modern composition which calls for it is Britten's *Noye's Fludde*, which was originally performed by children, under the beat of Charles Mackerras, in Orford Church, Suffolk, in 1958.

The **transverse** or **German flute** (henceforth referred to as 'flute') was certainly known to the Etruscans before the Christian era, and is thought to have originated in Central Asia. It seems to have come to Germany from Byzantium in the twelfth century, but after that it spread only gradually through Europe and with fluctuating success. In Spanish art it is seen in the thirteenth-century *Cantígas de Santa Maria* (Escorial Library, MS j.b.2, f.218v), and there are a good many French and Flemish illustrations of it from the following century, such as those in the *Romance of Alexander* illustrated by Jehan de Grise between 1338 and 1344. After 1400, however, it was seldom depicted in those latter parts, presumably due to the popularity of the recorder. It only returned to favour *c.* 1500, after which it finally

113 Flute played by David in the Theodore Psalter of Byzantine origin, dated 1066. *London, British Library, MS Add. 19352, f.189v.*

became established also in England, where it seems to have had no previous foothold at all. It was one of the many instruments played by the young Henry VIII, whose biographer Edward Halle (*d.* 1547) tells how, at 'Wyndsore', in the year 1510–11 he was

exercisyng hym selfe daily in shotyng, singing, daunsyng, wrastelyng, casting of the barre, plaiyng at the recorders, flute, virginals, and in settyng of songes, makyng of ballettes, and did set ii. goodly masses, every of them fyve partes, which were song oftentimes in hys chapel, and afterwardes in diverse other places.

The inventory of his instruments in 1547 included flutes made of 'woode', 'glasse', 'woode painted like glasse' and 'iuorie tipped with golde enameled blacke', besides 'phiphes of blacke Ibonie tipped withe Siluer'.

These early flutes were one-piece cylinders, with six fingerholes and no thumbhole. The 'phiphes', like Virdung's 'Zwerchpfeiff' and Agricola's 'Schweitzerpfeiffen' were early fifes with long, narrow bores, and they would normally have been played to the accompaniment of drums. The other flutes are likely to have been wider instruments suitable for consort music, such as the 'Querflöten' of Agricola and Praetorius, who both showed them in three different sizes. Those of Praetorius gave the bottom notes as *g* (bass), *d'* (alto or tenor) and *a'* (discant), when their respective holes were all covered by fingers; the bass flute was built in two sections.

By *c.* 1650 the flute had changed considerably, and probably at the hands of the same craftsmen (Jean Hotteterre and his companions) who had altered the recorder. It had a natural scale of D, as in the older alto or tenor instrument, and was built in three parts: a cylindrical head joint, a conical body joint, and a small foot joint which could be either cylindrical or conical and held a key for the bottom *e*^b'. The tuning could be remedied to a certain extent by adjusting the length where the parts met, but a more satisfactory method appeared *c.* 1720. This involved the division of the body joint into two sections, the upper of which could be replaced by one of several alternative lengths, known as the *corps de réchange*. Later in the century these themselves had become redundant due to the addition of a tuning slide, and extra keys had been added to produce a bottom *c'* and *c*[#]'. Intonation problems over other chromatic notes were at first remedied by new finger holes, and later by more keys. Johann Joachim Quantz, whose *Essay of a Method for Playing the Transverse Flute* (1752) is a valuable document on playing and musical style in general,

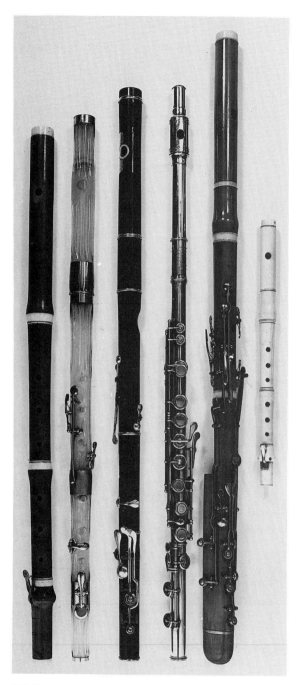

invented an extra key to give the difference between $e^{b\prime}$ and $d^{\#\prime}$, but it was not widely adopted. Such was the experimentation of the time that by 1800 there were in use flutes with keys ranging in number from one to eight.

The flute had by now ousted the recorder for the reasons given on pages 211–13. One of its most distinguished exponents was the Emperor Frederick the Great of Prussia, who was himself a pupil of Quantz, and his playing was described by Dr Burney after a concert in the palace of Sans Souci in 1772:

The concert began by a German flute concerto, in which his majesty executed the solo parts with great precision; his *embouchure* was clear and even, his finger brilliant, and his taste pure and simple. I was much pleased, and even surprised with the neatness of his execution in the *allegros*, as well as by his expression and feeling in the *adagio*; in short, his performance surpassed, in many particulars, any thing I had ever heard among *Dilettanti*, or even professors. His majesty played three long and difficult concertos successively, and all with equal perfection.

The nineteenth century saw radical changes which were aimed at improving tone and intonation, and involved many different mechanisms in which the keys were either 'open' or 'closed' when at rest. A stronger sound than before was produced from the flutes with large finger holes which were designed by the Charles Nicholsons, father and son; these were built by T. Prowse from 1822 onwards, and were sold by Clementi & Co. of London. Nicholson Junior, who was a virtuoso performer, was heard in 1831 by Theobald Boehm, a goldsmith, jeweller and flautist from Munich, who had already made some very beautiful flutes. Boehm saw the advantage of larger holes, and incorporated them into his design of the following year. This flute, like its immediate predecessor, had a conical body joint, but, due to the elaborate key mechanism, this was now in one piece. Its value was recognized abroad, and from 1843 onwards it was made in London by Rudall and Rose, and in Paris by Clair Godefroy the Elder. In 1844 Berlioz declared in his *Treatise on Instrumentation* that the flute,

114 Flutes, showing the progress made in less than 100 years. From left to right, the instruments are made by Cahusac, London, *c.* 1785; Laurent, Paris, early 19th century; Clementi & Co., London, *c.* 1825 (built by T. Prowse to Nicholson's design); Rudall, Rose, Carte & Co., London, 1857–71; I. Ziegler, Vienna, *c.* 1840 (with a downward extension to *g*), and a piccolo, late 18th century. *London, Royal College of Music.*

for a long time so imperfect in many respects, has now achieved such perfection and evenness of tone that no further improvement remains to be desired.

Nevertheless, in 1847 Boehm produced a further design, which won a first prize at London's Great Exhibition of 1851. Its chief innovation was the return to a cylindrical body, but with a slightly tapering head, generally described as 'parabolic'. The holes, which were larger than before, could not be covered by the fingers alone, so were provided with keys in the form of padded lids. The placing of the holes now depended on acoustic principles rather than the convenience of the player's fingers. This had already been apparent on the 1832 flute, and had been advocated as early as 1803 by the German flautist Dr. H.W. Pottgeisser. Many of Boehm's flutes were from now onwards made of silver.

Boehm's mechanism necessitated a new fingering system, which discouraged many musicians from adopting it. Hence other designs appeared, some of them attempting to improve on the old conical eight-keyed flute, and others, such as that of Richard Carte in 1867, combining the best features of the old instrument and those of the Boehm flute. The Carte instrument is still used by some British flautists, while the 'Reform Flute' by Schwedler of Leipzig (*c.* 1885) has been developed until now in Germany. Throughout the western world, however, the Boehm flute is the one most often played today.

While the normal flute gives *c'* as its lowest note, various contrivances have managed to extend its range downwards, although still keeping to the basic pitch. Larger flutes have included the alto and tenor sizes in G and F respectively, and basses in C such as the Albisiphon created *c.* 1911 by Abelardo Albisi of Milan. Of smaller instruments the **fife** represents the continuation of the Renaissance **Schweitzerpfeiff** with its narrow bore, having become smaller through the years and now having its lowest note at *b*♭′ or *c″*. The orchestral **piccolo**, which generally starts at *c″* or *d″*, was made in three sections with one key in the eighteenth century and was later adapted to the Boehm mechanism, but it has since reverted to having a conical bore. Conical flutes of simple design have long been used in civilian bands.

Reed instruments are much older than transverse flutes, being well documented as far back as the third millennium BC, when a pair of silver pipes was buried in the 'Royal Cemetery' at Ur. A cylindrical pipe with double reed was later termed **aulos** by the Greeks and **tibia** by the Romans, and according to *The Learned Banquet* ('Deipnosophistes') by Athenaeus of Naucratis, writing in the second century AD,

there were special *auloi* for each mode, so that at the Games all the *auleti* had to have an *aulos* for each mode.

He added that Pronomius of Thebes (born *c.* 475 BC) could play in several modes on one aulos because it had more holes than usual, with ferrules to cover those which were not needed. The aulos or tibia which was seen most often in the visual arts of Antiquity consisted of two pipes played together, and in the Phrygian version one of them curved upwards at the end.

In the Middle Ages double reed instruments were occasionally cylindrical but more often conical, and were given the Latin name *calamellus* from *calamus*, a reed. Their English name **shawm** was derived from that of the eastern *zurna*, an instrument which is said to have terrified the Crusaders, and still survives. In Europe there were three chief ways of arranging the mouthpiece. All of these used a reed fixed onto a staple, which in surviving folk shawms is generally made of metal. The simplest method was for the staple to be inserted directly into the top end of the instrument in the manner that can be seen in the bagpipe chanter or in the modern Breton *bombarde*. The second way was similar to this but with a flat circular disc loosely fitted around the staple so that the player's lips could rest against it. This survives in many types of eastern zurna, and can be seen on a shawm held by an angel on the Minstrels' Gallery at Exeter Cathedral. The third way was a late medieval development from the disc principle, involving a shaped wooden block known as the *pirouette*, which held the staple, and itself was set into the top of the instrument. In

116 Shawm, with a pirouette and double key. Detail from the Flemish painting *Mary Queen of Heaven*, by the Master of the St Lucy Legend, *c.* 1485. *Washington, National Gallery of Art, Samuel H. Kress Collection.*

the first two methods the reed often went right into the performer's mouth and was not controlled by his lips, so little or no nuance could be obtained. In the third way, however, the lips could exert more control over the reed, thus ensuring some degree of articulation and expression. (The disc is also sometimes known as a pirouette.)

From the twelfth century onwards the shawm was often portrayed in art, although at first it was quite short. Then it gradually grew longer, and from the late fourteenth century onwards the instrument was often played in groups of three sizes, which were described by Tinctoris, *c.* 1487, as 'suprema', 'tenor' (commonly called 'bombarde') and 'contra-tenor'. (Large sizes had a key for the lowest note, which was protected by a barrel-shaped *fontanelle*.) Other instruments with which it played included trumpets, sackbuts (trombones), bagpipes, tabors and nakers. The word *wait* applied to a shawm or its player when in the context of civic duties, or in the service of the nobility. According to the *Black Book* of his household, Edward IV had

A WAYTE, that ny3htly, from Mighelmasse til Shere Thursday, pipeth the wache within this court iiij

ances in art music was the instrument now known as the **basse de musette**, a very large shawm made in Switzerland during the eighteenth century and often played there with church choirs.

For the origin of the oboe we look again to the work of Jean Hotteterre the Elder at the *Grande Ecurie* of Louis XIV. His work on the refined form of bagpipes known as the **musette** must have filled him with a desire to civilize the shawm, and the result appeared in the late 1650s, possibly being played in public for the first time by Hotteterre himself and Michel Philidor II, in Lully's music for the ballet *L'Amour Malade* in 1657. This new *hautbois* differed from its progenitor in being built in three sections, in having a narrower bore and a narrower reed (with no pirouette), and a thumb hole, which had been absent from most shawms. There were three keys, two of them being alternatives for the little finger of either hand, but after *c.* 1750 one of these

tymes, and in the somer ny3ghtes iij tymes; and he to make bon gayte, and euery chambre dore and office, as well as fyre as for other pikers or perelliz.

Praetorius, who used the word 'Pommer' for any shawm with a key, described sizes from the great bass ('bombardone') in *F'* up to the small discant, this latter being the only one to which he actually gave the word 'Schalmeye'. The great bass had four keys, and on the larger sizes of shawm the reed was held in a crook. The word *douçaine*, which appears frequently in medieval and Renaissance literature, is thought to have meant a soft reed instrument, possibly with a cylindrical bore.

From the late Middle Ages the French and English terms *hautbois* and *hautboye* were often used for shawms, and some confusion must have arisen when they were also applied to the new **oboe**. After its arrival the shawm continued in use for many years, gradually becoming used mainly for folk music. One of its latest appear-

117 Oboe, around the base of which are carved scenes of dancers and musicians (see plate 227); Dutch, 17th century. *London, Victoria and Albert Museum.*

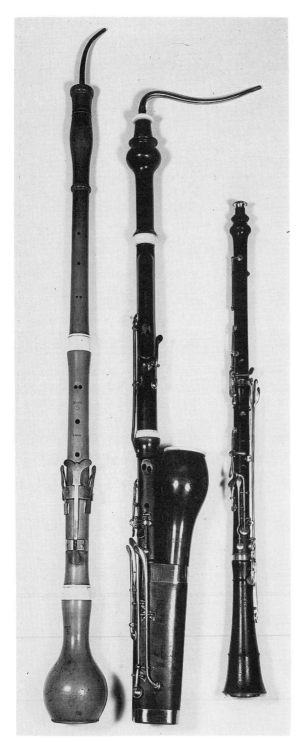

became redundant as by then most performers played with the left hand above the right. When all the holes and the bottom key were depressed, the lowest note of the oboe was c', while the second key gave $d^{\#}{}'$. Many instruments had alternative upper joints for adjusting the pitch. In the quest for better intonation the third and fourth holes were doubled to suit enharmonic changes, and extra keys were added towards the end of the eighteenth century by such makers as Jakob Grundmann and Carl Grenser of Dresden. Such was the oboe from the time of Lully and Purcell to that of the young Beethoven. In Beethoven's later years, however, the number of keys had increased to 13 in instruments designed by the Viennese player Josef Sellner and made by Stefan Koch. Their instrument was the basis for the type played in Germanic countries during the nineteenth century, with only gradual modifications.

In France, however, radical changes were made for refinement. The outline of the oboe became more simple, and the bore was narrowed further. One of the first craftsmen to work on adapting the mechanism was Henri Brod (1799–1839), who had studied on a four-keyed oboe and recognized its deficiencies. The German-born Guillaume Triébert (1770–1848) settled in Paris, and with his sons Charles Louis (1810–76) and Frédéric (1813–78) set to work to revise every part of the instrument in successive different 'systems'. Their traditions were later carried on by their foreman François Lorée (d. 1902), whose development of the Triébert 'Système 6' into 'Système A6' became known as the 'Conservatoire model', being used in the classes of Georges Gillet at the Paris Conservatoire from 1882. Among other designers connected to the Triébert firm were Appolon Marie-Rose Barret, whose 1862 mechanism made possible the same fingering for each octave. Independent work was done by Louis Auguste Buffet, who in 1844 patented an oboe adapted to the Boehm mechanism, aided by Boehm himself. With its large holes and large tone it was unacceptable to many French artists, although for a time it was used in military bands. It was, however, further developed by the Spanish-born Pierre-Joachim (Pedro) Soler who

118 Oboes, from left to right by M. Lot, Paris, *c.* 1775–83 (tenor); Triébert, Paris, *c.* 1825 (baritone or bass); Tabard, Lyon, *c.* 1835–40. *London, Royal College of Music.*

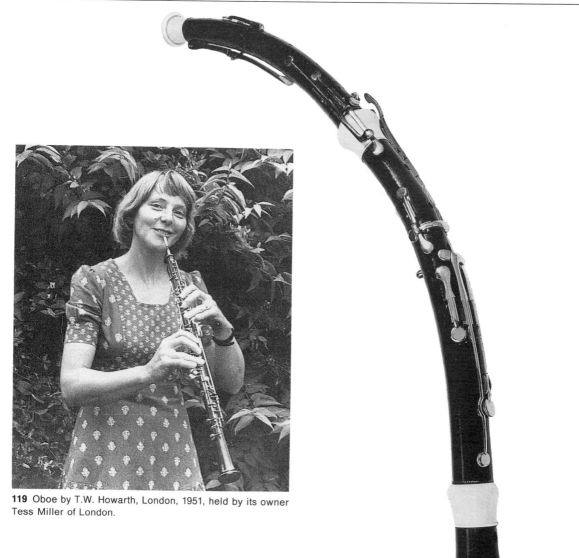

119 Oboe by T.W. Howarth, London, 1951, held by its owner Tess Miller of London.

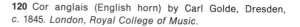

120 Cor anglais (English horn) by Carl Golde, Dresden, *c.* 1845. *London, Royal College of Music.*

also worked in Paris, and by the London-based Antoine Lavigne, whose instruments descended to *a*. In the twentieth century the French tradition has been carried on by Adolphe Lorée, the son of François, while the Austrian oboe has continued, although with less success than before. The German firm of Heckel has welded together the best characteristics of both schools.

Since the early days of the oboe, other sizes have existed than the treble in C, the nearest being the **oboe d'amore** in A, which was used particularly during the time of Bach. Tenor oboes in F or G went by such names as *haute-contre de hautbois*, *taille*, etc, and possibly included

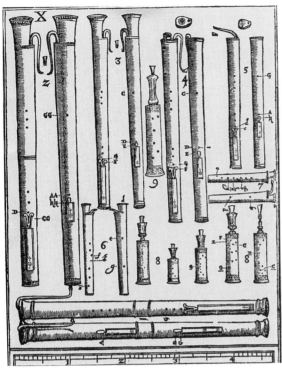

121 1, Bass sordun 2-7, curtalls ('Fagotten'); 8, racketts. Praetorius, *Theatrum Instrumentorum*, 1620, plate X.

Deux hautbois de forêt garnis en cuivre, ayant chacun trois corps, qui servent à hausser et baisser le ton, et une petite boette où il y a douze hanches; ils son de la façon de Bizet

which appeared in an inventory, dated 1780, of instruments in the King's Library at Versailles. (Charles Bizey was a mid-eighteenth-century oboe maker in Paris.) These may have been some form of **oboe da caccia**, which when called for by Bach was normally curved, and it retained this shape under the name **cor anglais** from the time of Gluck's *Alceste* (1776). Brod made it in a straight form from 1839, although this took time to become established. The bass (baritone) oboe in C often bent back on itself towards the bell, as did some of the tenor instruments. A contra-bass oboe was devised in the late eighteenth century by Christophe Delusse of Paris, but it had a limited career due to competition from the bassoon. High oboes have been in great demand

for military music. An instrument of the oboe family but of very different proportions is the **Heckelphone**, which was made in 1904 by William Heckel as a result of Wagner's request in 1879 for an instrument which 'should combine the character of the oboe with the soft but powerful tones of the Alphorn', the latter being a very long horn traditionally associated with Alpine regions.

During the Renaissance period there appeared several new families of low-pitched double reed instruments. That most resembling the shawm was the **bassanello**, which was said by Praetorius to have been invented by Iohann (Giovanni) Bassano of Venice, although this has been disputed by subsequent authorities. Praetorius added that 'the cantus size – the smallest – comes across very well on the tenor line of a consort piece, played together with various other instruments.' In contrast to this long instrument were those of the **rackett** family, also known as **Wurstfagott** (sausage bassoon). The rackett was a short, wide cylinder containing cylindrical tubing which bent back on itself nine times, and one owned by Praetorius, while only 11 inches (27 cm) deep, descended in pitch to C'. A 'sixteenth-century set of racketts made in the form of dragons can be seen today in the Kunsthistorisches Museum, Vienna, and they are typical of the disguised instruments made for *intermedi*, such as those mentioned on page 203. Like the rackett, the **sordun** (and its relative the **courtaut**) also had a cylindrical bore, but this was doubled back only once. It was closed at the bottom, and, according to Praetorius, it gave a sound similar to that of the crumhorn (page 130).

Of more lasting importance because of its historical development was the **curtall** or **dulcian**, which in Italy was covered by the term **fagotto**. Like the sordun it had a double reed on a crook and a bore bent back once, but this bore was conical. Of the two **Doppel-fagotten** mentioned by Praetorius, one descended to F' and the other to G', as the former produced a better B flat and the latter a better B natural. The most usual size was the **Chorist Faggott**, which descended to C, and was often used in church. Figure 222 shows a curtall being played in company with two

122 *The Bassoon Player* by Harmen Hals (1611–69). This is one of the earliest pictures of the bassoon after it had developed from the curtall, so its dark colouring is frustrating to the organologist of today. *Aachen, Suermondt Museum.*

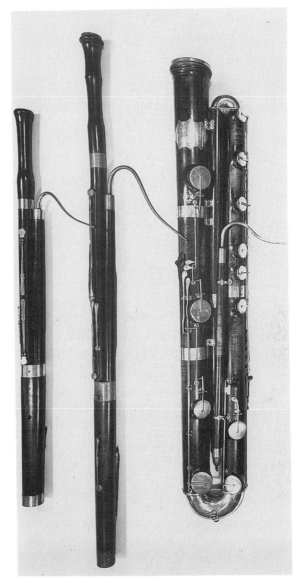

123 Bassoons, from left to right: (?) English, late 18th century; Quart-bassoon marked '2/Samme/London', *c.* 1853; Contra-bassophon by Alfred Morton, London, *c.* 1876. *London, Royal College of Music.*

long shawms, a cornett and sackbut to accompany choristers of the Abbey of Montserrat. The instrument seems to have originated in one piece in the late sixteenth century, but during the years which followed it gradually came to be built in two or more sections. By the late seventeenth century it had been divided into four main parts; from the butt there emerged the tenor ('wing') and bass ('long') joins, and projecting from the latter the bell which made possible the lowest note $B^{b\prime}$. It is believed that this change may have been the work of the Hotteterre circle.

The resulting instrument became known as the **bassoon**, although for a time it was also covered by the words *curtall* and *dulcian*, and also *fagotto*, which has never gone out of use. Early bassoons had much wider reeds than those of today, and in instruments by Johann Christoph Denner (1655–1707), his son

124 *William Beale Wotton*, professor of bassoon at the Royal College of Music, painted by Arnold Willins in 1898. *London, Royal College of Music.*

Jacob (*d.* 1735) and their contemporaries, there were three keys. A fourth had appeared before 1750, and it was for such an instrument that Mozart wrote his Bassoon Concerto in 1774. By 1800 there were six keys, but in spite of very good instruments by Grundmann and members of the Grenser family, it was not possible to play smoothly in all tonalities. This problem was tackled by Carl Almenräder, who around 1820 produced a bassoon with 15 keys, but at the expense of its tone. From 1831 he worked in partnership with Johann Adam Heckel, whose son Wilhelm considerably widened the bore. Successive members of the Heckel family have continued the business, and the firm now produces some of the best bassoons in the world. Boehm applied his principles to the bassoon with the help of Frédéric Triébert, producing an instrument which won a prize at the London Exhibition of 1862, although its vast cost prevented it from being widely adopted. The best French bassoons of today are by the firm of Buffet-Crampon in Paris,

125 Contrebasse-à-anche, French, late 19th century. *London, Horniman Museum.*

126 Bladder-pipe played by a shepherd in an *Altarpiece of the Virgin Mary* (detail from the scene of an angel appearing to St Joachim), Venetian School, probably late 14th century. *London, National Gallery.*

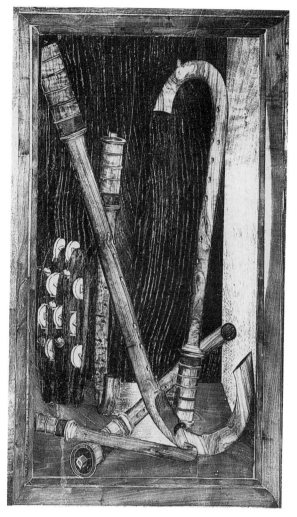

127 Crumhorns and timbrel, in an intarsia panel by Fra Giovanni Barile da Siena, 1513–21. *Rome, Vatican, Stanza della Segnatura.*

according to Anthony Baines (*Woodwind Instruments and their History*), who, in comparing the relative merits of the German and French bassoons, wrote that while the French instrument is 'more subtle and vocal', the Heckel bassoon is 'more uniformly effective in the orchestra'. Professor Giles Brindley's electrified Logical Bassoon (p. 106–7) has made radical changes in line with technological developments of the twentieth century.

During its history the different sizes of bassoon have included the **tenoroon**, which is pitched a fourth or fifth higher than the usual instrument, and the **contrabassoon (double bassoon)** which descends to $B^{b''}$. On 6 August 1739 the *London Daily Post and General Advertiser* announced that in Marylebone Gardens, London, there would be played

Two Grand or Double Bassoons, made by Mr. Stanesby, jun. the Greatness of whose sound surpasses that of any

other Base Instrument whatsoever. Never performed before.

Thomas Stanesby (1692–1754), who with his father of the same name was one of the greatest English makers of wind instruments, may have made this instrument at the request of Handel, who used it early in 1740 in his *L'Allegro, il Penseroso ed il Moderato*. A shorter and more bulky instrument was the **Contrabassophon**, which was invented by Heinrich J. Haseneier of Coblenz in 1847. It was played a good deal in England, and appeared in the Handel Festival of 1871.

Related to the oboe and bassoon is the likewise conically-bored **Sarrusophone**, which was created by the French bandmaster Sarrus and patented by P.L. Gautrot of Paris in 1856. Made of brass and with a double reed, its smaller sizes (now obsolete) were straight, while the larger ones somewhat resembled the bassoon and contrabassoon in shape. Like the saxophone, which inspired it, the sarrusophone has been used to a great extent in military bands, as have other double-reed brass instruments such as the **contrabasse-à-anche**, which was played mainly on the Continent during the latter part of the nineteenth century.

During the Middle Ages certain pipes were fitted with a bladder which acted as an air reservoir above the double reed. Today they are called **bladder-pipes**. In the late fifteenth century there emerged a new class of instruments which had no bladder, but the reed was covered by a wooden cap containing a narrow mouth hole. The most spectacular of these was the cylindrically-bored **crumhorn** which curved, horn-like, at its lower end, and was made in different sizes for consort playing. Henry VIII possessed a good many of them, and it is known that 13 of his collection were sent to him by the Flemish scribe Pierre van den Hove (who used the name 'Alamire'), as a cover for passing on information about the activities of certain English exiles abroad. Bearing in mind that the crumhorn was still being played in the *Grande Ecurie* at Versailles in 1690, it must have lasted about 200 years, but its main period of popularity was from *c.* 1500 to *c.* 1650.

Other reed-cap instruments included the conical **Rauschpfeife**, which was virtually a covered shawm, the **corna muse** which appeared to be straight and was covered below, producing a soft sound, and the similar-looking **Schryari** or

128 Rauschpfeifen (right) and shawms (left), in a woodcut attributed to Albrecht Altdorfer, from *The Triumph of Maximilian,* 1526, plate 79.

129 Clarinets, from left to right by I. Scherer, ?Paris, *c.* 1750; Cramer & Co., London, *c.* 1830–40 (in B flat); Wood & Ivy, London, 1836–47 (in E flat); Metzler & Co., London, 1842–7 (in C); and bass clarinet by Maino & Orsi, Milan, late 19th century. *London, Royal College of Music.*

Schreierpfeifen which, by having open ends, sounded, according to Praetorius, 'strong and fresh in sound'. An inventory taken at the castle of Cassel on 24 February 1613 included four different sizes of Schryari besides 'l Krumbhorn case with 8 Krumbhörner of different sizes', and a *Strach*, described here as being a 'long straight instrument, basset to the Krumbhörner'.

Instruments with only a single reed came late to European art music, although in primitive forms they had been known from Antiquity. In the medieval **hornpipe** (still extant today as a folk instrument), which itself could be a single or double instrument, the one or two reeds were often encased in horn, while the opposite end of the wooden pipe was terminated in an expanding bell, also made of horn. The single reed also made a brief appearance in the **Phagotus**, an instrument related to bagpipes, which was made by Canon Afranio of Ferrara (1480–c. 1565), but it is significant that such reeds were mentioned neither by Praetorius nor by Mersenne.

In the late seventeenth century, however, a new instrument called the **chalumeau** came onto the musical scene. (It should not be confused with the shawm, which has often used the same name in France.) This was a cylindrical pipe with seven fingerholes, a thumbhole, sometimes one or two keys, and a single beating reed fixed to the upper side of the mouthpiece. Its disadvantage lay in its range of less than one and a half octaves, and it could not overblow.

This problem was solved *c.* 1700 by Johann Christoph Denner of Nuremberg, and in doing so he created the **clarinet**. By altering the position and size of the keyed holes, he made playable the third and fifth harmonics, which sound a twelfth and eighteenth respectively above the fundamental. (When the reed is held between the player's lips the clarinet acts as a stopped pipe, and as such it cannot sound harmonics at the octave. The subsequent development of the instrument was aimed at making playable all the notes between the bottom and the top, and on smoothing out as far as possible their difference of tone.) Apart from their single reed and two keys, Denner's clarinets looked very much like

130 Bass clarinet by Nicola Papalini, Chiaravalle, *c.* 1815. *Boston, Mass., Museum of Fine Arts.*

treble recorders, and they were built in three parts. Gradually new keys were added to fill in the missing notes, so that by the time of Mozart's maturity there were five, and by 1790 there were six. (Because of the difficulties of fingering, clarinets were made as transposing instruments in different pitches.) The instrument was now fully chromatic, but the notes were of uneven quality. This was considerably remedied by the Russian-born Ivan Müller, who, in *c.* 1812, made a 13-keyed clarinet with improved intonation due to its holes being placed more correctly than before. His fingering system enabled performance in any key, and he claimed that alternative instruments were no longer necessary. Among other makers to facilitate awkward jumps was Adolphe Sax of Brussels, who also extended the range of pitch downwards.

Inevitably there appeared a 'Boehm clarinet', although Boehm himself was not involved with its production. This was the work of Hyacinthe Klosé and Auguste Buffet between 1839 and 1843. With further attention to the positioning of holes, to the type of their keys, and to economy of fingering, they devised the clarinet which is among the most used in America and western Europe today. Many professional clarinettists still like to use alternative instruments in A and B flat, which, with their downward extensions, actually sound $c^{\sharp}$ and d for their lowest notes.

Larger instruments included the late eighteenth-century **clarinette d'amour**, which had its mouthpiece attached to a crook, and was distinguished by a bulbous bell; it was succeeded by the **alto clarinet** in F or E flat around 1820. The **bass clarinet** has been designed in very

131 Basset horn, of a type used in the music of Mozart; probably Viennese, *c.* 1780. *Nuremberg, Germanisches Nationalmuseum.*

132 Saxophone, in the 'Mark 7' tenor model by H. Selmer, Paris, 1976.

133 Bagpipes (right) played with a pipe-and-tabor in the border of a Flemish Book of Hours, *c.* 1300. *London, British Library, MS Stowe 17, f.31.*

varied ways, resembling a curtall or bassoon *c.* 1800, and appearing in a snake-like form in Italy about ten years later. Adolphe Sax made straight ones with the bell facing downwards in contrast to its previous position (*c.* 1845), but more recent designs have turned it up again. Many designs have appeared for a **contrabass clarinet**, notably the **Bathyphon** patented by W. Wieprecht and E. Skorra of Berlin in 1839, the **Pedal Clarinet** of Fontaine-Besson of Paris in 1889, and current models by the firms of Selmer and Buffet.

Of earlier vintage was the **basset horn**, attributed to A. and M. Mayrhofer of Passau, *c.* 1770. Its early shape was curved, then angular, and later on straight, with its distinguishing feature being a 'box' in which the tubing doubled back on itself to save the overall length; its lowest note was *F*. The composers with which it is chiefly associated are Mozart, Mendelssohn and Richard Strauss, and between their respective eras it was used to a considerable extent in military bands. Berlioz, in his suggestions for 'the finest concert orchestra' (p. 219), suggested the use of 'one basset-horn or one bass clarinet'.

During the nineteenth century there appeared several single-reed instruments with a conical bore. The most important was the **Saxophone**, which was invented by Adolphe Sax around 1842; it occurs in various sizes of which the smallest are straight and the largest have an upturned bell and a crook. It has been used a great deal in military and jazz bands, and for occasional special effects in orchestral music. A

wooden relative is the **tarogato**, which, originally a double-reed folk instrument from Hungary, was later adapted for a single-reed mouthpiece, and was called for in the final act of Wagner's *Tristan*.

Last but by no means least come the **bagpipes**, which combine characteristics of all the reed instruments mentioned above. In the *Orationes* of Dio Chrysostom (born *c.* 40 AD) we are told that the Emperor Nero could 'play the pipes, both by means of his lips and by tucking a skin beneath his armpits'. From that time onwards information about the bagpipes is scanty, and it is not until the Middle Ages that their history becomes more clear. In the ninth-century letter from 'Jerome' to 'Dardanus' (see p. 28) one interpretation of the word 'chorus' is of a bag from which project a mouthpipe and a chanter. This is illustrated in the many manuscripts containing the letter, and from the twelfth century the instrument appears

134 Musette from 18th-century France. *London, Royal College of Music.*

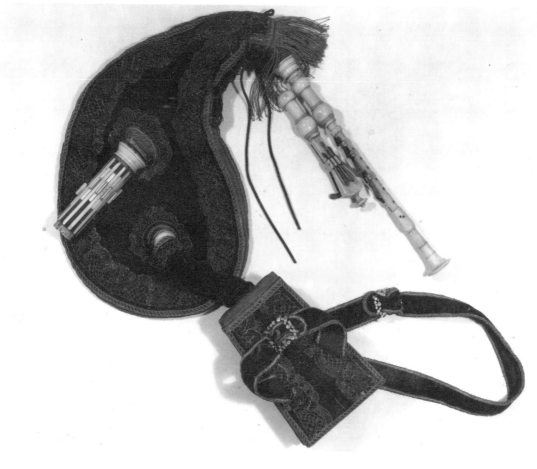

135 Bagpipers of the Argyll and Sutherland Highlanders at the Military Exhibition of 1890. *London, Mansell Collection.*

in independent sources, one example being a carving at the Spanish Abbey of Ripoll. While this simple bagpipe continued in use for some time, the most usual medieval type had appeared by *c.* 1250. This had the bag, mouthpipe and chanter as before, but also a drone pipe, which became one of the most important characteristics of the instrument. Athough the *Cantigas de Santa Maria* manuscript shows on f. 313v a bagpipe with four drones, these are exceptional, and it was not until the fifteenth century that two or more drone pipes became frequent. Bellows were applied to Irish bagpipes before 1600, and have since been used in the French *musette*, the Northumbrian *small-pipe*, and the Bohemian *dudy*, to name but a few. The **musette**, which was played by the artificially rustic French nobility during the reign of Louis XIV and later, and was improved by Jean Hotteterre the Elder, had two ivory or ebony cylindrical chanters with silver keys, and a cylinder containing four interchangeable drones; moreover, all its reeds were double. The bagpipes best known today are perhaps those of Scotland, which in their large type have a mouthpipe, chanter and three drones, but numerous other varieties can be found as folk instruments in different parts of Europe.

The role of the bagpipe in history has been one of the most varied among instruments. A favourite for shepherds to play while guarding their sheep, it has also been played to accompany such activities as dancing, acrobatics, and tournaments, and processions for weddings, funerals and pilgrimages, besides amusing the dilettante noblemen mentioned above. From the Middle Ages onwards it has been used for military purposes, and today massed bands of pipers play to the world during the Edinburgh International Festival. An instrument of great importance in its own right, it has, however, remained outside the confines of the symphony orchestra, except in such rare cases as the *Peasant Wedding* composed in 1755 by Leopold Mozart.

VI

The Brass Families

The 'brass' instruments, like those of the 'woodwind' families, have during their history been made from a great variety of materials. In all cases their sound is generated by the vibrating lips of the player, often against a cup-shaped mouthpiece. Allowing for many hybrids, they can broadly be divided into two basic types: those with a conical bore comprising horns, and those with a cylindrical bore, namely trumpets.

From the earliest sound-producing horns, those of animals, there emerged two main lines of descent. One consisted of instruments which officially gave only the notes from the harmonic series (although altering the embouchure and covering the bell with the hand could produce other notes), while the other comprised those with fingerholes. Due to their close connection with the woodwind instruments, this latter group will be treated first.

Because the simple animal horn did not naturally sound adjacent notes of the harmonic series, fingerholes were added to it at an early date, and from the Romanesque period onwards it was often depicted thus in the hands of shepherds. It was later imitated in wood and became an instrument of art music with the name **cornett** (Italian **cornetto**, German **Zinck**), being already known in this form before 1400. Many examples have survived from the sixteenth century onwards, some being of wood covered with leather, and others being of ivory or ebony; its sizes were treble, tenor and bass (this is thought to have been the English **lysarden**), with an occasional high **cornettino**. While some were straight, most were curved, and the exotic snake-like shape of the larger ones avoided too great a distance between the fingerholes. Most cornetts, of whatever shape, needed a separate mouthpiece, but in some of the straight ones this was actually turned in the top part of the instrument, and could not be seen from outside. This type was known as the **mute cornett**, as it made a softer sound. During the Renaissance and early Baroque periods, cornetts were frequently played with church choirs, as they sounded not unlike the human voice. Their popularity eventually waned with the ascendancy of the oboe.

Somewhat similar to the bass cornett, but with a much wider conical bore and thinner walls was the **serpent**, which, according to the Abbé Leboeuf (*Mémoire concernant l'histoire ecclésiastique et civile d'Auxerre*, Paris, 1743), was invented by Canon Edmé Guillaume of Auxerre around 1590. Early examples had just six or seven fingerholes, but up to fourteen keys were added after 1800. One of the serpent's chief uses was described by Burney during his French tour of 1770:

In the French churches there is an instrument on

136 Horn with fingerholes, from a Book of Hours made in Milan, *c.* 1494 for the Sforza family. *London, British Library, MS Add. 34294, f.34v.*

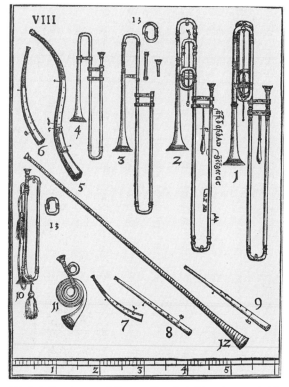

137 1–4 Trombones; 5–9 cornetts, straight and curved; 10, trumpet; 11, hunting trumpet; 12, wooden trumpet; 13, trumpet crook. Praetorius, *Theatrum Instrumentorum,* 1620, plate VIII.

each side of the choir, called the serpent, from its shape, I suppose, for it undulates like one. This gives the *tone* in chanting, and plays the base when they sing in parts. It is often ill-played, but if judiciously used, would have a good effect. It is, however, in general overblown, and too powerful for the voices it accompanies; otherwise, it mixes with them better than the organ, as it can augment or diminish a sound with more delicacy, and is less likely to overpower or destroy by a bad temperament, that perfect one, of which the voice only is capable.

A picture of it being played in Autun Cathedral can be seen in figure 234, and a contrabass serpent called the **Anaconda** was played in Almondbury Church for many years by Joseph and Richard Wood who made it *c.* 1840.

The serpent was also used in military bands and in orchestras, either in its own right or as a substitute for the bassoon family, as happened when it deputized for the double bassoon in a performance of Haydn's *Creation* at the Paris Opéra in 1800. Although it gave way to the ophicleide after *c.* 1830, it was still widely used later in the century. Related to it were the V-shaped copper or brass **bass horn** and the wooden **Russian bassoon**, which had a dragon's-head bell, both of which flourished in similar conditions to the serpent during the nineteenth century.

The principle of adding keys to instruments of metal was applied to the singly-coiled copper **bugle horn** and patented by Joseph Haliday of Dublin in 1810. This **keyed bugle** in C or B flat was very popular until the middle of the century, particularly in Britain and America. A larger form, the **ophicleide**, was invented by Halary of Paris in 1817 (patented in 1821) and made of brass, somewhat resembling a bassoon in shape. The most usual size, pitched in C or B flat, was frequently used as a bass to the brass instruments of the orchestra by such composers as Mendelssohn and Berlioz, and it only became obsolete with the final acceptance of the orchestral tuba. Both the keyed bugle and the ophicleide were prominent in military music, and can be seen in the long frieze commemorating the Duke of Wellington's funeral in 1852, where the bands of

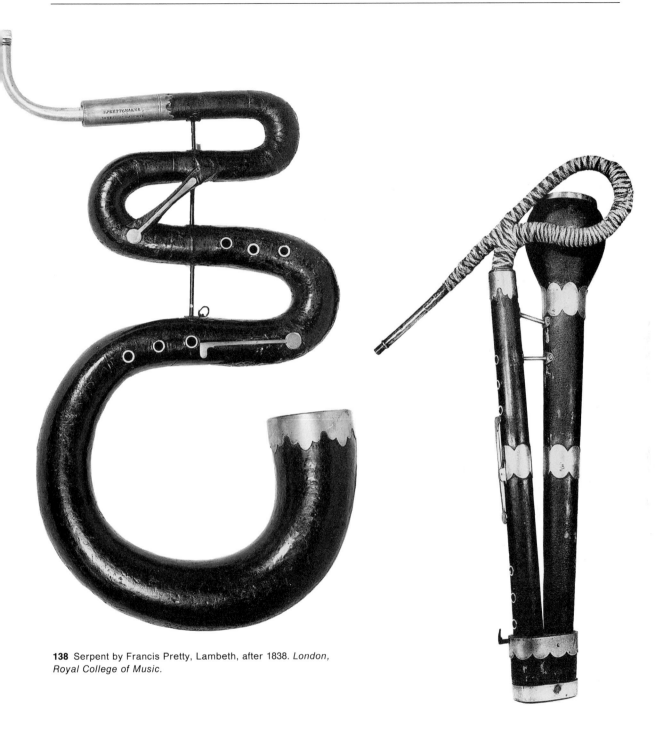

138 Serpent by Francis Pretty, Lambeth, after 1838. *London, Royal College of Music.*

139 Bass horn, possibly by Astor, London, early 19th century. *London, Horniman Museum.*

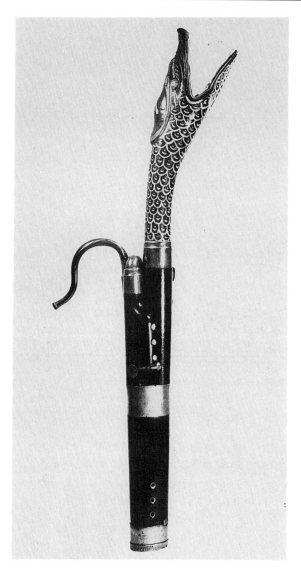

140 Russian bassoon by Jeantet, Lyon, *c.* 1825. *London, Horniman Museum.*

different regiments contain very varied instruments. (This is at Apsley House, London, the Wellington Museum.) The ophicleide appears in a photograph of the Crediton Town Band taken in 1862 by William Hector (plate 201 in the author's *Musical Instruments of the West*).

Simple **horns** without fingerholes, and with the mouthpiece carved out of the body itself, go back to remote Antiquity. Some were used mainly for outdoor signalling, while others, such as the Jewish **shofar** (a ram or goat horn), had ritual purposes. Long before the advent of Christianity, however, they had inspired the making of metal horns, with perhaps the most spectacular being the Bronze Age **lurs** which have been discovered in Scandinavian peat bogs. These bronze instruments were played in pairs, each of the two being tuned to the same basic note, and their flat disc at the wide end is seen to a lesser extent on horns of about the same period excavated in Ireland. It is not known whether they played in unison or in parts, or whether they used all the harmonics which were attainable. However, a glimpse of their great potential was heard on 25 August 1972, when two modern players dressed as ancient Danes gave an enthralling virtuoso performance after the closing dinner of the International Musicological Society's congress at Copenhagen.

The almost circular Roman **cornu** (fig. 198), which was often played with the long tuba and the hydraulis, was held in such a way that its bell was in the uppermost position, high above the player's shoulder. It was frequently depicted in the arts, one of the many examples in Rome itself being on Trajan's Column. The Roman **buccina** has not yet been sufficiently identified, but it seems to have been some kind of animal horn which in the later stages was covered in brass. Anthony Baines (*Brass Instruments*, pp. 68–9) has suggested that the Byzantine **boukina** may have been the 'cavalry salpinx' of 'leather and thin wood' which, according to Procopius in *The History of the Wars*, VI, xxiii, was used in the army of Belisarius in 540.

In the Dark Ages and the early medieval period, animal horns were again the most used in Europe, the most distinguished of them being

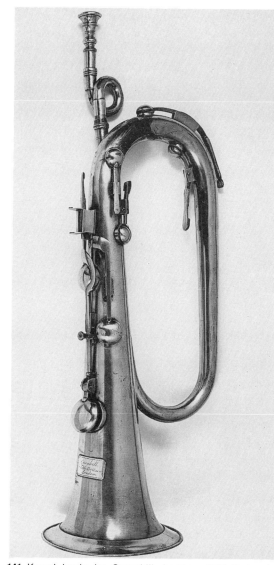

141 Keyed bugle by Greenhill, London, 1824–9. *'ondon, Royal College of Music.*

142 Bass ophicleide, on the title page of *Solfège-Méthode pour l' Ophicleide Basse*, by V. Caussinus, Paris, *c*. 1840. *London, British Library, h.2295.a.*

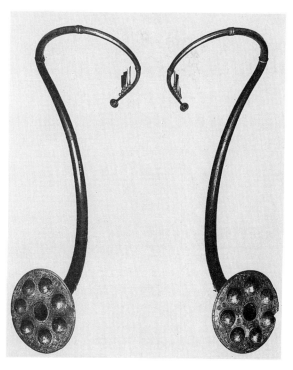

143 Lurs from the Bronze Age, discovered at Brudevaelte Moor, North Sealand, Denmark. *Copenhagen, Danish National Museum.*

144 Horn in its most simple form, from a margin of the Luttrell Psalter, made in England *c.* 1325–35. *London, British Library, MS Add. 42130, f.43v.*

the carved ivory **oliphant**, which was made by Byzantine and Moorish craftsmen, mainly in the eleventh century, and much associated with warriors. Larger **horns of metal** were again widespread by the late fourteenth century, being well represented on a misericord of 1379 in Worcester Cathedral, where a huntsman's horn curves round most of his body. A vivid description of one of the medieval uses of horns is given in Froissart's *Chronicles* concerning an expedition of the Bishop of Durham against the Scots:

The Scots infantry all carry horns slung on their shoulders, in the manner of hunters. The horns are all of different sizes, and when they are all blown together, in different keys, they can be heard four miles away by day, and six miles away by night, to the terror and consternation of their enemies, and the great delight of themselves. The Scots commanders now ordered music of this kind to be played. The bishop was less than half a mile away when this happened, and the noise was as if all the devils in Hell had gathered together. Drums were also beaten, and the English, who had never heard anything like it before, were very much frightened. The noise stopped abruptly and then, when the English were only half a mile away, started up again. However, the bishop advanced steadily to within two bowshots of the Scots, who began to make more noise than ever, while the bishop was able to see the strength of the Scots position. After some deliberation, the English knights found it inadvisable to attack, for defeat seemed more probable than victory. They therefore returned to Newcastle.

It was for hunting and military purposes that horns were mainly used for the next three hundred years, with their shapes varying from straight to any degree of curvature. Tightly coiled horns lasted from the fifteenth century to the early twentieth, but it was the large seventeenth-century horn with one or two coils which led to the orchestral **French horn** of today. This was wide enough to carry over the shoulder, and some of its best examples are by the Crétien family of Vernon in Normandy. Horn music was played by a string orchestra in Cavalli's opera *Le Nozze di Teti e di Peleo* (1639), and from the time of

Lully's ballet *La Princesse d'Elide* (1664) horns themselves were increasingly used for fanfare effects in dramatic performances. Franz Anton, Count von Sporck, heard such hunting horns at the Court of Louis XIV while doing the Grand Tour in 1680–82, and introduced them to Bohemia on his return. Soon afterwards they were known in Vienna.

It was there that Michael Leichnamschneider was responsible for turning the horn into a truly orchestral instrument, by reducing its size to create a more sonorous tone, and, not later than 1703, by the addition of crooks. These were coils of different lengths, which, when added to the main tube, lengthened it and therefore lowered the basic pitch, although not increasing the number of available notes. All orchestral horn music up to *c.* 1750 was theoretically restricted to notes of the harmonic series, although in practice the lower harmonics could be lowered still further in pitch by the 'falset' technique of relaxing the embouchure.

In the mid eighteenth century horn-playing was revolutionized by hand-stopping, in which notes other than the natural harmonics could be produced by the performer inserting his hand into the bell of the instrument, to a greater or lesser degree. This meant that a complete scale was now available, although with a difference of *timbre* between the natural and stopped notes. Up

145 Two French horns played with handhorn technique, two violins, viola and bass, on the title page of Mozart's *A Musical Joke*, K.522, published posthumously in 1801. *London, British Library, Hirsch IV.128.*

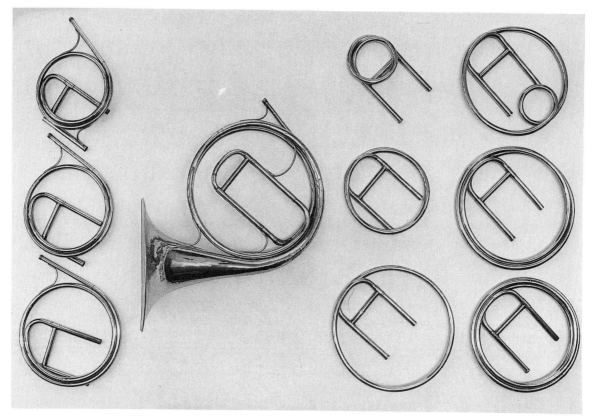

146 Inventionshorn with its crooks, by Gustav Pfretzschner, Neukirchen, *c. 1840. Copenhagen, Musikhistorisk Museum.*

to this time the French horn had normally been played with the bell pointing upwards, but to accommodate the hand the position was now reversed. A player much associated with this technique, even if he did not invent it, was the Bohemian-born Anton Joseph Hampl, who worked in Dresden. From his time, at least until that of Brahms, composers wrote for the handhorn, which itself went through several modifications. In the earliest surviving crooked horns (dating from the mid eighteenth century), one or more crooks were added between the main body of the instrument and the master crook, which held the mouthpiece. According to the number of crooks added, the bell was at a different distance from the player's mouth. This was inconvenient for hand-stopping, so around 1753 Hampl devised a new system by which the crooks were added at the centre of the instrument and the

mouthpiece remained at the same distance from the hand. The resulting **Inventionshorn** was first made by Johann Werner of Dresden, and later by Johann Gottfried Haltenhof of Hanau-am-Mayn, whose instruments contained a tuning slide for adjusting the pitch to that of other instruments. A strengthened type of Inventions-horn was the *Cor Solo*, designed by Joseph Raoux of Paris *c.* 1780, especially for the use of virtuosi. This had crooks for G, F, E, E flat and D, the keys most needed for solo horn music. Orchestral horns, however, needed at least nine crooks, and so, to avoid the inconvenience of carrying them all around, there appeared **Omnitonic horns**, of which the earliest example is by J.-B. Dupont of Paris, and dates from *c.* 1815. This instrument is now kept at the Paris Conservatoire. Its basic principle is that detachable crooks are replaced by the necessary amount of tubing built into the main instrument, the correct amount for each fundamental pitch being opened up by a device which varied from one instrument to another.

147 French horn with valves, 19th century. *London, Horniman Museum.*

148 Cornet-à-pistons by Guichard, Breveté, Paris, before 1845. *London, Horniman Museum.*

149 Orchestral tuba in F, made by Boosey & Hawkes in 1955 for Gerard Hoffnung, who is seen playing it here.

The technique of handstopping, however, still needed to be used. Other methods of dispensing with detachable crooks had included the short-lived **Amor-schall**, invented *c.* 1766 by the Bohemian Kölbel who worked at St Petersburg. No example of this instrument is known to survive, but it is said to have had keys and a bulbous bell, to which was attached another bulbous shape containing small holes.

Of more lasting importance was the **valve horn**, which was foreshadowed as far back as 1788, when the Irishman Charles Clagget patented the 'Cromatic Trumpet and French Horn', but this double instrument disappeared after a few performances. In Berlin in 1818 Heinrich Stölzel of Saxony and Friedrich Blühmel of Silesia patented the use of valves, bringing together their own discoveries, of which Stölzel's had already been publicized in 1815. Their horns were furnished with two piston valves, each of which made available a greater length of tubing, and the pitch accordingly descended a semitone or tone as required. In the 1830s a third piston was added, which lowered the pitch by yet another semitone. Since then many types of valve have been invented, but those most used today are the rotary valves, apparently invented by Joseph Riedl of Vienna *c.* 1832, and the type of piston valve produced by Francois Périnet of Paris in 1839. In fact the valve horn was not widely used at first, as players and listeners preferred the sound of the natural horn, which was used until late in the century. The great advantage of the valve horn, however, was that the changes previously made by removing crooks between playing could now be effected during perform-ance, and the instrument was chromatic within itself. While the basic pitch of the horn has varied much during its history, it is nowadays a transposing instrument normally in F, or, in the double horn, adaptable from F to B flat.

The introduction of valves reformed not only the French horn, but also some of its minor relatives. The bugle with valves was known as the **flugel horn**, while the valved circular **posthorn** became the **cornet-à-pistons** or **cornopean** *c.* 1827 in the hands of Halary. There are many other 'horns', united by their conical bore and use of valves, but of very varying shapes and sizes, and confusing terminology. These include instruments going by the names of **euphonium**, **bombardon**, **alto**, **tenor**, **bari-tone** and **bass** (**tuba**) **horns**, and the family of **Saxhorns**, patented by Adolphe Sax in 1843. Their main use is in brass band music. Of the **tuba** family, the most important is the **bass tuba** in F, patented by Wilhelm Wieprecht and Johann Gottfried Moritz in 1835, which eventually super-seded the serpent, bass horn, Russian bassoon and ophicleide. The lowest tuba is the **sub-contrabass** in B flat. **Wagner**'s special '**tubas**' designed for *The Ring* have occasionally been used by other composers, notably Richard Strauss. Related to the tuba are the circular **helicon**, associated with Wieprecht and Ignaz Stowasser *c.* 1849, and a somewhat similar instrument with a very long bell which was invented by John Philip Sousa in 1898 became adopted by Amer-ican army bands under the name **Sousaphone**.

In contrast to the horn, the **trumpet** family normally has a cylindrical bore. Up to the Middle Ages, however, this was often conical, the charac-ter of the instrument appearing in its straight outline and expanding bell. It is well documented in ancient arts, and surviving specimens incude two from the tomb of Tutankhamun who reigned in Egypt from *c.* 1361–52 BC; one of these is of bronze and gold, and the other is of silver. The Greek **salpinx** and the Roman **tuba** were long trumpets, mainly cylindrical and with a flared bell. The Roman **lituus**, on the other hand, had a curved bell, at first being made from a reed pipe terminating in a horn, and later being fashioned in brass or bronze.

With the collapse of the Roman Empire the **trumpet**, like the organ, disappeared from most of Europe, and is next seen on a wide scale in the visual arts of the Middle Ages. Early examples are in the French ninth-century Apocalypse at Trier (Stadtbibliothek MS 31), and in a fresco of the Cathedral Baptistery at Novara, dating from *c.* 1000. From this time onwards the metal trumpet gradually spread again through Europe, its dis-tinctive pommels (bosses) and cylindrical bore

150 Two long trumpets played for a joust in the Smithfied Decretals, written in Italy but illustrated in England, c. 1325–30. *London, British Library, MS Roy, 10.E.iv, f.66.*

becoming established through eastern influence at about the time of the Third Crusade (1189–92). Such instruments, however, are not normally seen in English art until after 1200, their predecessors being long, straight and conical instruments very probably made of wood, as seen in the Tiberius Psalter (British Library MS Cotton Tib. C.vi, f.18v.) of c. 1050. Nevertheless even these are rare in English sources of the time, and most contemporary illustrations of the word 'tuba' (as in the Apocalypse) show an unmistakably curved horn.

Once it had become established, the true trumpet became one of the most important instruments on account of its use on ceremonial occasions, whether of peace or of war. While the names *trumpe* and *buisine* were often used for long trumpets, *trompete* and *clarion* for shorter ones and *beme* possibly for wooden ones, the matter has been considerably confused by poetic licence. Of certain value, however, is Maurice Byrne's

discovery, in documents of the Goldsmiths' Company, that in 1391 certain specified 'trompes' weighed more than 'clarions' (*Galpin Society Journal* XXIV, 1971, 63). The following excerpts show some of the contrasting ways in which these instruments fitted into society:

A barge shall mete you full right
With four and twenty ores full bright
With trompettes and with clarioune
The freshe water to rowe up and doune.
(Anon., *The Squire of Low Degree*, l.811–14: c. 1450.)

Tho saugh I in an other place
Stonden in a large space,
Of hem that maken blody soun
In trumpe, beme, and claryoun;
for in fight and blod-shedynge
Ys used gladly clarionynge.
(Chaucer, *The House of Fame*, l.1237–42; c. 1375.)

A trumpet of latten and brass, measuring about 154 cm in length, was excavated at Billingsgate, London, in 1984, and is now kept at the Museum of London.

By the middle of the fourteenth century

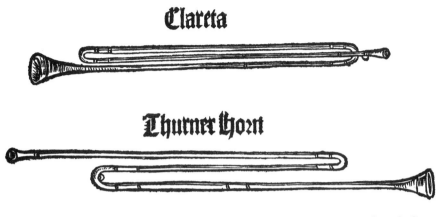

Clareta

Thurner Horn

Des selßenzweyten geschlechts der holen totē/ist die ander art von den instru-
menten/welchen der mensch durch sich selß nit winds genüg mag gebē oder dye
nyemant erplasen kan/das synd alle dye instrumenta/dar zů man plaspelg ha-
ben müß. **C**

151 'Clareta' and 'Thurner Horn' from Virdung's *Musica Getutscht,* 1511. The former may have been a slide trumpet, and the latter is known to have been played frequently on towers.

trumpets had become so long that some of them were bent back into a shape like a flattened letter *S*. These and the straight ones were often played together, a striking example being in a picture of the Battle of Agincourt (1415) from the St Albans Chronicle (London, Lambeth Palace, MS 6, f.243). About this time the instrument was also looped right over, one of its earliest depictions being in the wall paintings by Brother John of Northampton in the Chapter House at Westminster Abbey, dating from the 1390s. Virdung later described this form as 'Clareta'.

While the straight trumpet remained for heraldic purposes, folded ones became normal, and were generally pitched in D. Praetorius, however, said that

a short time ago it became the practice in many court orchestras either to use the trumpet in a lengthened form or to attach crook tubes to its front

to bring it down to C. On it the harmonic series was divided into two main registers, the *principale* (medium) and *clarino* (upper), with different players specializing in each, although there was no difference in the instruments themselves. Clarino playing, which uses the adjacent notes of the harmonic series, was used by Monteverdi in *Orfeo* (1607) and reached its zenith in the time of Bach, who immortalized it in his Second Brandenburg Concerto (1721). Later in the eighteenth century this high register was abandoned, and the trumpet was again used mainly for music of a fanfare type, whether in or out of the orchestra. It was now pitched in F or E flat. An invaluable guide to eighteenth-century trumpets, with their history, technique and social standing, can be found in the *Trumpeters' and Kettledrummers' Art* by Johann Ernst Altenburg, published at Halle in 1795.

The trumpet described so far, whether straight, folded, or sometimes even coiled, had produced the natural harmonics in whatever key it was built (or crooked). One of the first attempts to make it chromatic came in the Renaissance **slide trumpet**, in which the mouthpiece was fixed to a movable piece of tube. The player would hold this in one hand close to his mouth, and with the other hand he would pull the rest of the instrument further away, lowering the basic pitch possibly by as much as a perfect fourth. By this means the trumpet could play a wide range of chromatic notes, and was able to play with voices and other instruments in Renaissance polyphony, which the normal trumpet could hardly ever do, except in such pieces as Dufay's *Gloria 'ad modum tubae'* (see p. 192). A surviving Baroque *Zugtrompete* by Hans Veit of Naumberg, dated 1651 (now in the Institut für Musikforschung, Berlin), is thought to have been the type of instrument specified by Bach as the 'tromba da tirarsi'. In the late seventeenth century an English variety was known as the **flat trumpet** because it could play the 'flat' notes involved in minor keys. At the funeral solemnity of Queen Mary II in 1694 a Full Anthem by Purcell was 'accompanied with flat Mournfull Trumpets', according to the British Library MS Harl. 7340, p.521. This instrument which was described in detail by James Talbot between 1685 and 1701, was the predecessor of the English slide trumpet (normally in F) much associated with John Hyde in the late eighteenth century, and which lasted about 100 years. The French also made slide trumpets to a limited degree at this time.

Further attempts to make the chromatic notes playable included the **Stopftrompete** or **Trompette demilune** of the eighteenth and early nineteenth centuries, using handstopping techniques which, however, proved to be less successful than on the horn. Its French name came from the curved shape in which not only the main body, but also the crooks were built. A **keyed trumpet**, such as that by Joseph Riedl which was being played by the Viennese Anton Weidinger in 1801, is thought to have been the instrument for which Haydn wrote his Trumpet Concerto in 1796.

Mechanization of the trumpet, which can be traced back to Charles Clagget's invention of 1788 (p. 146), became permanent with the invention of valves, but only after they had been applied to the horn. Early references to **valve trumpets** include Wieprecht's use of them in a Prussian band in 1824, and Spontini's despatching of some from Germany to Paris two years later. For a long time, however, the natural trumpet was used unless the valve one was specified, and in England the slide trumpet was considered adequate for most of the century. The basic pitch of the valve trumpet varied considerably, that of F being the most usual in orchestral circles until *c.* 1910, since when it has been replaced by C or B flat, although alternatives are still available.

As the art of clarino playing had vanished before 1800, the modern revival of Baroque music has led to experiments to find a '**Bach**' **trumpet**. One of the first was produced by Julius Kosleck, who played it for Bach's Bicentenary in 1885; it consisted of a long buisine-line instrument with two valves. After further valve-trumpet attempts by C. Mahillon & Co. of Brussels in 1892, Werner

152 Trumpet made by William Bull of London in the late 17th century. *London, Museum of London.*

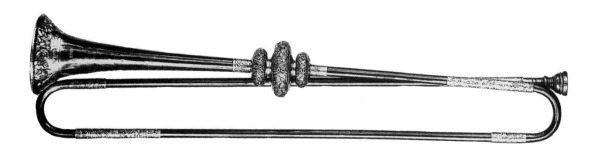

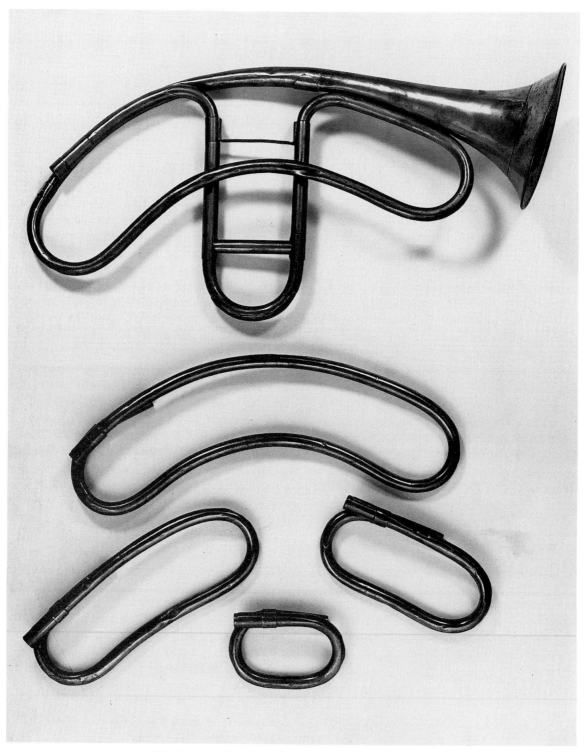

153 'Demilune' Trumpet with crooks, by Charles Kretzsch-
mann, Strasbourg, 1827–35. *London, Royal College of Music.*

154 Trumpets, from left to right: Keyed trumpet by W. Sandbach, London, 1812; slide trumpet by I. Kohler, London, 1860; valve trumpet by Conn, USA, 1976. *London, Royal Military School of Music, Kneller Hall. (The valve trumpet is owned by Bandsman J. Mitchell.)*

monarch entertained the Emperor Charles V in London in 1522,

> ...they passed to the Conduite in Cornehill where the strete was enclosed from side to side with ii gates to open and shitte, and over the gates wer arches with towers embattailed set with vanes and scutchions of the armes of the Emperor and the kyng, and over the arches were two towers, the one full of Trompettes and the other full of Shalmes and shagbuttes whiche played continually...

It is not known where the trombone originated, but the earliest recorded maker of them was Hans Neuschel II of Nuremberg, a town celebrated for its brass instruments. Neuschel made instruments for Maximilian I, and his portrait appears in *The Triumph of Maximilian* (1526) at the express wish of the Emperor himself, whose instructions had already been given in 1512. A tenor trombone by Georg Neuschel, the son of Hans II, is dated 1557, and now belongs to Dr René Clemencic of Vienna.

Like many other Renaissance and Baroque instruments, trombones were built in different sizes. Four were known to Praetorius, namely the **alto**, **tenor**, **bass** and **contrabass**, and a **soprano** was also used in the eighteenth century. The tenor in B flat was, and still is, the instrument most used, descending normally to *E*, while the contrabass was an octave lower. Praetorius said that with careful playing it could be made to go lower still, and it was sometimes supplied with crooks for that purpose, as were the other sizes. Chromatic music was no problem as trombones could play with the slide in seven different positions. During this early period the instruments were used to a great extent in church music, particularly in association with cornetts, and they were occasionally used for special effects in opera, a notable example being Monteverdi's *Orfeo* of 1607.

Around 1740 the bell was widened in order to produce a stronger sound, but already the instrument was loosing favour in many parts of Europe, and in England for a long time the only trombone players were to be found in the king's private band. In Germany and Austria, however, the instrument was played to a greater extent,

Menke of Leipzig *c.* 1934, and others, a new natural form described as **clarino** was produced in 1960 by Otto Steinkopf and Helmut Finke, based on a coiled trumpet of posthorn shape in a portrait of Bach's Leipzig trumpeter Gottfried Reiche (*d.* 1734).

In the fifteenth century the folded slide trumpet was adapted so that, instead of having a single movable tube with mouthpiece attached (although this type continued to be used) it had a two-legged slide which extended the back part of the instrument. This was the point at which the **trombone** developed from the trumpet, and it was to follow a very different path. The Italian word *trombone* was already in use before 1460, but the English and French preferred to call the instrument by some form of the word **sackbut**, and to the Germans it was **Posaune**. According to Edward Halle's *King Henry VIII*, when that

being incorporated into notable dramatic scores, such as Gluck's *Orfeo* (1762), Mozart's *Magic Flute* (1791) and Haydn's *Creation* (1798). Georg Wagenseil (1715–77) wrote one of the earliest trombone concertos. With Beethoven's use of the alto, tenor and bass instruments in his Fifth, Sixth and Ninth Symphonies, the trombone gradually gained a foothold in the symphony orchestra, at first being used for harmonic rather than melodic purposes. Later on the alto instrument was replaced by a second tenor playing in its high register. A contrabass was called for by Wagner in *The Ring* (1876), and it is still needed occasionally for other works. Although valves had been applied to certain trombones by 1830, these instruments came to be used mainly in military bands, as they are easier to play while marching. Most orchestral performers, however, still prefer to use the traditional instrument.

155 An angelic orchestra which includes, on the right, a bass trombone and tenor violin. Detail from *The Glory of the Angels* (early 17th century) by Ludovico Caracci. *Bologna, Church of San Paolo Maggiore.*

VII
Free Reed Instruments

A free reed is a small tongue of metal, of which one end is attached to a frame while the other vibrates freely through pressure or suction of air. The pitch depends on its length and thickness. (It should not be confused with the type of reed used in the regal, which was somewhat similar in shape but fixed to beat against its frame, and was therefore not 'free'.) Although the principle of the free reed was probably discovered in remote Antiquity by the slitting of a blade of grass, the earliest specially constructed instrument to which it was applied was the Chinese *sheng* or Japanese *sho*, which is still played in the Far East after at least 3000 years. Its first reeds are thought to have been made of bamboo.

Free reeds did not become properly established in Europe until the late eighteenth century, by which time a great deal of experimentation had taken place. This seems to have been fuelled by those travellers who would bring back or send a sho or sheng from the Far East, such as the Jesuit Père Joseph Amiot, who sent a sheng from China to Paris in 1777. Already, however, the experimentation had started, although two of the earliest results have apparently not survived. The first was the **Organino**, based on the regal, which was made by the Italian Filippo Testi in 1700, and the other was also a keyboard instrument, said to have been played on in the middle of the

century by Johann Wilde of St Petersburg, the inventor of the nail violin. Later products included the **Organochordium** made between 1782–9 by the Danish organ-builder Kirschnigk, and here a claviorganum with free reeds was combined with the mechanism of a piano. This was seen by the Abbé Georg Joseph Vogler, who, eager for novelty, had free reeds incorporated into church organs and also into his transportable organ called 'Orchestrion' (not to be confused with those mentioned in Chapter IX), with which he toured Europe from 1789 onwards. One of the earliest reed organs in America was made by Ebenezer Goodrich, an organ builder of Boston, *c.* 1809.

From about this time organs were built with free reeds and no pipes in order to save space; as, however, there were so many of them, only a few can be mentioned here. One of the earliest was the **Orgue expressif** devised by Gabriel-Joseph Grenié of Paris in 1810, and that was followed in 1821 by the **Physharmonica** of Anton Häckl in Vienna (this name was also applied to related instruments by other makers). Here the organ was connected to a piano and sounded with it, and such an instrument was involved in one of the most horrific musical experiences of Berlioz (see p. 220). In England one of the first reed organs was the **Royal Seraphine**, made *c.* 1830 by John Green of London, and in that year a

156 Harmonium by Mason & Hamlin, Boston, 1878. *Portsmouth, City Museum and Art Gallery.*

new Parisian development came with the **Poïki-lorgue** of Aristide Cavaillé-Coll. In all these instruments the bellows were worked by one or two pedals, as they were in the **Harmonium** made by Alexandre-François Debain in 1840. This was distinguished by having four registers from 1842 onwards, and other devices were added for graduating the dynamics; similar instruments under the same name were made by the competitive firms of Jacob Alexandre and Victor Mustel, who were responsible for enlarging the range of sound effects.

In most of the European reed organs the reeds vibrated through pressure of air as opposed to suction. This latter technique, however, was preferred in America, where in 1846 a patent for it was granted to Jeremiah Carhart of Buffalo, New York (although he was not the originator of the idea), and in 1856 he received the patent for mass-producing free reeds. Since that time the number of registers has considerably increased, and a knee-operated swell was incorporated into organs by the Boston firm of Mason & Hamlin (fig. 156), which since 1860 has supplied numerous organs to Europe, and was one of several firms to include two or three manuals in its later models. Nowadays small organs are made with air provided by an electric blower, giving the performer a chance to play with his feet on pedals.

Although the harmonium is used in its own right in domestic circles, it is perhaps most useful when deputizing for other instruments, whether it be for a church organ or in an amateur orchestra. The author will never forget playing in a thrilling school performance of Beethoven's *Egmont* Overture in 1948; nearly all the wind parts were supplied by a small organ and two harmoniums, as few of the right wind instruments were readily available there in the post-war period.

European **mouth organs** date back to 1821, when Friedrich Buschmann started to experiment in Berlin and produced the **Aura**, which was the ancestor of today's **Harmonica**. At first it had 15 notes, but later five more were added, and they were sounded by alternative pressure and suction through one mouth hole. Meanwhile in 1829 Charles Wheatstone of London made his **Symphonium**, which consisted of a box with one mouth hole and finger buttons to control the

157 Harmonica with carved ivory covers, Viennese, 1880–85. Trossingen, Matth. Hohner AG.

158 Accordion (Gola 454 model) by Hohner.

flow of air to the brass reeds. Buschmann's instrument became known as the **Mundharmonica (mouth harmonica)**, and one of these was taken by the clockmaker Christian Messner to his home village of Trossingen between the Black Forest and the Alps. There he started to make his own version of the instrument, to be followed in 1855 by Christian Weiss and in 1857 by Matthias Hohner, whose firm eventually absorbed the others and has made Trossingen the chief centre for mouth organs. Today the simplest harmonicas are still diatonic, like the early ones, but since the 1920s a tuning slide has been added to the larger models to make them chromatic. Other types include those which provide chordal accompaniments to the diatonic instruments, and compound harmonicas in as many as six keys. The virtuosity of Larry Adler and others has raised the harmonica to the dignity of a concert soloist and has inspired the writing of concertos for it by such eminent composers as Vaughan Williams. A more recent development by Hohner is the **Melodica** (*c.* 1959), which has one mouthpiece leading to a more-or-less rectangular case in which the reeds are controlled either by buttons or by a piano-type keyboard. It is much used in schools and is, incidentally, a very good deputy for the conical **trumpet** used in toy symphonies, when the single free reed in that instrument is out of order.

The **accordion** dates back to the diatonic **Handaoline** of 1821, in which Buschmann added handblown bellows and a keyboard of buttons to his Aura. This was followed in 1829 by the **Accordion** of Cyrillus Demian of Vienna. Here the bellows were terminated at each end by a

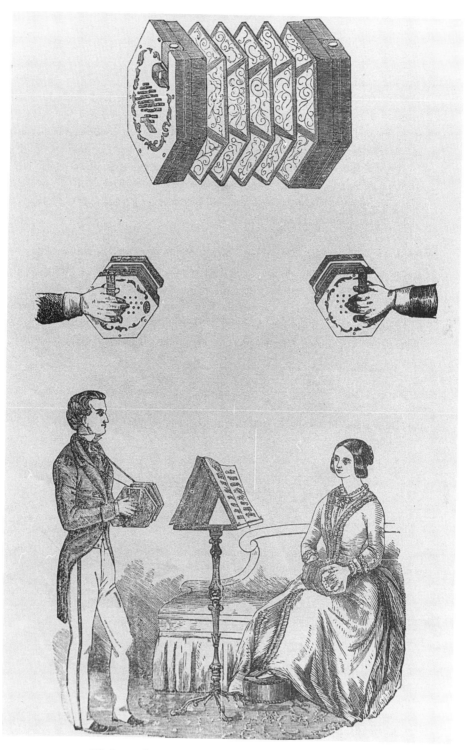

159 Concertinas, as seen in the frontispiece to *Chidley's Instructions for the Concertina, c. 1854. London, Royal College of Music.*

box containing reeds which were controlled by finger buttons, those of the right hand playing a diatonic melody and those of the left a simple chordal accompaniment. Since the 1850s the accordion has been chromatic. Mariano Dallape of Stradella in Italy substituted piano keys for the right-hand buttons on certain models, giving rise to the name **piano accordion**, and an **organ accordion** with a keyboard of three octaves was produced by M Busson of France. Other developments have included the addition of stops and couplers and a great number of bass chords, while some of the most expressive (but not necessarily the best) have electronic effects such as vibrato and the sounds of orchestral instruments.

The **Concertina** was the result of Charles Wheatstone's applying the bellows of the accordion to his own Symphonium, a process which was completed in 1844. Between the buttons of both hands a chromatic scale could be played, but it was not until the later 'duet system' that each hand alone was completely chromatic. During the nineteenth century the concertina attracted virtuosi such as the London-based Giulio Regondi who was already an expert on the **Mélophone** (a guitar-shaped instrument with free reeds, bellows and a keyboard, invented by the Parisian clockmaker Leclerc). His two concertos are among numerous compositions for the concertina which include, besides chamber music in which it is played with more usual instruments, an *Adagio for Eight Concertinas in E* by Edouard Silas, one-time professor of harmony at the Guildhall School of Music, London.

VIII
Percussion Instruments

Percussion instruments are those which by their nature involve a striking or clashing action. They can be divided into three main categories: *idiophones*, which when played give out their own natural sound, *membranophones*, which depend for their pitch on a membrane stretched over a resonator, and *chordophones*, involving struck strings. Besides these, there will also be treated here some shaken, plucked and rubbed idiophones which by their musical context fit best into this chapter. Membranophones will be considered first, as, apart from the piano, they include the percussion instruments of greatest historical importance, namely drums.

The antiquity of **drums** cannot be doubted, as various different shapes and sizes (some of them very large indeed) can be found in Mesoptamian art dating from the third millennium BC. In Europe they have been of three main types: cylindrical drums in which both ends of the cylinder are normally covered with a membrane; frame drums in which the diameter of the head is longer than the length of the side, and one or both ends are covered; and bowl-shaped drums which are covered only on top.

The last-mentioned have in the long run been the most important in European art music under the general name **kettledrums**. Although the Babylonians had very large instruments of kettle-drum shape *c.* 1100 BC, and fig. 160 shows that the Greeks had shallow bowl-shaped drums in the sixth century AD, the continuous European history of the orchestral timpani only goes back to the thirteenth century AD, when the Arabic *naqqâra* were adopted by the Crusaders. Joinville, in his *Life of St Louis*, (completed in 1309), tells us that at the battle of Mansourah on 8 February 1250 'King Louis came up at the head of his battalions, with a great noise of shouting, trumpets and nakers' ('...a grand noyse et a grand bruit de trompes et de nacaires'). These **nakers** were small kettle drums played in pairs, of which each one was tuned to a different note. According to the visual arts they seem to have arrived in England *c.* 1300, and one 'nakarier' was mentioned in the payroll of minstrels at the Feast of Westminster in 1306. In England they were normally on a belt round the performer's waist, but on the Continent they were sometimes placed on the back of a servant or an animal, while the drummer walked behind wielding the sticks.

In the fifteenth century larger paired drums also came from the East, being used particularly by cavalry regiments where one drum was suspended on each side of a horse. Praetorius gave evidence of their having tuning screws in the seventeenth century, at which time the known pitch was generally *d* or *c* for the tonic and *A* or

160 Drums and pipes played at Pharoah's feast in a 6th-century Greek illustration from *The Book of Genesis*, chapter 40. *Vienna, Österreichische Nationalbibliothek, Cod. theol. graec.31, f.34.*

161 Nakers, played in the margin of *The Romance of Alexander*, illustrated by Jehan de Grise in Flanders, 1338–44. *Oxford, Bodleian Library, MS Bodl. 264, f.149v.*

G respectively for the dominant below, to suit the pitch of the trumpets. By 1700 these cavalry drums were often used with trumpets in orchestral works of a ceremonial nature, and were called **timpani**. As their orchestral use increased, so they were adapted for it. For instance, greater scope was allowed to the harmony by tuning them to a fifth instead of a fourth (i.e. to the tonic with the dominant *above*) as was sometimes done from the time of Bach onwards. Gradually other intervals were specified within the limits of the two drums, reaching the extreme of an octave in Beethoven's Eighth and Ninth Symphonies. Berlioz experimented to a considerable degree, announcing in his *Treatise on Instrumentation* that:

to obtain a certain number of chords in three, four and five parts, more or less doubled, and furthermore to achieve the striking effect of very close rolls, I have employed in my grand Requiem Mass eight pairs of differently-tuned kettledrums and ten drummers.

Such numbers were unusual, however; since the time of Weber three drums have often been used, while four, five or more are exceptional. Other investigations by Berlioz included the use of drumsticks with ends of wood, wood covered with leather, and sponge.

Until the time of Beethoven and Weber the

tuning depended on the adjusting of square-headed screws with a separate tuning key. This lengthy process then gave way to built-in T-shaped screws which could be manipulated more easily and enabled the pitch to be changed, if necessary, between or even within movements, provided the performer had sufficient rest from playing. Experiments to simplify the tuning still further included a device produced by Gerhard Cramer of Munich in 1812; it consisted of a central screw which could turn all the others at once.

From 1843 onwards different systems have involved the use of a pedal, which not only simplifies tuning but makes possible such musical devices as *glissandi*. Although such machine drums

are regularly used in orchestras today, hand-tuned timpani are still frequently played.

In Greek and Roman times the frame drum was called **tympanon** and **tympanum** respectively, and its chief use seems to have been in rites honouring Cybele and Dionysus. Whatever may have happened to them in the Dark Ages, such drums were known again in Romanesque Europe, exemplified by a carving on a capital of *c.* 1100 in the cloister of the abbey of Moissac. Gradually more shapes emerged, some of them being in primitive forms. A barrel, for instance, forms the resonator of the cylindrical drum in the much-reproduced picture of 'profane' instruments in the twelfth-century MS B.18, f.1 at St John's College, Cambridge (which, incidentally, was for long thought to be English, but is now known to come from Rheims). Its shape, however, may have been inspired by the long cylindrical drum which had come from the East to Byzantium,

162 Kettle drums played by one of many musical angels in a Book of Hours made in Milan for the Sforza family, *c.* 1494. *London, British Library, MS Add. 34294, f.29v.*

where by that time it was already highly developed. From the thirteenth century onwards, European drums included not only the single-headed frame drum known today as the **tambour**, but also the double-headed one of similar shape, and the long cylindrical drum which were both covered by the name **tabor**. These were often played with the three-holed pipe (see page 113). The tabor often had a snare, and a fourteenth-century carved stall front in Lincoln Cathedral shows it to have been tunable by that time in England (a practice which had long been known in the East). Each pair of adjacent cords passing diagonally from one side to the other was threaded through a small piece of leather which could be pushed up or down, thus tightening or loosening the tension and so raising or lowering the pitch. The medieval instrument was some-

163 Timpani, from the *Musikalisches Theatrum* of Johann Christoph Weigel, Nuremberg, before 1740, plate 15.

164 Tympanum, played with tibia (left) and cymbals (right) for dancers on a vase painted by Polignotus, *c.* 440–430 BC.

times hit with two sticks which were either straight or shaped at the end, but more often there was only one stick, even when no pipe was involved. A fifteenth-century Dutch manuscript in the Bodleian Library (MS Douce 248, f.13) shows the stick of a pipe-and-tabor combination to be decorated with small bells.

It is worth noting that the word *symphony* (while generally applied to an instrument of the hurdy-gurdy family) was sometimes used for the medieval tabor. John of Trevisa's translation of *De Proprietatibus Rerum* (see page 20) leaves no doubt over the matter:

The Symphonye is an Instrument of Musyk: and is made of an holowe tree closyd in lether in eyther syde And Mynstralles betyth it wyth styckes And by accorde of hyghe and lowe therof comyth full swete notes.

The description seems to suggest that this particular type of drum could be tuned.

From this time onwards the tabor grew much larger and was often held down at the side of the performer, hence the name **side drum**. (While the word 'drum' is today used in a generic sense, it apparently only came into the English language in the sixteenth century.) As this was frequently played with the fife it became an important ingredient of military bands, and it has played an increasing part in the orchestra since the time of Handel, who called for it in the *Music for the Royal Fireworks* of 1749. Other forms of side drum include the snareless **tenor drum**, dating from the 1830s and played with soft beaters, and the large **bass drum** (at first called **long drum**) which appeared in the orchestra in the eighteenth century to play in Turkish style music. This also had no snare. It was enlarged soon after 1800, and now has a prominent place in the orchestra, being set in a frame in such a way that it can be turned to any suitable position. In 1857 Messrs Distin of London patented their **Monster Bass Drum** which, having a diameter of eight feet (2.44 m), was used only for very special occasions, such as the Handel Festival in 1865. Before its appearance in the first Hoffnung Concert in London in 1956, a door of the Royal Festival

165 Tabor (tunable) and nakers played by angels designed by Agostino di Duccio, *c.* 1450–57. *Rimini, Tempio Malatestiano (Church of San Francesco).*

166 Drum used as a table in *Soldiers playing cards* by Baron Jan August Hendrick Leys, 1849. *London, Wallace Collection*.

167 Bass drum, side drum, single and paired cymbals, with pedal timpani in the foreground. *London, Royal College of Music*.

Hall had to be removed to let it in.

A two-headed drum with a square frame was known in medieval Europe, and appears particularly in carvings of France and Spain. It is well represented in the arch sculptures (*c.* 1300) in the sacristy of Bayonne Cathedral, and is still found in Spain, notably Galicia, as a folk instrument under the name *pandeiróo*. This version contains bells which jingle inside.

The tympanon or tympanum of Greece and Rome sometimes had jingles on its frame, and in this form was later described as **timbrel** or **tambourine**. It only became widespread in European art from the late thirteenth century onwards, and several different kinds existed. Although the frame normally held jingles in the form of thin metal discs, these were sometimes replaced by small bells, but they could also be found together, particularly in Renaissance Italy. Sometimes there was a snare, but another Italian

168 Timbrel and pipe played by angels designed by Agostino di Duccio, *c.* 1450-57. *Rimini, Tempio Malatestiano (Church of San Francesco).*

169 Cymbals played by angels designed by Agostino di Duccio, *c.* 1450–57. *Rimini, Tempio Malatestiano (Church of San Francesco).*

170 Clappers accompanying a rebec on a 12th-century capital. *Barcelona, Church of Santa Maria de l'Estany.*

characteristic was to have no membrane at all and the instrument was then only shaken. The average tambourine was, and is, normally struck by the hand or the fingers. The Baroque period was one of the times when it was unfashionable in art music (as it had been in fifteenth-century France and Flanders), but it reappeared when 'Turkish' music became popular in the late eighteenth century, and has been a fairly regular member of the orchestral percussion department ever since.

Among the oldest idiophones in art music are the round **cymbals**, of which several bronze pairs survive from Antiquity, ranging in size from small finger-cymbals to others of 16 inches (40.6 cm) in diameter, as seen in the City Museum at Pompeii. Cymbals of classical Greece and Rome, and also those of medieval Europe in general, were either deep in shape or almost flat with a slight central dome, like those of today. Being traditionally associated with Turkey, they have, since 1623, been made predominantly by the Armenian family of Zildjian, at first in Constantinople and now in America. While the earlier method of playing seems to have involved clashing them directly together (as shown so often in the

visual arts), more recent techniques have included brushing them against each other, hitting them with drumsticks (hard or soft) and, in Bartok's Sonata for Two Pianos and Percussion (1937), tapping them very quietly with the blade of a penknife. A large orchestral cymbal is now often suspended on a pole, and sometimes connected to a bass drum so that one performer can easily play on both. Berlioz said of the cymbals:

Combined with the high tones of the piccolo and with the strokes of the kettledrum, it is particularly suited to scenes of unbridled wildness or to the extreme frenzy of a bacchanalian orgy.

Related to the single cymbal is the **gong**, a metal disc with its rim bent inwards. Although it is particularly connected with the Far East, a Roman example dating from the first or second century AD was excavated in Wiltshire and can now be seen in the Devizes Museum. The use of the gong in European orchestras seems to date from the eighteenth century, when Gossec called for it in his *Funeral Music for Mirabeau* (1791). It is also known by the name of **tam-tam**.

Very small cymbals described as **crotales** were often fixed to a forked piece of flexible wood or metal to form **clappers**, and as such were portrayed in the arts from ancient Egypt to the early Middle Ages. Other clappers of equal antiquity were made only of wood. In the Romanesque period clappers made of wooden blocks were associated particularly with Spain, but from *c.* 1300 they spread over most of Europe, similar instruments sometimes being made of bone. It is only from the fifteenth century that clear pictures emerge of the smaller and rounder **castanets** which are still connected so much with Spanish music. Single and paired wooden blocks (the latter called **Chinese**, or **temple blocks**) are often beaten with sticks in contemporary music.

The **triangle** has a comparatively short history. Its simplest form, that of a plain metal triangle hit with a beater, can be seen in the thirteenth-century stained glass of León Cathedral, but it does not appear frequently in the arts of northern Europe until well after 1300. The earliest English picture of one which has yet come to light is in the mid-fourteenth-century glass of the Lady Chapel of Ely Cathedral. This instrument is most unusual, as it is shaped like a stirrup, has small bells hanging from the lower bar, and is hit with a hammer. More often there were metal rings suspended from the bar, a custom which continued for several hundred years. The triangle is another of the instruments which, adopted mainly from the Turkish Janissary bands, entered orchestral scores in the eighteenth century, and has been increasingly used ever since.

Shaken idiophones are so numerous that only a few can be mentioned here. Among the most simple is the **rattle** consisting of a gourd filled with seeds or pebbles, now the **maraca** of American Indians. It appears with other instruments in the arts of medieval Spain, and has now moved into the orchestral world by being included in such works as Messiaen's *Turangalîla Symphony*.

The Egyptian **sistrum**, which was used by the Romans in the cult of Isis, consisted of a metal frame across which were stretched loose bars sometimes holding jingles, the whole instru-

171 Triangle-player balancing two candles on a rod held in his mouth. Detail from an early 14th-century Flemish Book of Hours. *Cambridge, Trinity College, MS B.11.22, f.148.*

172 Sistrum, played by the Egyptian goddess Isis in a Roman statue. *Rome, Museo Capitolino.*

174 Chimebells hit by hammers of different types, from the Winchcombe Bible, made in England, *c.* 1130-40. *Dublin, Trinity College, MS 53, f.151.*

173 Jingling Johnny of unknown origin. In 1812 it was captured by the 88th Connaught Rangers from the French, who in turn had taken it from the Moors. *London, Royal Military School of Music, Kneller Hall.*

ment being shaken from a handle below. At the temple of Amon-Mut-Khons, a relief in the great colonnade of King Amenhotep III (1402–1364 BC) shows acrobats or dancers performing to the sounds of four sistra. The sistrum spread to Greece and Rome, and an example from Pompeii is preserved in the Museo Nazionale at Naples. Its nearest medieval equivalent was the triangle with jingles or bells. **Small bells**, however, were often worn by medieval people (particularly jesters) on their clothes, as can be seen in many pictures such as that of the Shaftesbury Psalter, dating from *c.* 1130–40 (British Library MS Lans. 383, f.15v; illustrated in Mary Remnant, *Musical Instruments of the West*, fig. 178). In contrast to this somewhat wild picture, where the bells are attached to the costume of a bear, the will of Alice Barbour of Salisbury, dated 1407, says 'I bequeath to my son John . . . my fifth ring of gold and a green girdle appareled with bells'.

The **Turkish Crescent** or **Jingling Johnny** (known in France as the **chapeau chinois**) is known to have existed in the sixteenth century, and became one of the most spectacular instruments surrounding the Turkish sultan. It consisted basically of a pole on which were fixed

175 Chimebells played by David in the initial E(xultate Deo) while his minstrels play trumpet and harp. From the Ormesby Psalter, this part made in England, *c. 1310–20. Oxford, Bodleian Library, MS Douce 366, f.109.*

various metal ornaments, one of them resembling a Chinese hat, and above it a Turkish crescent. The sounds were produced by numerous small bells or other jingling devices when the instrument was shaken. European regiments made great efforts to acquire Jingling Johnnies. One of those at the Royal Military School of Music, Kneller Hall, London (fig. 173), was captured from the Moors by the French, who themselves lost it in 1812 to the 88th Connaught Rangers. Berlioz recommended four of them for his gigantic orchestra which never materialized (page 220).

Idiophones can be tuned by being made in different sizes. Bells, for instance, which each give out one basic note, become part of a melodic instrument when several are arranged together in a prepared sequence. Such were the **chimebells (cymbala)** which can be seen in the visual arts dating from the eleventh century to *c.* 1500. They were arranged in varying numbers on a rod or frame, and the performer hit them with two hammers. These were generally of metal, but it is possible that the ends may have been tempered by a strip of leather or other softer substance which could not be visible in a picture. The Winchcombe Bible shows two very different ham-

mers, one apparently of wood, and the other deliberately covered at each end with something which would make a contrasting sound. Several manuscripts of the period give the tuning as diatonic but with an added B flat, which is part of the 'soft' hexachord starting on F. A noteworthy and much-reproduced example is that from the York Psalter (Glasgow University Library, MS Hunter 229, f.21v), dating from *c.* 1170, where 15 bells are played by two performers, each of whom wields two hammers. Although it has been suggested by Hélène La Rue (in 'The Problem of the Cymbala') that chimebells did not normally exist during the Middle Ages, the present writer feels very strongly that they would not have been illustrated for about 500 years without being made for performance. Anyone who has had the good fortune to play on them knows what an eminently satisfying musical instrument they are.

The keyboard **carillon**, which appeared in the Netherlands some time after 1500, must have had its origins based on the idea of chimebells. Here church bells in a tower were controlled by a keyboard, of which the notes were so wide that each had to be played by the whole hand, and many carillons had pedals. (They could also be worked mechanically, as is seen in chapter IX.) This strenuous occupation was described in some detail by Dr Burney when he visited Amsterdam in 1772:

At noon I attended M Pothoff to the tower of the *Stad-huys*, or town-house, of which he is *carilloneur*; it is a drudgery unworthy of such a genius...he executed with his two hands passages that would be very difficult to play with the ten fingers; shakes, beats, swift divisions, triplets, and even *arpeggios* he has contrived to vanquish...I never heard a greater variety of passages, in so short a time; he produced effects by the *pianos* and *fortes*, and the *crescendo* in the shake, both as to loudness and velocity, which I did not think possible upon an instrument that seemed to require little other merit than force in the performer.

In contrast to this technique is that of playing **handbells**, where each person can ring no more

176 Carillon at the Cathedral of Notre Dame, Antwerp. Marin Mersenne, *Harmonicorum Libri*, Paris, 1636, p.160. *London, Royal College of Music.*

today are the **tubophone** in which horizontal tubes are struck (similar to fig. 177), and **tubular bells** in which they are suspended vertically from a frame. The latter are often used as a substitute for real 'church' bells which appear in certain scores, such as Britten's opera *The Turn of the Screw* and Messiaen's *Turangalîla Symphony*. In 1886 Auguste Mustel invented the **celesta**, another keyboard form of glockenspiel, in which metal bars are hit by soft hammers and there is a sustaining pedal. One of its earliest parts was in Tchaikovsky's 'Dance of the Sugar-Plum Fairy' in the *Nutcracker Suite* of 1892. The **lyra-glockenspiel** consists of a portable lyre-shaped frame into which are fitted the bars or other tuned shapes. It has been much used in continental military bands since the nineteenth century, and also appears in such grand processions as that of the Munich Beer Festival. Other tuned bells include sets of **sleigh bells** at different pitches, which were strikingly used by Mozart in his *Sleigh Ride* dance, K. 605.

Related to the glockenspiel is the **xylophone**, which is of primitive origins and can still be found as a folk instrument in many parts of the world. It consists of tuned bars of wood (arranged nowadays like a keyboard) which are hit with sticks or hammers, and has been known in Europe at least since the sixteenth century when Hans Holbein the Younger showed it being played by a skeleton in his series of woodcuts *The Dance of Death* (1523). Nevertheless it was apparently not written into orchestral scores until 1874, when Saint-Saëns used it in his *Danse macabre*. Before that time not even Berlioz had specified it, in spite of performances around Europe by the Russian Jew Gusikow, who had so much impressed Mendelssohn. Today the orchestral xylophone is arranged to resemble a piano keyboard, with a separate resonator beneath each note, and a range of about four octaves from c'. An octave lower is the **marimba**, another form of xylophone based on folk instruments, and this also has resonators. A further development is the **vibraphone**, devised *c.* 1920 by Hermann Winterhoff of the Leedy Drum Co. in America. Here the bars are of a light metal alloy, and the

than four bells and the skill lies in the co-ordination between the different performers.

Under the name **glockenspiel**, bell-like sounds have long been produced by varying lengths of metal or glass arranged in strips or tubes, and struck either with beaters or by means of a keyboard. Figure 177 shows an instrument containing horizontal tubes which allow for two diatonic octaves and are hit by a stick; it is played with more usual instruments of the period at an event of national celebration in 1609. Both Handel in *Saul* (1739) and Mozart in *The Magic Flute* (1791) wrote for instruments which gave the effect of bells by means of a keyboard. Alternatives

instrument is distinguished by a clockwork or electric mechanism which activates a fan giving a vibrato effect to the sound; it also has dampers.

From the late Middle Ages there are pictures of **musical glasses**, built in different sizes and sometimes tuned by water filled to different levels. At first they were struck, as shown in the stained glass made *c.* 1447 by John Pruddle for the Beauchamp Chapel at Warwick, but later on there was developed a technique of rubbing the edge of each glass with a dampened finger. In London in 1746 Gluck played a concerto which he had written for 26 drinking glasses and orchestra. In 1762 Benjamin Franklin caused the glasses to revolve by means of a treadle, and called his instrument the **Glass Harmonica**; however, although works were written for it by Mozart, Beethoven and others, it had an adverse effect on the nerves of the performers, and was not widely adopted.

Mention has already been made of instruments used for special effects, such as sleigh bells. Others include the **anvil**, which was illustrated by Praetorius in 1620, and was prominent in Wagner's *Das Rheingold* (first performed in 1869) where 18 are called for. When real anvils are not available, other metal contraptions can provide a substitute sound. The **wind machine** is a revolving barrel-shape friction instrument, with the sound getting higher or lower according to the speed at which it turns. Other effects include a huge strip of metal which when shaken gives the effect of **thunder**, hinged wooden blocks which when clapped together sound like a **whip**, and a machine to create the sound of **breaking glass**.

An idiophone which fits into a category all of its own is the **Jew's harp**. Neither Jewish nor a harp, it is a metal frame placed against the mouth of the player who flicks its metal tongue with his finger, and by altering the position of his mouth, causes the sounding of the harmonic series. Several examples have been dug up in cemeteries from Roman times onwards. For a long time it was thought that one of the angels on the Minstrels' Gallery at Exeter Cathedral was playing a Jew's harp. In 1976, however, when the paint was

177 An early form of glockenspiel, played by the boy on the right in a group of musicians at celebrations in honour of La Trève, by Van de Venne, 1609. *Paris, Musée du Louvre.*

being renovated by Anna Hulbert, it was found that the instrument in question had actually been a trumpet which later got broken off just beyond the mouthpiece. A good Renaissance illustration of a Jew's harp being played can be seen in *The Triumph of Maximilian*, where the performer is one of the fools of the Emperor's Court.

Most chordophones are plucked or bowed, or played by means of a keyboard with a plucking or striking mechanism. Relatively few are struck directly by a beater held by the performer. The most simple of these is a **string drum** seen in continental art from the fourteenth century onwards, but rarely, if ever, in English sources. Described by Jean Charlier de Gerson (1363–1429) in his *Tractatus de Canticis* (1423) as 'chorus', its shape was based on that of the monochord, with two or more strings generally tuned to the tonic and dominant. These were struck by a wooden stick to provide a rhythmical drone accompaniment to other instruments, most often the three-holed pipe, and in this combination it can still be found in southern France under the names **tambourin de Béarn** and **tambourin basque**. A similar folk instrument to have sur-

178 Tuned percussion instruments in an informal setting. Left, from back to front: marimba, vibraphone, glockenspiel; centre, from back to front: tubular bells, tubophone; right, cowbells, gongs. *Percussion Services Ltd., 17–23 Vale Royal, London, N.7.*

vived in Hungary is the **gardon**, which is made in a shape resembling that of a cello.

More important historically is the **dulcimer**, which started life as a psaltery hit with beaters, instead of being plucked. This method is shown on the ivory cover of the Melissenda Psalter (British Library MS Eg. 1139), which was made by Byzantine craftsmen in Jerusalem between 1131–43. Although an early European example seems to be in a carving of *c.* 1300 in the south doorway of St Martin's Church at Colmar, the dulcimer is not widespread in European art until

the fifteenth century. At this time the strings were single or double, and parallel to each other in the same plane. Some instruments had a bridge dividing the strings so that they each gave a different note on either side of it. Already before the time of Praetorius the courses had become triple, (as they had in the Persian *santur* about 300 years earlier), and another bridge had appeared. When this was at the right-hand end of the instrument its strings had the longest possible sounding length and gave the lowest notes. The strings passed alternately over one bridge and under another, sloping in such a way that the performer had greater freedom for striking than before. Gradually more bridges (or sets of small ones) were used to suit individual tuning requirements, the range of pitch was extended, and the instrument became fully chromatic. One of the

179 Glass harmonica made in Germany, *c.* 1780. *London, Horniman Museum.*

180 Pipe and string drum similar to the tambourin de Béarn. Detail from a Book of Hours made in Milan for the Sforza family, *c.* 1494. *London, British Library, MS Add. 34294, f.36v.*

181 Dulcimer, in the form of a rectangular box (for another shape see plate 111). Detail from *The Virgin and Child* by Giovanni Baccati (*fl.* 1445–80). *Perugia, Galleria Nazionale dell' Umbria.*

182 Cimbalom by V.J. Schunda of Budapest, 1887; played by its owner, John Leach of London.

greatest innovators was the German virtuoso Pantaleon Hebenstreit (*c.* 1667–1750), who enlarged the dulcimer to over nine feet (2.74 m) in length, and gave it gut as well as metal strings. He toured Europe playing his own compositions on it, and caused Louis XIV to christen it the **Pantaleone**. Nevertheless, because of the great cost of its strings, this instrument was already in a dilapidated state when Burney saw it in Dresden in 1772, and the dulcimer never became a regular member of the musical scene in western Europe. It was used mainly for special effects, such as when Samuel Pepys heard it being played 'among the Fidlers' for a puppet show in Covent Garden on 23 May 1662. In Germanic countries, however, it has long been used for folk music under the name **Hackbrett** (chopping board), and in eastern Europe, particularly in Hungary where its specialist performers have tended to be Jews and gipsies, it is called **cimbalom**. The cimbalom was developed in the late nineteenth century by V.J. Schunda of Budapest, who gave it a range of four octaves, stood it on legs, and devised a damper mechanism operated by means of a pedal. In recent years this instrument has been used to a considerable extent in the concert orchestra, with one of its most notable compositions being the *Háry János* suite by Kodály.

IX
Mechanical Instruments

'An Instrumente that goethe with a whele without playinge uppon' was among Henry VIII's instruments in 1547, but the idea was not new. Music without a performer was already known in Biblical times, when King David was fascinated by the sound of the north wind playing on the strings of his lyre, and in the tenth century St Dunstan was accused of sorcery because his harp played by itself. In later times instruments were made with the sole purpose of sounding in the wind, prominent among them being the gut-strung **Aeolian harp** and the **glass chimes**.

Wind power was often helped by water. Archimedes (*c.* 287–212 BC) is said to have made a statue of an aulos player standing on a box, and when water was poured through its cistern, air was forced upwards through a tube in the player's body, emerging through his mouth into the reed of the aulos. Ktesibios, the inventor of the organ, made singing birds which apparently worked on the same principle, and in later times the Byzantine Emperor Theophilus (AD 829–42) had a golden tree with birds singing in its branches, although it is not clear how this worked.

Church bells were first mechanized with the invention of clockwork in the Middle Ages. Then came the discovery that a barrel or cylinder, fitted with carefully-placed pegs or pins, could set in motion the hammers to hit the bells. The number of bells was gradually increased, resulting by the sixteenth century in large automatic **carillons** in the towers of churches and town halls, particularly in the Low Countries, where they are still famous. In 1772 Burney described the carillon at the Royal Palace in Amsterdam as having a brass cylinder weighing 4474 pounds (*c.* 2030 kg), and pinned with 7200 iron studs.

The next important instrument to be mechanized was the **organ**, in which the pins on the barrel led to the sounding of the pipes. The oldest surviving instrument of this type is the Salzburg *Hornwerk*, which was built in 1502 for the Hohensalzburg Castle, and is still playing after various restorations. Among its earliest pieces were three *Alten Choral* by Caspar Glanner, who died not later than 1577. Originally it had one cylinder, but Leopold Mozart added others, including on them some of his own tunes. While the cylinder of this instrument is turned by a handle, other Renaissance mechanical instruments were powered by water, such as that of the Villa d'Este at Tivoli, and the only surviving example, at Hellbrun near Salzburg. Detailed drawings of such organs were given by Athanasius Kircher in his *Musurgia Universalis*, which was published at Rome in 1650 (fig. 183).

In contrast to single instruments were those in which several were played at once by one person. In the museum of musical wonders built

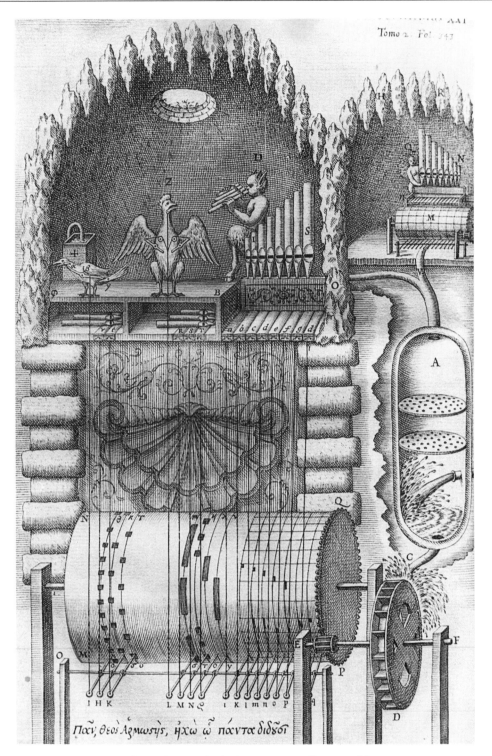

183 Design for a mechanical organ powered by water; Athanasius Kircher, *Musurgia Universalis*, Rome, 1650. *London, Royal College of Music.*

XI

The Use of Instruments

It is only within the last three centuries that composers have, with anything approaching regularity, specified the exact instruments to be used in a given piece of music. Before that time instruments played a considerable part in the functions of daily life, whether as signals, as toys, for the private enjoyment of the players, or for the enrichment of special events, both sacred and secular; the choice of instruments, however, depended on what was available and suitable for the occasion, and only on rare occasions did the composer leave instructions for the instrumentation, even though at the time he may have had particular ideas in mind.

From verbal descriptions and from the visual arts, we see that in ancient Greece and Rome the kithara and lyre often accompanied the voice, while wind and percussion instruments were associated more with dancing and pagan rites. Lucretius tells us that at a feast in honour of the goddess Cybele,

the taut drums throb to the beat of the palms, the hollow cymbals clash around them, the trumpets sound their harsh threat, and the Phrygian rhythm of the tibia stirs the soul.

(*De Rerum Natura*, ii, 618–20.)

Organs were sometimes used in honour of the gods, as witnessed by the occasion when one was played at a festival honouring Apollo at Delphi in 90 BC (p. 97). They were also performed to enliven the fights of gladiators in the circus, and there they were accompanied by the cornu and tuba, both instruments of war.

For the centuries following the collapse of the Roman Empire we know little about the development of instrumentation, although there is enough evidence to show that the voice was generally accompanied by a stringed instrument, and that horns were used on ceremonial occasions. By the Romanesque period, however, two very important developments had occurred. One was the acceptance of the organ by the Christian Church, and the other was the widespread use of the bow.

The Church's attitude to the use of instruments in the liturgy has fluctuated throughout the ages, largely due to changing musical conditions. Hence the slow adoption of the organ because of its earlier pagan associations. By the twelfth century, however, it was well established in the more important churches (see p. 98ff.), while those who could not afford it may have had an organistrum instead. According to Honorius of Autun, in the same period, chimebells and larger bells were, like the organ, used to serve God: 'ut organis, cymbalis & campanis Deo serviamus' (*Commentarius in Ps.* 80,4). On the other hand the Cistercian St Ailred of Rievaulx said that the sound of organ pipes and bellows and the bells

184 The combined harpsichord and bagpipes created by Michele Todini in 17th-century Rome. *New York, Metropolitan Museum of Art.*

by Michele Todini (*fl. c.* 1650–*c.* 1681) in the Palazzo Verospi, Rome, the novelties included a combination of bagpipes and harpsichord (fig. 184), besides a harpsichord and three spinets sounding from one keyboard. Handel is said to have played the organ through the keys of a harpsichord during performances of his oratorios. Related to such devices is the way in which manual organs were embellished by mechanical instruments, a striking example being that made in 1724-5 for the Garrison Church in Berlin, as described by Dr Burney:

I found a large organ in this church, built by Joachim Wagner; it is remarkable for compass, having 50 keys in the manuals, and for its number of pipes, amounting to 3220; but still more so, for the ornaments and machinery of the case, which are in the old Teutonic taste and extremely curious.

At each wing is a kettle drum, which is beat by an angel placed behind it, whose motion the organist regulates by a pedal; at the top of the pyramid, or middle column of pipes, there are two figures, representing Fame, spreading their wings, when the drums are beat, and raising them as high as the top of the pyramid; each of these figures sounds a trumpet, and then takes its flight.

There are likewise two suns, which move to the sound of the cymbals, and the wind obliges them to cross the clouds; during which time, two eagles take their flight, as naturally as if they were alive.

Among the completely mechanical instruments which appeared in the eighteenth century were small cylinder organs for teaching birds to sing. The **Serinette** was for canaries, the **Perroquette** for parrots and the **Merline** for bullfinches and blackbirds, and the music recorded on their pins included works by Lully and François Couperin. **Flötenuhr** or **flute clocks** were clocks containing a cylinder and organ pipes, which gave a flute-like sound. A keen maker of these was Primitivus Němec, librarian and cellist to Prince Esterhazy, and composers who wrote pieces especially for them included C.P.E. Bach, Haydn, Mozart and Beethoven. Flute clocks are therefore very valuable evidence of how these composers expected their ornaments to be performed. A larger instrument, known in the more specific sense as the **barrel organ**, emerged around 1800 and was used a great deal in churches, particularly in England. Diderot, in his 'Projet d'un nouvel orgue' (*Mémoires sur differents sujets de mathématiques*, The Hague, 1748), wished that they could be more widespread 'in order to eliminate indifferent organists'. They were not, however, restricted to the performance of hymns and psalms, as many barrels were pinned with popular songs. Charles Dickens, in his essay

185 Bird organ played by the boy in *The Graham Children* by William Hogarth, 1742. *London, National Gallery.*

Crossing the Channel, wrote:

And now that Hazebroucke slumbers certain kilometres ahead, recall the summer evening when your dusty feet strolling up from the station tended hap-hazard to a Fair there, where the oldest inhabitants were circling round and round a barrel organ on hobby horses, with the greatest gravity . . . .

The cylinder **musical box** was initiated by the Swiss watchmaker Antoine Favre in 1796, and enjoyed great popularity for over a hundred years. Its most usual mechanism involved a pinned cylinder and a metal comb with tuned teeth, the sound being produced when a pin on the cylinder plucks a tooth of the comb. While this type of musical box still continues to be made (its mechanism often enhances such objects as cuckoo clocks, cigarette boxes, Toby jugs, and revolving fruit bowls), it was to some extent displaced by instruments of the **Symphonion** and **Polyphon** type, which appeared *c.* 1890. Instead of a cylinder they had changeable metal

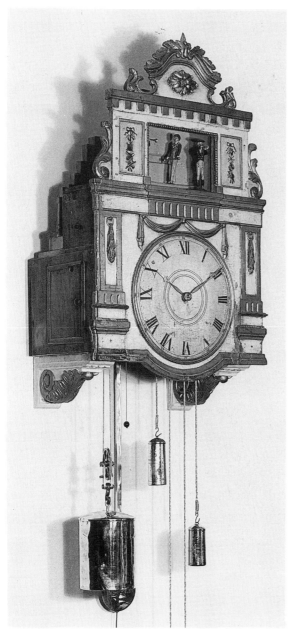

187 Barrel organ by Broderip & Wilkinson, London, *c.* 1805. *London, Royal College of Music.*

186 Flute clock from the Black Forest, *c.* 1790. *Utrecht, National Museum van Speelklok tot Pierement.*

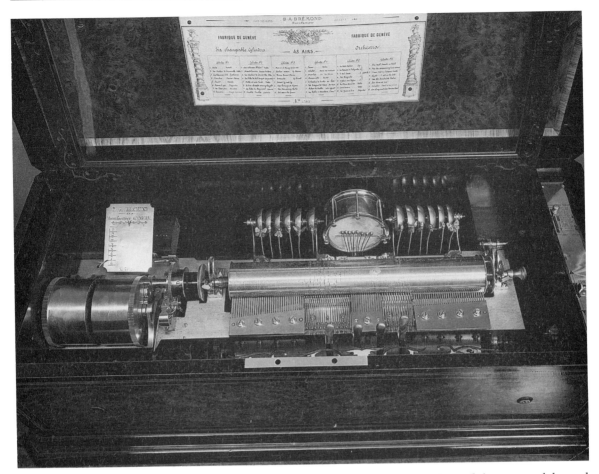

188 Orchestral musical box by B.A. Brémond & Co., Switzerland, *c.* 1885–90. *Liverpool City Museum.*

discs stamped with projections which plucked at the comb. These, however, did not last long due to the early twentieth-century development of the **Phonograph** and later **Gramophone** which, under its modern title of 'record-player', is still with us today as a means of reproducing prerecorded sound.

Meanwhile the change to more expressive and dramatic music in the late eighteenth century had brought into fashion large mechanical organs which imitated as many instruments as possible and were covered by the general name **orchestrion**. They are said to have been invented by J.G. Strasser, a clockmaker of St Petersburg, between 1789 and 1801, and were worked by the cylinder mechanism. One of the most celebrated was the **Panharmonicon** of Johann N. Mälzel of Vienna, which gave the sounds of strings, wind and percussion instruments. Having promised to make a hearing aid for Beethoven, Mälzel then asked him to write a composition for this instrument, and the result was *Wellington's Victory or the Battle of Victoria* in 1813. The Panharmonicon was, however, soon to be outdone by the **Componium** (1821) of Dietrich Nicolaus Winkel of Amsterdam, who was enraged that Mälzel had poached his own idea of the *Metronome*. The Componium (which is now in the museum of the Brussels Conservatoire) was not only an orchestrion with nine stops and a triangle and drum, but it also contained a composing mechanism which made variations on whatever tune was fed into it, the ingenuity being such that to exhaust all the possibilities would take 138 billion years. A later

development to the orchestrion family was the substitution, by Michael Welte of Freiburg in Breisgau (1807–80), of pneumatic action instead of the older pinned barrel method. Here the sounds were determined by the suction of air through a perforated paper roll which could easily be changed. The successor to the orchestrion is the Dutch **street organ** which can still be seen being pushed round old towns such as Delft, and is well represented in the Museum 'Van Speelklok tot Pierement' of mechanical instruments at Utrecht.

Among the most celebrated makers of mechanical instruments were the Kaufmann family of Dresden. In 1851 they demonstrated to Queen Victoria at Buckingham Palace their **Harmon-ichord** (similar to an upright grand piano but with the friction of a cylinder against strings of wire); their artificial **Trumpeter** whose instru-

189 Instruments made by Friedrich Kaufmann and his family, on the occasion of their demonstration to Queen Victoria at Buckingham Palace in 1851. From left to right are the Harmonichord, Chordaulodion, Orchestrion, Automaton Trumpeter and Symphonion. *The Illustrated London News, 5 July, 1851*.

ment contained free reeds and could play more than one note at a time; their **Chordaulodion** which gave the sounds of flutes and strings; their **Symphonion** which imitated various instruments with piano accompaniment, and their **Orchestrion**. This last contained both kettle and military drums and a triangle, besides effects for flutes, flageolets, clarinets, cornets, bugles, trumpets, bassoons, oboes, trombones, etc.

In contrast to these giants was the **Organette**, a small reed organ with pneumatic mechanism, which was first popularized in America in the

1880s. Inevitably it led to larger instruments of the same type, one of the best being the **Orchestrelle** produced by the Aeolian Company from *c.* 1898.

Like the organ, the **piano** also went through the pinned barrel stage, being operated by a handle or by clockwork. A great change came in the late nineteenth century when pneumatic action was added to it in America (possibly by E.S. Votey), one of the most popular types being the **Pianola** of the Orchestrelle Company. At first this 'piano player' was a separate device, containing a perforated paper roll. It was pushed up to the keyboard of an ordinary piano, and when its air passed through the holes in the paper, 'fingers' played appropriate notes on the keyboard. The next stage was the 'player piano', where the pneumatic action and paper roll were built into the piano itself, and the hammers were hit by pressure of air within. In these early designs there were devices by which a human being could control the interpretation, the general idea being well conveyed in an advertisement for the *Apollo Piano Player* - 'You supply the Expression and Soul. We supply the Technique'. The final stage came when the actual interpretations of great pianists were recorded on the rolls, as represented by the *Duo-Art Pianola* produced by the Aeolian Company from *c.* 1898 onwards (see fig. 237).

Because of the technical difficulties involved, the mechanization of bowed instruments has been comparatively rare, with a notable example being the electro-magnetically-controlled **Virtuosa** produced in America in 1908, while pneumatic instruments included Stransky's **Violina** (1911) and the **Violiniste** of E. Aubry and G. Boreau (1920). Nevertheless, a remarkable demonstration was given to the Paris Conservatoire by M. Mareppe, in the form of an automaton violinist who played with a live orchestra and could obey the conductor. An account by the eye-witness M Bruyère, made known in 1840, said that among other things,

he struck into a cadenza, in which the harmonics, double and single, arpeggios on the four strings, and saltos, for which Paganini was so celebrated, were introduced with the greatest effect; and after a close shake of eight bars, commenced the coda, a prestissimo movement, played in three parts throughout; this part of the performance was perfectly magical. I have heard the great Italian, and still greater Norwegian, Ole Bull; I have heard the best of music, but never heard such sounds as then saluted my ear. It began pianissimo, rising by a gradual crescendo to a pitch beyond belief, and then died away, leaving the audience absolutely enchanted...

We have already seen how the mechanical instruments of the past were displaced by the gramophone. Now, however, they are rapidly becoming collectors' pieces, ranging from singing birds in snuff-boxes to gigantic orchestrions, and innocent-looking pieces of furniture such as the armchair belonging to King Frederick of Würtemberg, which played when anyone sat on it....

X

Instruments in the Twentieth Century

The twentieth century is a short time within the 5000 years covered by this book, yet it deserves special attention on account of its greater variety of instruments and their treatment than that of any previous period in history. There follows here a brief summary of the main categories involved, but not, due to lack of space, a description of all the new instruments and methods of sound production which have appeared since 1900.

The instruments most played today are still those of the average symphony orchestra, besides, of course, the piano and organ, all of them continuing their gradual processes of evolution, and exemplified by the **New Violin Family** described on pp. 69–70.

There is also a revival of interest in old instruments, which was pioneered in the early years of the century by Canon Francis Galpin and Arnold Dolmetsch. Since the early 1950s this has steadily gathered momentum, but for a long time there was insufficient knowledge as to which instruments should be used for the music of different periods. Seventeenth-century viols, for instance, were often used in the performance of twelfth and thirteenth-century music, and the crumhorn in particular has been misrepresented. Because its sound was unusual to most people in the 1960s and 70s, audiences gladly believed that it was 'authentic' for any medieval music, although it seems to have come into existence only in the late fifteenth century. During the last ten years the situation has improved considerably, as more musicians are trying to use the right kind of instruments in their performances of music of any period from the early Middle Ages to the nineteenth century and beyond. Others, however, still aim to give a good entertainment regardless of historical exactitude, and provided that this is honestly done, it is comparatively harmless. The danger is when the audience is led to think that it is genuine.

The sounds of the past are also being explored by the composers of modern music, not only for their historical value, but also because some of their very varied timbres blend well into the modern idiom; an early example of this trend is Frank Martin's Harpsichord concerto of 1952.

So much for ordinary instruments in their ordinary or revived conditions. One of the characteristics of modern music is their increasing use in extraordinary ways. The idea is not new. In the seventeenth century Carlo Farina called for the bow stick to be bounced on the violin strings (*col legno*) and for its hairs to play very close to the bridge (*sul ponticello*), which at that time may well have been regarded as outlandish. Today the *avant-garde* composers are exploring every possible way of making sounds come from an instrument. String players have to bow with the stick and hair together, to strike the strings with the wood of the bow between the bridge and the

190 Traditional instruments in their mid 20th-century forms, played by members of the Melos Ensemble: Emanuel Hurwitz (violin), Neill Sanders (French horn), Gervase de Peyer (clarinet), William Waterhouse (bassoon), Cecil Aronowitz (viola), Adrian Beers (double bass) and Terence Weil (cello).

tailpiece, and to bow with excessive pressure 'so that the string creaks and jars'. Many instruments have to be 'scraped'. The woodwind and brass players are instructed to remove their reed or mouthpiece and blow through it separately, or to blow down the rest of the instrument without it, or just to rattle the keys without blowing at all. Harpists are told to 'play with the fingernails on the sounding-board', while pianists pluck the piano strings with their fingernails or play on them with drumsticks. The possibilities are unending. Often an instrument is 'prepared' by the presence of extraneous objects. While some of these methods jar one's nerves either by the sound they make or just by the very thought of potential damage to the instrument, others, when

used by serious composers, can produce some very wonderful effects, and each piece of music must be judged on its merits. It is generally best to *see* these works being performed, as the visual aspect adds much to the overall effect.

There has been a great increase in the use of percussion instruments, with those such as cowbells, African drums and Chinese wood blocks being already of some antiquity although they have not been used for long in western art music. Solo pieces often require considerable versatility and virtuosity, and bear witness to the ever-growing number of expert percussionists. A typical example is Stockhausen's *Zyklus* of 1959, in which one person alone plays on a marimba-phone (steel marimba), guero (scraper), 2 wood-drums, a bunch of bells, side drum, 4 tom-toms, 2 cymbals, a Hi-hat (cymbals worked by a pedal), at least 2 triangles, a vibraphone, 4 cowbells, a gong and a tam-tam.

The use of electricity in music has had far-reaching effects and is manifest in numerous

191 Among the many groups playing music on period instruments is the London Serpent Trio: Andrew Van der Beek, Christopher Monk and Alan Lumsden, seen here at the Egyptian Tombs, Highgate Cemetery, London.

ways. The least obvious is when it eases the performance of existing instruments, with a notable example being the organ, which no longer needs one or more human beings to work the bellows. Somewhat related to this is the electrical actuation of the fans attached to the resonators of the vibraphone. In both these cases the performer's action is the same with or without electricity, which does not of itself affect the sound of the music. Professor Giles Brindley's **Logical Bassoon** and **Logical Contrabassoon** are instruments adapted, in the words of the inventor, 'to replace the mechanical linkage between the fingers and the note-holes by an electrical one', the aim being 'to preserve the timbre of the best notes, improve that of inferior notes, and make

the player's task easier' (*Galpin Society Journal*, xxi, 1968, 152). While the timbre of the best notes is preserved, and the player still blows through a reed and controls the pitch by means of his fingers, the instrument's appearance has nevertheless changed a good deal from that of the traditional bassoon.

Another category involves the use of microphones to enlarge the sound of a natural instrument. Here the sound is altered to a certain extent, whether in the process of making a recording or in rendering the instrument more audible in a concert hall. This latter method has aroused much controversy when applied to such quiet instruments as the clavichord.

Further instruments, although retaining their original performing action, are adapted by built-in loudspeakers and amplifiers. These include the **Neo-Bechstein piano**, invented by Wilhelm Nernst in 1936. Retaining its keys, hammers,

192 Piano, played with a drumstick by Robert Sherlaw Johnson, a noted exponent of new techniques.

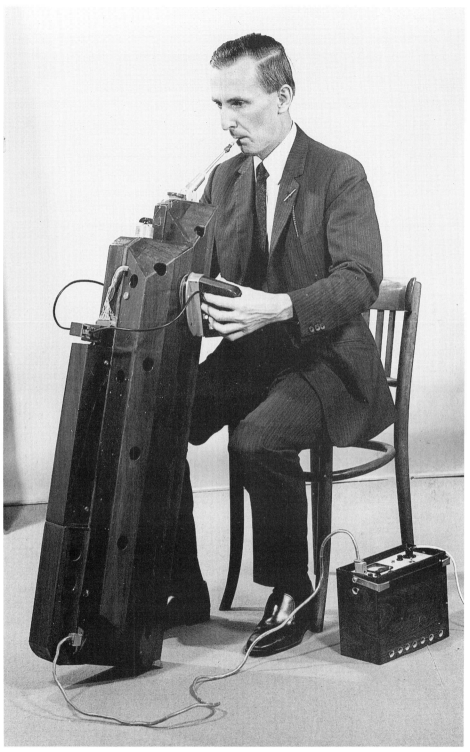

193 The Logical Contrabassoon, played by its inventor,
Professor Giles Brindley.

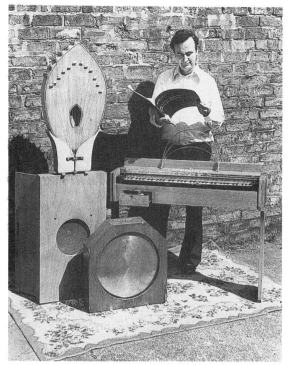

194 The ondes Martenot, with its owner, John Morton, standing behind the keyboard. The *palme* is placed on top of the *principale*, with the *métallique* in front.

195 Thaddeus Cahill's Telharmonium, the earliest electronic instrument. *The Illustrated London News, 23 February, 1907.*

strings and sustaining pedal, it has 18 microphones which take the place of the soundboard, and an amplifier controlled by the left pedal. The **electric guitar**, which also dates from the 1930s, (although it has been through many developments since then) is another instrument which bears some resemblance to its prototype by keeping its strings and fretted fingerboard, but the sound is quite different, and when magnified too much it becomes a public nuisance.

The largest category of electrical instruments is that in which frequencies are generated by electronic means, and magnified in different ways. Some of them, such as Lev Theremin's **Theremin** (*c.* 1924), Friedrich Trautwein's **Trautonium** (1930) and Maurice Martenot's **ondes Martenot** (c. 1928) are only melodic, sounding just one note at a time. One of the simplest shapes is that of the Theremin, which to the casual eye consists of a cabinet from which a metal rod projects upwards. By moving his hand towards or away from the rod, the player can raise or lower the pitch respectively. Too much glissando can be avoided by the use of control buttons. The ondes Martenot is nowadays in four distinct parts, one containing keyboard and controls, and the other three being diffusers of the sound. They are the *principal*, which gives the most natural sound of the instrument, the *métallique* which by means of a gong creates a metallic resonance, and the *palme*, across which are stretched 24 strings. These give the effect of a viola or cello in legato pasages, but of a harp when the playing is glissando, and their very beautiful effects are produced when a ring on the performer's right index finger pulls a ribbon along the length of the keyboard. The actual type of touch and the required dynamics are controlled by a small key in a drawer below.

The polyphonic instruments, those which can play more than one note at a time, included the oldest electronic instrument of all, the **Telharmonium** invented by Thaddeus Cahill in 1906 and erected in New York. Its gigantic machinery, which was controlled from a keyboard, was intended to produce music which could be played by telephone to those who wished to hear it. Unfortunately the plan had to be dropped, as the

196 The Hammond 'Monarch', an electronic organ which, according to its 1976 advertisement, can 'create millions of sound variations to suit any musical mood or style'.

197 The E.M.S. (London) 'Synthi 100' studio synthesizer. *Electronic Music Studios.*

sounds interfered with the normal telephone wires. Later electronic organs appeared in the 1930s and have since been in great demand due to their relatively low cost and small size as compared to pipe organs, being used in churches, private houses, cinemas, schools and other institutions. One of the most frequently played is the **Hammond Organ**, which has two manuals, a pedal-board, and the means of producing innumerable different types of sound.

All the instruments previously described have normally depended for their musical result on a single performer playing at a certain time. Since the Second World War a new process has been set in motion – that of mixing sounds to be used as required. Under the title *musique concrète* this can be done at the minimum by two tape recorders, but the subject has now been developed to such an extent that complete electronic studios are built to contain the necessary equipment. A prominent item is the **synthesizer**, a machine which can produce any sound for which it has been prepared. Certain models retain a visual connection with music by the presence of one or two keyboards, but others would not be recognized by the ordinary person as having anything to do with music. Nevertheless their potentialities for generating and synthesizing sounds are immense, and together with tape recorders, microphones, amplifiers, oscillators and other gadgets of the electronic studio, they provide stimulus to many composers, who often use their sounds together with those of 'live' instruments. Their overall value can only be judged at a later date in the light of history.

XI

The Use of Instruments

I t is only within the last three centuries that composers have, with anything approaching regularity, specified the exact instruments to be used in a given piece of music. Before that time instruments played a considerable part in the functions of daily life, whether as signals, as toys, for the private enjoyment of the players, or for the enrichment of special events, both sacred and secular; the choice of instruments, however, depended on what was available and suitable for the occasion, and only on rare occasions did the composer leave instructions for the instrumentation, even though at the time he may have had particular ideas in mind.

From verbal descriptions and from the visual arts, we see that in ancient Greece and Rome the kithara and lyre often accompanied the voice, while wind and percussion instruments were associated more with dancing and pagan rites. Lucretius tells us that at a feast in honour of the goddess Cybele,

the taut drums throb to the beat of the palms, the hollow cymbals clash around them, the trumpets sound their harsh threat, and the Phrygian rhythm of the tibia stirs the soul.

(De Rerum Natura, ii, 618–20.)

Organs were sometimes used in honour of the gods, as witnessed by the occasion when one was played at a festival honouring Apollo at Delphi

in 90 BC (p. 97). They were also performed to enliven the fights of gladiators in the circus, and there they were accompanied by the cornu and tuba, both instruments of war.

For the centuries following the collapse of the Roman Empire we know little about the development of instrumentation, although there is enough evidence to show that the voice was generally accompanied by a stringed instrument, and that horns were used on ceremonial occasions. By the Romanesque period, however, two very important developments had occurred. One was the acceptance of the organ by the Christian Church, and the other was the widespread use of the bow.

The Church's attitude to the use of instruments in the liturgy has fluctuated throughout the ages, largely due to changing musical conditions. Hence the slow adoption of the organ because of its earlier pagan associations. By the twelfth century, however, it was well established in the more important churches (see p. 98ff.), while those who could not afford it may have had an organistrum instead. According to Honorius of Autun, in the same period, chimebells and larger bells were, like the organ, used to serve God: 'ut organis, cymbalis & campanis Deo serviamus' (*Commentarius in Ps.* 80,4). On the other hand the Cistercian St Ailred of Rievaulx said that the sound of organ pipes and bellows and the bells

198 A gladiatorial fight enlivened by a tuba, two cornua and a hydraulis. Detail of a Roman mosaic of the 1st century AD, from a villa at Dar Buk Ammera, neat Zliten, Libya. *Tripoli Museum.*

199 Organistrum or symphony, organ and chimebells, in a picture representing church instruments, from the Rutland Psalter, f.97v., made in England, mid-13th century. *London, British Library, MS Add. 62925, f.97v.*

'caused the ordinary people to stand with wondering faces, trembling and amazed' (*Speculum Caritatis*). Ailred, however, was a member of the Cistercian order, which preferred to serve God with the utmost simplicity, and he would not have approved of a charter made by Raoul d'Argences, Abbot of Fécamp from 1190 to 1220, to allow the local *confrérie des jongleurs* to perform on their instruments in the Abbey church. In a possible attempt to represent the more usual church instruments soon after that time, the artist of the thirteenth-century Rutland Psalter depicted one of the best medieval representations of the organ, together with 13 chimebells and an organistrum or symphony (fig. 199).

By 1500, trumpets, shawms, cornetts and sackbuts often enriched the liturgy for special events, either playing on their own or doubling the voices. Dufay's four-part *Gloria 'ad modum tubae'* is one of several pieces where textless parts are playable on trumpets, but as yet it was rare for such instruments to be specified. The words 'ad modum' might just imply vocal imitation of the sound of trumpets, but figure 200 does show trumpeters and singers performing together, in a manuscript dating from Dufay's lifetime. Since the Reformation the multiplicity of religions has

200 In the initial C(antate domino) two trumpets accompany three clerical singers in the presence of David, while a portative organ (presumably his) sits on the ground. In the border are, clockwise from top left, a mandora (gittern), trumpet, pipe, harp, lute, three (?) recorders, hornpipe, shawm psaltery and bagpipes. *Oxford, Bodleian Library, MS Douce 18, f.157.*

led to even greater diversity of instrumental practice than before, so for the rest of this chapter any reference to liturgical music will be within its purely musical context.

There are a good many medieval references to instruments being played in church on completely un-liturgical occasions, such as when Edward I heard 14 minstrels playing before the statue of Our Lady in the crypt of Canterbury Cathedral on 6 June 1297. A later occasion concerns the Princess Eleanor, sister of Edward III, when she was travelling from London to Holland in 1332 to marry the Count of Guelders. She stopped at St Paul's Cathedral to leave an offering at the great *Crux Borealis* in the North Chapel, and her subsequent expense accounts reveal payments

to several fiddlers ('diuersis vidulatoribus') who played there. Portable instruments were often used in processions, particularly outside a church when the organ could not be heard. When Duccio's celebrated painting the *Maesta* was taken into the cathedral at Siena on 9 June 1311, it was accompanied by the sounds of trumpets, shawms and nakers, as befitted a great occasion. Gentile Bellini's *Procession of the Relic of the Cross in the Piazza San Marco* of 1496 includes two groups of musicians. Accompanying the cleri-

201 The choir of the Emperor Maximilian I, supported by the cornett player Augustin Sobinger and the trombone player Stewdl, in an engraving by Hans Burgkmair. *The Triumph of Maximilian*, 1526, plate 26.

202 David plays the harp and one of his minstrels the rebec, together with a juggler. Detail from St Augustine's *Commentary on the Psalms* (1–50), written *c.* 1070–1100 at Christ Church, Canterbury, by monks brought from the Norman Abbey of Bec by Archbishop Lanfranc. *Cambridge, Trinity College, MS B.5.26, f.1.*

for bagpipe players ('enflabotz') at Puivert, in sport and laughter.' Medieval methods of accompanying a monophonic song or dance (provided it was suitable for such treatment) included doubling the melody, playing in heterophony around it, droning below or above it, playing it at a set interval apart, or playing solo passages at the beginning and end, with an interlude between each verse. In the *Tristan* of Gottfried von Strassburg, for instance, we read that:

Tristan ... drew his snatches and preludes, his haunting initial flourishes so sweetly from his harp and made them so melodious with lovely string music, that all came running in, calling one another.

The treatment, however, would vary according to circumstances, and one of the most unusual descriptions must surely be from Thomas of Celano's *Second Life of St Francis of Assisi* (chapter xc), where we are told that St Francis would

pick up a stick from the ground and putting it on his left arm, would draw across it, as across a fiddle, a little bow bent by means of a string; and going through the motions of playing, he would sing in French about his Lord.

cal singers just in front of the relic are players of the harp, lute and rebec, while in the distance a band of trumpet and shawm players holds together the whole congregation.

Very little secular music has survived from before the twelfth century, and no completely instrumental pieces are known from before the thirteenth. This was the time when most minstrels could not read or write words, let alone music, so most of what they played was passed on from one person to another, or improvized on the spur of the moment and never played again. This accounts to a great extent for the lack of early instrumental dance music, although certain songs, such as *Tuit cil qui sunt enamourat, viegnent dançar* (which may come from the court of Eleanor of Aquitaine), were intended for dancing and would often have involved instruments. A rare suggested specification in a Troubadour song occurs in Peire d'Alvernhe's satirical *Chantarai d'aquestz trobadors*, which ends with the words 'This poem was made

203 David plays a fiddle on his lap, surrounded by minstrels playing, from left to right: lute, portative (?) organ, panpipes, horn and psaltery; other instruments are out of the picture. Detail from a capital, *c.* 1100, in the porch of *Jaca Cathedral, Spain.*

204 David plays a psaltery-harp while his minstrels play a tabor, horn and one-armed bowed lyre (with curved or pointed bridge), from an early 12th-century Italian Psalter. *Paris, Bibliotheque Nationale, MS Lat. 2508, f.IIv.*

205 Harp, double pipe, medieval viol and rebec, played by David and his minstrels in an English Psalter, c. 1190–1200. *Cambridge, St John's College, MS K.30, f.86.*

Christopher Page, in his book *Voices and Instruments of the Middle Ages*, has made a valuable contribution to our knowledge of the extent to which instruments were used to accompany songs at this period.

The earliest known instrumental dances, both monophonic and polyphonic, date from the thirteenth century, as also do some three-part textless motets in French sources. One of these is called *In seculum viellatoris*, suggesting that a musically literate fiddler or medieval viol player had either composed the work, or was to play the tenor part, which was based on the melody for the words 'in seculum' from the Easter Gradual *Hec dies*.

The oldest known keyboard pieces have survived in the so-called Robertsbridge Fragment, which consists of two leaves dating from *c.* 1325–50 and bound into a register from Robertsbridge Abbey (British Library MS Add. 28550, ff. 43 and 44). They contain dances and motet arrangements, some sacred and some secular, and

206 Fiddle and gittern (citole) played together for dancing in the initial D(eus), from an English Book of Hours, *c. 1260–90. London, British Library, MS Eg. 1151, f.47.*

207 Minstrels at a feast, playing a fiddle, symphony, harp and psaltery. The psaltery player appears to be giving a beat. Detail from a French *Bible Moralisée, c. 1250–75. London, British Library, MS Harl. 1527, f.36v.*

208 Harp and fiddle played by David and a minstrel. This combination of instruments occurs frequently, but in this case both are inaccurately depicted. From the 13th-century Bible of the Abbey of Foucarmont, f.115. *Neufchatel-en-Bray, Musée Municipal.*

as these show respectively the styles of Italy and France, it has been suggested that they were collected by an Englishman. The great problem is what instrument they were written for. On the whole, they are too intricate to be divided among different performers, and are best controlled by one mind, and the only two possible instruments for that in fourteenth-century England were the organ and the chekker. Athough the latter was known in England *c.* 1360, we have insufficient knowledge of its capabilities. One necessary requirement for the Robertsbridge Fragment was that the instrument should be chromatic, as among its pieces are the notes F, C and G sharp, and B and E flat. The other necessity was that

209 King Alfonso X 'The Wise' of Castile with his courtiers, including players of the fiddle and gittern (citole), late 13th century. *Escorial Library, MS j.b.2. (b.I.2), f.29.*

the keys should be narrow, as some of the music is very fast. The present writer has never seen a fourteenth-century English representation of an organ which satisfies those requirements, although there are some from the Continent. Could it be that the scribe, or the person for whom he wrote out the music, collected it while on the Continent and then could not find a suitable instrument to play it on at home?

From this period onwards, songs written by such composers as Guillaume de Machaut and Francesco Landini contained textless parts which seem to indicate instrumental participation with the voice. There is, however, a school of thought which suggests that these parts were only vocalized. However, before 1400 the Monk of Salzburg referred somewhat ambiguously to the use of 'das Nachthorn', 'das Taghorn', 'das Kchuhorn' and 'die Trumpet' in connection with certain songs, but for another, *Zart libste frau in liber acht*, he makes it clear that a bumbarde is to play the lowest part, 'Das ist der pumhart dar zu'. The Monk's example, however, was not generally followed, and we have to search for descriptions

of events to find out how music was actually performed. These can be tantalizing. The chroniclers of the celebrated Feast of the Pheasant, held at Lille by Philip the Good, Duke of Burgundy, on 17 February 1454, tell us of two trumpeters on horseback, of a model church containing singers, an organ and a bell, and of a pie (if the word 'pasté' really did mean a pie, apart from its various other meanings), containing 28 musicians. From the church came singing and organ music and the bell, and from the pie the sounds of a German cornett, of a quartet of recorders, of a lady called Paquette singing with two fiddles and a lute, and of many other items, but we are not told of the music they played. For the two pieces which *are* mentioned by name, there is no reference to instruments.

By this time it was customary to play in groups of either loud (*haut*) or soft (*bas*) instruments. The former type would include trumpets, shawms and bagpipes, while among the latter would be harps, lutes, fiddles, portative organs, recorders and other instruments suitable for indoor use. Many of them were extending their compass downwards (influenced by the descent of the human voice into the bass register in the mid-fifteenth century), with the result that by about 1500 there were certain families of different sizes aiming at some

210 Minstrels who should entertain a king, playing (centre) a harp and organ, and (border, left to right) bagpipes, timbrel, gittern (citole), fiddle, double pipe, shawm, crowd, pipe-and-tabor, gong and portative organ. From *De nobilitatibus, sapientiis, et prudentiis regum*, composed by Walter de Milemete for Edward III in 1326–7. *Oxford, Christ Church, MS 92, f.43.*

211 Three instrumens of the gittern (citole) family accompany singers in a 14th-century Italian Apocalypse. *London, British Library, MS Add. 47672, f.471.*

212 Singers accompany themselves on a psaltery (*mezzo-canone*) and mandora (gittern), from a manuscript of *The Romance of King Meliadus* written for Louis II, titular King of Naples, between 1352–62. *London, British Library, MS Add. 12228, f.222v.*

213 A singer accompanies himself on a portative organ, while around him are a mandora (gittern), lute, two shawms, clock with bell, symphony, rebec and bow, harp, (?) recorder, psaltery, bagpipes, pipe-and-tabor, cymbals, trumpet and panpipes. From the *Roman de la Rose, Valencia University Library*.

214 Angels play a harp and recorder together in a 15th-century Flemish Book of Hours. *London, British Library, MS Eg. 2125, f.157v.*

215 Angels play a portative organ and harp by the Virgin and Child, carved in wood below a window on the front of a 15th-century house used by monks travelling in the direction of Bury St Edmunds and Walsingham. *Newport, Essex, Monk's Barn.*

216 Two trumpets, lute and fiddle played at *The Marriage of Our Lady* by Sano di Pietro, 15th century. *Rome, Pinacoteca Vaticana.*

217 Trumpeters and shawm players leading a procession, seen on a dish made at Caffagiolo in the late 15th century. *Rouen, Musée des Antiquités.*

218 In a scene based on a lost Norwich Mystery Play, a singer accompanies himself on a lute during the Resurrection of the Innocents; early 16th-century roof boss in the north transept of *Norwich Cathedral.*

kind of standardization. When instruments of one family were played together the group was called a *whole consort*, while a *broken consort* was the continuation of the apparently older method of grouping together instruments of different tone qualities. Little of the consort music written during the sixteenth century had specified instrumentation, but we do know that instruments were used on certain occasions with the composers' consent. For instance, at the celebrations for the marriage of Cosimo I, Duke of Florence, to Eleanora of Toledo in 1539, Francesco Corteccia's music for the *intermedi* included:

a) the song *Vattene almo riposo* sung by 'Dawn', accompanied by a harpsichord, organ, recorder, harp, voices of birds and a bass viol;

b) the song *Vientene almo riposo* sung by 'Night', accompanied by four trombones;

c) the song *Bacco, Bacco e u o e* sung by 20 bacchantes playing a drum, rebec, cornett, two crumhorns, a straight trumpet, a harp and a straight cornett, all of which were hidden among bones, branches and other disguises.

Towards the end of the century more compositions were written for suggested or specified instruments. The first volume of Giovanni Gabri-

219 An orchestra of (left) string and (right) wind players, with triangle. Detail from the title page of Elias Nikolaus Ammerbach's *Ein New Kunstlich Tabulaturbuch*, Nuremberg, 1575. *Munich, Bayerische Staatsbibliothek.*

eli's *Sacrae Symphoniae* (1597), which are mainly 'for voices or instruments', includes the completely instrumental *Sonata Pian' e Forte*, where, as the title suggests, instructions are given for playing loud or soft. Its two 'choirs' consist of (a) one cornett and three trombones, and (b) one 'violino' (actually a viola, as it descends below the violin register) and three trombones. These instruments, besides an organ and 'fagotto' (curtall or dulcian), appear more frequently, and often with independent parts, in the second volume, which was published posthumously in 1615. They are, incidentally, the instruments which, apart from the organ, appear most often in the sacred music of the Baroque period.

The chief partsong of the Elizabethan age, the madrigal, was normally written out for voices. It could, however, also be doubled by instruments or played by them alone, as indicated by the frequent direction 'Apt for voyces or viols'. An

220 Singers accompanied by an organ and trumpet in the German MS *Splendor Solis*, 1582. *London, British Library, MS Harl. 3469, f.27.*

important landmark in the history of chamber music came with *The First Booke of Consort Lessons* published by Thomas Morley in 1599, for a flute, treble viol, bass viol, cittern, pandora and treble lute, without voices. These instruments can be seen playing together for the wedding festivities of Sir Henry Unton, in the painting of his life history dating from soon after his death in 1596. In another scene Sir Henry himself is seen playing in a consort of viols (fig. 224).

A good impression of the music which went on in an English country house at this period can be gleaned from an inventory made in 1603 at Hengrave Hall, Suffolk, the home of the Kytson family who for many years employed the composer John Wilbye:

In ye chamber where ye musicyons play: Instrewments and Books of Musicke.

Itm, one borded chest, with locke and key, wth vj vialls	iiij li
Itm, one borded chest, with six violenns	iij li
Itm, one case of recorders, in nomber vij	xls
Itm, iiij cornutes, one being a mute cornute	xs
Itm, one great base lewte, and a meane lewte, both wth out cases	xxxs
Itm, one trebble lute, and a meane lute with cases	xls

Itm, one bandore, and a sitherne with a dooble case	xxxs
Itm, two sackboots, wth ther cases	xxxs
Itm, three hoeboys, wth a curtall and a lysarden	xxs
Itm, two flewtes, wth out cases	ijs vjd
Itm, one payer of little virginalls	xs
Itm, one wind instrument like a virginall	xxs
Itm, two lewting books covered with lether	
Itm, vj bookes covered with pchement. cont^g vj setts in a book, with songs of iiij, v, vi, vii, and viii partes	ijs
Itm, v books covered wth pchement, cont^g iij setts in a book, wth songs of v ptes,	iijs
Itm, vj books, covered wth pchement, cont^g ij setts in a book, with English songs of iiij, v, and vj partes	iijs
Itm, v books, covered wth pchement, wth pavines galliards measures, and cuntry dances	vs
Itm, v books of levaultoes and corrantoes	vjd
Itm, v old bookes, covered wth pchment, wth songes of v partes	vjd
Itm, iiij books covered wth pchment, wth songes of iiij partes	vjd
Itm, v bookes covered wth blacke lether	ijs
Itm, v books covered wth pchment, wth pavines and galliards for the consert	iijs
Itm, one great booke w^h came from Cadis covered wth redd lether, and gylt	xs
Itm, v books cont^g one sett of Italyan fa-laes	xviijd
Itm, one great payer of dooble virginalls. In the parlour	xxxs
Itm, one payer of great orgaynes. In the Church	vli
Itm, hangings of blewe and yellow saye complete	iijs
Itm, one long bord with ij tressels	ijs
Itm, one long joyned forme and one playne forme	ijs

It was from consorts such as those mentioned above that the earliest opera and oratorio orches-

221 Three choirs of instrumentalists playing in the
polychoral tradition derived from Venice. Praetorius,
Theatrum Instrumentorum, 1620, title page.

222 Singing choristers accompanied by a cornett, two
shawms, trombone and curtall, in *The Virgin of Montserrat*
by Juan Ricci (1600–81). *Barcelona, Abbey of Montserrat.*

tras were formed. Emilio de Cavalieri's Introduction to the *Rappresentazione di Anima e di Corpo* (1600) suggests the suitability of such instruments as a double harp, harpsichord and chitarrone to be played behind the scenes, while at a given point a Spanish tambourine and Spanish guitar may be played on the stage by actors. This work is noteworthy, not only for being the earliest known oratorio, but also for containing one of the earliest known figured bass parts for the continuo, itself a recent development associated with that group of Florentine poets and musicians known as the *Camerata*. Monteverdi, in his opera *Orfeo*, which was first performed in Mantua in

1607, calls clearly for:
Duoi Gravicembani
Duoi contrabassi de Viola
Dieci viole da brazzo
Un Arpa Doppia
Duoi violini piccoli alla Francese
Duoi Chitaroni
Duoi Organi di legno
Tre bassi da gamba
Quattro Tromboni
Un Regale
Duoi Cornetti
Un flautino alla Vigesima Seconda
Un Clarino con tre trombe Sordine

223 Angel musicians playing a cornett, violin and organ, in a 17th-century wall painting by Clemente Maioli. *Ferrara, Church of Santa Maria dei Teatini.*

This is not just an assembly of any instruments which happened to be around. They were carefully selected to suit the dramatic effects required, a striking example being the use of the regal when Charon, the ferryman of the Underworld, challenges Orpheus at the shores of the river Styx. The aria 'Possente Spirto' demonstrates the virtuosity of its players in the respective obbligato sections for two violins, two cornetts, and the double harp.

Compositions using a basic string orchestra (of the violin rather than the viol family), although rare at this time, can be traced back at least to 1581, when *Circé, ou le Balet comique de la Royne* was performed at the French Court to celebrate the marriage of the King's sister to the Duc de Joyeuse. This includes dances, written by Lambert de Beaulieu, which were played by ten 'violons' which were actually different sizes of the

violin family. Thus was set the tradition for the famous *Vingt-quatre Violons du Roi* established in 1626 by Louis XIII for his entertainment. The idea was adopted by Charles II on his accession to the English throne in 1660 (although instruments of the violin family had been played at the Court since the time of Henry VIII), and according to Pepys this new band played at the Coronation banquet on 23 April 1661: 'I took a great deal of pleasure to... hear the Musique of all sorts; but above all, the 24 violins'. In the words of Roger North, they 'disbanded all the old English music at once', although Henry Purcell wrote viol fantasias as late as 1680 and William Lawes had composed 'Sonatas' for violins before 1645. Meanwhile in France Lully had created in 1656 a select group, *Les Petits Violons*, which became renowned for its uniformity of

224 Two groups of musicians from *The Life of Sir Henry Unton*, painted after his death in 1596 by an unknown artist.On the left Sir Henry (right) plays in a consort of five viols, and on the right a broken consort consists of (left to right) a violin, flute, lute, cittern, bass viol and pandora. *London, National Portrait Gallery.*

bowing and general orchestral discipline. This was the basic orchestra (arranged for five string parts–see p. 67) used for his operas and ballets with wind instruments added for special effects such as rustic or war-like scenes. In the ballet *Alcidiane* (1658), for instance, shepherds and shepherdesses danced to the sound of woodwind instruments, the music being directed by Lully who was dressed as a faun. The wind players came from the bands of the *Grand Ecurie* at Versailles, which by 1690, consisted of:

Les trompettes
Les fifres et tambourins ou tambours
Les joueurs de violons, hautbois, saqueboutes et cornets
Les cromornes et trompettes marines
Les hautbois et musettes de Poitou.

After the oboe appeared, as a result of refinements to the shawm by Jean Hotteterre and his colleagues, its first documented appearance in a specific part seems to have been in Robert Cambert's opera *Pomone* of 1671, although it is known to have been played in Lully's music for *L'amour malade* of 1657 (p. 123). From that time it became a frequent member of the orchestra and of chamber music, generally supported on the continuo line by the newly developed bassoon.

A typical late seventeenth-century ceremonial

225 Singers accompanied by a rebec (or kit), ?sordun, and lute, with a cornett on the ground by the lute case. Detail from *A Festival in a Palace Garden* by Sebastian Vrancx (1573–1647). *Copenhagen, Royal Museum of Fine Arts.*

226 A string orchestra (perhaps containing some of 'The King's Twenty-Four Violins') playing in Westminster Hall during the banquet celebrating James II's Coronation on 23 April, 1685. Francis Sandford, *The History of the Coronation of...James II,* London, 1687, after p. 118 *London, British Library.*

orchestra is that for Purcell's Ode for St Cecilia's Day, *Hail bright Cecilia*, which was first performed at a public concert in the Stationers' Hall, London, in 1692. The choruses are joined by strings, oboes, trumpets, kettle drums and continuo, while the solo voices are accompanied either by the continuo alone, or by it with any of the above-mentioned instruments, or by recorders, selected according to the mood of each movement.

While so much instrumental music was still connected with dancing, drama or singing, the seventeenth century saw great advances in purely instrumental forms and techniques. The old fantasias and canzonas, which so often reflected the Renaissance equality of voices, gave way to

sonatas, in which there was more scope for instrumental freedom and virtuosity above the supporting continuo. Although some of these works, and particularly trio sonatas, still allowed for a choice of instrument, others were restricted by their idiom to one in particular. Such works are those violin sonatas by Biber and Corelli which, by their double stopping alone, regardless of other devices, preclude performance on a recorder, flute or oboe.

It could be said that an instrument comes of age when a concerto is written for it. After Stradella and Corelli had paved the way with the concerto grosso, with its contrast of large and small instrumental groups, the solo concerto emerged in the works of Torelli and other composers working at the church of San Petronio, Bologna. The first solo concertos, which were written before 1700, were mainly for the trumpet and violin, by then two of the most experienced instruments in current use. Soon afterwards, Vivaldi was teaching in Venice at the *Ospedale*

della Pietà, a girls' orphanage which produced very competent musicians. He not only provided them and others with a new repertoire, but also did great service to the instruments themselves, by the works which he wrote for them. These included solo concertos for the violin, viola d'amore, cello, mandolin, flute, recorder, piccolo, oboe and bassoon, besides double concertos which also featured the lute, theorbo, horn and organ, as well as many concerti grossi, sonatas and other instrumental pieces. J.S. Bach used several concertos by Vivaldi as models for his own, transforming, for instance, a Vivaldi concerto for four violins into one for four harpsichords (*c.* 1733).

Much of Bach's instrumental music was written when he was *Kapellmeister* at the Court of Prince Leopold of Anhalt Köthen, whose orchestra in 1717 included players of the violin, cello, viola da gamba, bassoon, trumpet and drum. It had no regular French horns, as these instruments were comparatively rare in orchestras. Gradually more pieces were written to include them, so freelance horn players travelled around in pairs, playing where they could, and 'die beyden Waldhornisten' who visited Köthen in 1722 may have taken part in a performance of Bach's First Brandenberg Concerto. In this, and in other *concerti grossi* dedicated to the Margrave Christian Ludwig of Brandenberg in 1721, Bach used instruments which were, or were fast becoming, regular members of the orchestra. In the Fifth Brandenberg Concerto he raised the role of the harpsichord to that of soloist, placing it in the small concertino group with the solo flute and violin, and giving it a magnificent cadenza. It was in his sacred music that Bach exploited the tone qualities of some of the more introspective instruments. In the *St John Passion* for instance, the *arioso* 'Betrachte meine Seel' is sung to the obbligato accompaniment of two viole d'amore and a lute. It was in sacred music, too, that the usual keyboard continuo instrument was the organ. This instrument's part as a concerto soloist seems to have originated in Handel's oratorios, where concertos could be played on an organ, harp or harpsichord between the acts.

227 A quartet of three oboes and a bassoon, played on the bell of the 17th-century Dutch oboe shown in plate 117. *London, Victoria and Albert Museum.*

Bach and Handel represented the culmination of an era, both in their writing and in their use of instruments. Yet already during their lifetimes changes were taking place which radically altered the character of music. These changes were associated chiefly with Mannheim, Paris and Vienna, and were reflected particularly in early Germanic symphonies and Parisian operas. Counterpoint was to a great extent abandoned, together with the figured bass continuo part, although written-out or improvised keyboard parts remained with some orchestras until well after 1800. The bass viola da gamba, which had outlived most of the other viols by about a century, was not suited to the new music, and gave way to increasing pressure from the cello, which had already emerged from the larger bass violin before 1700. The transverse flute, which

CONCERTATO

228 A concerto played on harpsichord, strings, oboes and horns. *Zurich Musicalische Neu-Jahrs-Geschenke*, 1744, plate LX. *London, British Library, Hirsch IV.1135, p.473.*

had long been used as an alternative to the recorder, finally took precedence in the middle of the eighteenth century, partly due to the renowned musicianship of the Emperor Frederick the Great, and also because of its greatly suitability in the new 'expressive' music where the frequent crescendi and diminuendi would have wrought havoc with the intonation of a recorder. Horns, which had previously been used a great deal in the clarino register, were now brought down to a lower level where they provided a mellow texture which blended well with the other instruments. Timpani, the chief percussion instruments of the Baroque period, were joined for special effects by the triangle, cymbals and the bass drum, which had recently been popularized by the Turkish Janissary bands, and also by the tambourine.

The Court of the Elector Carl Theodor at Mannheim contained an orchestra under Johann Stamitz and his successor Christian Cannabich which was the most celebrated since that of Lully. In 1756 it consisted of

10 first violins, 10 second violins, 4 violas, 4 cellos, 4 double basses, 2 flutes, 2 oboes, 2 bassoons, 4 horns, 1 trumpet and 2 timpani.

Clarinets were used as extras or instead of other instruments, and Stamitz himself wrote one of the earliest clarinet concertos, perhaps slightly after those of his fellow German Melchior Molter, which are dated 1747. The discipline and attack of the Mannheim orchestra, together with its cultivation of dynamic ranges, caused Dr Burney to describe it in 1772 as 'an army of generals'. He did, however, note

an imperfection in this band, common to all others that I have ever yet heard... the want of truth in the wind instruments. I know that it is natural for these instruments to be out of tune, but some of that art and diligence which those great performers have manifested in vanquishing difficulties of other kinds, would surely be well employed in correcting this leaven, which so much sours and corrupts all harmony. This was rather too plainly the case tonight, with the bassoons and hautbois, which were rather too sharp at the beginning, and continued growing sharper to the end of the opera.

229 A choral work, performed with strings and organ. *Zurich Musicalische Neu-Jahrs-Geschenke*, 1769, plate LXXXV. *London, British Library, Hirsch IV.1135, p.(279).*

It was in outdoor music that wind instruments could sound their best, unhampered by a hot room or orchestral pit. On the way to Mannheim Burney had passed through Darmstadt, where he

was so fortunate, as to alight from my chaise just as the landgrave's guards were coming on parade. I never heard military music that pleased me more; the instruments were, four hautboys, four clarinets, six trumpets, three on each side the hautboys and clarinets, and these were flanked by two bassoons on each side; so that the line consisted of eighteen musicians; in the rear of these were cornets and clarions.

The whole had an admirable effect, it was exremely animating, and though trumpets and clarions are usually too shrill and piercing, when heard in a small place, yet here, the parade or square where they mounted guard is so spacious that the sound has room to expand in all directions, which prevents the ear from being hurt by too violent a shock.

230 The flute, recorder and cello are played respectively by the Scottish 9th Earl of Cassilis, the Irish Lord Charlemont and the Welsh Mr Phelps. Behind them, and possibly singing, is Mr Ward, an Englishman. The four were painted by Sir Joshua Reynolds in Rome in 1751, when they were doing the Grand Tour. *Dublin, National Gallery of Ireland.*

Earlier in the year he had also been pleased with varied bands at Ghent:

the one was an extra-band of professed musicians, consisting of two hautbois, two clarinets, two bassoons, and two French horns; the other were enlisted men and boys, belonging to the regiments; the number of these amounted to twenty. There were four trumpets, three fifes, two hautbois, two clarinets, two *tambours de basques* [tambourines], two French horns, one crotolo or cymbal, three side-drums, and one great kettle-drum. All these sonorous instruments, in the open air, have a very animated and pleasing effect.

Apart from military bands, the performers of outdoor music included serenading parties (see p. 15), itinerant musicians and students. Some of the latter were taught at music schools attached to Jesuit colleges, and Burney describes how he heard them in the streets of Munich:

they performed some full pieces very well: there were violins, hautboys, French horns, a violoncello, and bassoon. I was informed, that they were obliged

frequently to perform thus in the streets, to convince the public, at whose expense they are maintained, of the proficency they make in their musical studies.

Such outdoor music encouraged complete independence of parts, as a keyboard instrument was not always available to fill in the harmony. A portable harp, however, was sometimes used in street music.

The gradual rejection of the continuo was also evident in chamber music, where trio sonatas gave way to trios and quartets without an accompanying keyboard instrument. Already Alessandro Scarlatti (1660–1725) had written, during the last years of his life, *Sonate a quattro: Due Violini, Violetta e Violoncello – senza cembalo.* These could be performed by one or more players to each part, as could the early string quartets of Haydn, of which the first dates from before 1755. Of the wind instruments, oboes and flutes were already well experienced in chamber music, while bassoons had been used mainly as part of the continuo. Now the greater independence for these

231 A military band consisting of horns, oboes and bassoons. Detail from *Zurich Musicalische Neu-Jahrs-Geschenke*, 1759, plate LXXV. *British Library, Hirsch IV.1135, p. 593.*

and other instruments resulted in such works as the *Sonata a quattro* for two horns and two bassoons by Johann Wilhelm Hertel (1727–89). A new development was the appearance of sonatas for piano with easy accompaniment for the violin, as composed by Johann Christian Bach and published in London in 1773. It was for Mozart to place the two on a more equal footing, where they have remained ever since, with the piano gradually being joined by other instrumental partners as specified by each composer.

While more and more music was being written for wind instruments, it still depended to a great extent on the resources available. Gluck's original version of *Orfeo*, which was produced in Vienna in 1762, included the old chalumeaux, but in the Paris version of 1774 they were replaced by clarinets, as these had been established in the French capital for at least twenty-five years. When Haydn entered the service of Prince Paul Anton Esterhazy in 1759, the orchestra consisted of 2 flutes, 2 oboes, one bassoon, 2 horns and strings, while another bassoon, besides trumpets and timpani, could be co-opted. Hence most of his early symphonies used these instruments, and it was only after the court's acquisition of two more horn players in 1763 that he was sometimes able to incorporate four horns into his works, the first time being in the Symphony no. 13 of that year. (Some of the woodwind players could play more than one instrument, as they do today, so the two cor anglais parts in no. 22, 'The Philosopher', of 1764 would have been played by the oboists.) Mozart was also restricted during his early years in Salzburg, and it was after his visits to Mannheim and Paris in 1777–8 that he incorporated clarinets into his symphonies, the first one being no. 31, 'The Paris' Symphony, written for a *concert spirituel* in that city in 1778. Haydn, although using them in other works, did not write for clarinets in a symphony until his 99th, dating from his visit to London in 1794–5. His 'Nelson' Mass provides an example of orchestration restricted by sheer economic con-

232 The orchestra for Haydn's opera *L'Incontro improviso*, performed at Esterháza in 1775. *Munich, Theatermuseum.*

siderations during a time of crisis. Written during wartime in 1798 and then called *Missa in Angustiis* (it was later performed before Lord Nelson during his visit to Austria in 1800), it was originally scored only for strings, three trumpets, timpani and organ. The organ played partly as a continuo instrument and partly as a complete substitute for the woodwind and horns which would otherwise have been included.

The average orchestra around 1800 comprised first and second violins, violas, cellos, double basses, 2 flutes, 2 oboes, 2 clarinets, 2 bassoons, 2 horns, 2 trumpets and 2 timpani. It was generally 'conducted' by the leading violinist with his bow, or, if there was one, sometimes by the keyboard player. (Although the piano was fading out in its orchestral capacity as successor to the harpsichord continuo, it was rapidly gaining ground as a concerto soloist.) Up to this time the trombone, piccolo and contrabassoon had been called for through the dramatic needs of opera and oratorio, but it was only from the time of Beethoven's Fifth Symphony (1805–7) that they became frequent members of the concert orchestra, being joined in the Ninth Symphony (1824) by the triangle, cymbals and bass drum of the 'Turkish' music. Beethoven did not set out to use some of the very new instruments which already existed during his lifetime, but to explore to the full the known qualities of those that were well established. For instance, the double basses, which hitherto had been used mainly to double the cellos in the earlier music, were now given some very difficult sections due to Beethoven's belief that what could be done by Dragonetti might also be done by others. The cellos and violas had more melodic parts than before, and all the bowed strings were made to play in higher positions, not only by Beethoven but also by such contemporaries as Schubert and Weber, whose opera *Der Freischütz* inspired orchestrators for many years to come. Weber was also responsible for the introduction of the third kettledrum, although it was not immediately adopted elsewhere. Four horns became normal, and further use was made of hand-stopping them. It is not certain, however, whether the elaborate solo for

fourth horn in the slow movement of Beethoven's Ninth Symphony used this technique, or whether it involved an early use of the valved instrument.

In contrast to this there should be mentioned an exploitation of hunting horns in bands, which had already been popular for nearly 50 years when Spohr heard one at St Petersburg in 1803, and described it in his autobiography:

During Lent, when no public performances are allowed, the Court Theatre gave two big concerts a week in the Steiner Theatre, at which all the virtuosos of the Court Orchestra... appeared. The orchestra, at the first concert, consisted of thirty-six violins and twenty basses and doubled winds. In addition to this, and as reinforcement for the chorus, were forty hornists of the Imperial Band, of whom each individual had to play only one tone. They served as an organ, and gave strength and security to the singing of the chorus, whose parts they doubled. In certain small solo passages the effect was overwhelming. Between the first and second parts of the second concerto, these same hornists played an overture of Gluck, with a speed and exactitude that would have been difficult enough for string players and seemed sheerly miraculous as done by hornists, each of them playing only a single tone. It is hardly credible that they could accomplish the most rapid passages with the utmost clarity, and I, for one, would not believe it possible had I not heard it with my own ears. And yet, understandably enough, the adagio of the overture made a greater effect than the allegro for it remains a kind of monstrosity to drill fast pasages into these living organ pipes, and one cannot help thinking of the disciplinary methods by which it must have been achieved.

It is to a great extent with wind instruments that the subsequent development of orchestration is involved. In the early years of the century, orchestras and bands were often reinforced by a serpent, Russian bassoon or bass horn in the lower parts. Of uncertain intonation, they were joined or superseded by the ophicleide after this large form of keyed bugle was patented in 1821. Horns, trumpets and cornets were revolutionized after the invention of valves in Berlin (p. 146), and after Spontini had sent some valved instruments to Paris in 1826 they were gradually included in the scores of French composers, one of the earliest instances being a valved trumpet in the opera *Les Francs Juges* (1827) by Berlioz. Nevertheless it was a long time before they were widely adopted, with most players preferring the valveless instruments to which they were accustomed. The invention of the orchestral tuba (complete with valves) *c.* 1835 gave the strongest bass yet to the other brass families, and it was quickly adopted in Germany. However, it took longer to become established in England and France, where the ophicleide persisted until the 1860s and even then was preserved for a time in outdoor bands (see the author's *Musical Instruments of the West*, plate 201). In military music new sounds came on the scene with tenor and alto horns, saxhorns and helicons, and a prominent part was given to the cornopean or cornet-à-pistons. Meanwhile the cor anglais, which had previously been used only on rare occasions in the orchestra, now took a more permanent place and was strikingly acknowledged by its long solo in the *Roman Carnival* overture by Berlioz. The basset horn, which also dated back to the eighteenth century and had often been used by Mozart, was called for by Mendelssohn and a few other composers, but it did not become a regular member of the orchestra due to the appearance of the bass clarinet. The saxophone, dating from 1840 and used in certain orchestral works, has been restricted mainly to bands and light music, as has the somewhat later sarrusophone.

Berlioz was very much concerned with the balance of instrumental forces, and realized that, while the number of strings was fairly static, their relative strength was being reduced due to the increasing number of wind instruments. In his *Treatise on Instrumentation* (1843) he listed the requirements for 'the finest concert orchestra' as being:

21 first violins
20 second violins,
18 violas,
8 first violoncellos,
7 second violoncellos,
10 double basses,
4 harps

233 A theatre band, directed by its violinist. Behind him are played a serpent, ophicleide, trombone with dragon's head and drum. From 'La Parodie de la Vestale', *Chants et Chansons Populaires de la France*, II, 1843. *London, British Library, Hirsch M.108.*

2 small flutes,
2 large flutes,
2 oboes,
1 English horn,
2 clarinets,
1 basset-horn or 1 bass clarinet,
4 bassoons,
4 valve horns,
2 valve trumpets,
2 cornets with pistons (or cylinders),
3 trombones (1 alto, 2 tenor) or 3 tenor trombones,
1 bass trombone,
1 ophicleide in B flat (or 1 bass tuba),
2 pairs of kettledrums with 4 drummers,
1 bass drum,
1 pair of cymbals

Not quite content, he also devised a plan for an orchestra of 465 instrumentalists which would include 30 harps and 30 pianos. Among the different sound effects it might produce, he described

combining the low tones of the ophicleides, bass tubas and French horns into a small band, joined with the pedal tones of the tenor trombones, the lowest of the bass trombones and the 16' stop of the organ – profoundly grave, religious and calm expression in *piano*

and

combining the 30 harps with the entire mass of stringed instruments playing pizzicato into a large orchestra, thus forming a new gigantic harp with 934 strings – graceful, brilliant and voluptuous expression in all shadings

besides

combining the 30 pianofortes with the 6 sets of small bells, the 12 pairs of ancient cymbals, the 6 triangles

(which might be tuned in different keys like cymbals) and the 4 crescents into a metallic percussion orchestra – gay and brilliant expression in *mezzoforte*

and

combining the French horns, trumpets, cornets, trombones and ophicleides into a small band – pompous and brilliant expression in *forte*

For this 'small band' there were 16 French horns (of which 6 were to have valves), 8 trumpets, 6 cornets, 4 alto trombones, 6 tenor trombones, 2 bass trombones and 3 ophicleides. This orchestra never came into existence, as it was only intended to be tried out for one performance, and, as Berlioz said, it would have needed a hall specially designed for the occasion. On seeing the care taken over his treatise, one can imagine his frustration when, at a party in Vienna, he heard his *Roman Carnival* overture

arranged for two pianos (eight hands) and physharmonica. When its turn came, I was near the door which opened onto the room where the five performers were seated. they began the first allegro much too slowly. The andante was passable; but the

234 A double bass and large serpent played near the organ in Autun Cathedral, in a retrospective impression by M. Bourguignon, early 20th century. *Autun Cathedral, 71.131.50.*

moment the allegro was resumed, at an even more dragging pace then before, I turned scarlet, the blood rushed to my head and, unable to contain my impatience, I shouted out: 'This is the carnival, not Lent. You make it sound like Good Friday in Rome.' The hilarity of the audience at this outburst may be imagined. It was impossible to restore silence, and the rest of the overture was performed in a buzz of laughter and conversation, amid which my five interpreters pursued their placid course imperturbably to the end.
(Berlioz, *Memoirs*)

Berlioz was unique in his use of instruments and his theories as to what could be done with them. Other composers of his time were not so advanced in this respect; Wagner, for instance, called not so much for a wide variety of instruments as for larger numbers of each than were customary, with great emphasis on the brass. (In his early works he wrote for natural and valved horns together, but he later discarded the valveless type.) In *Die Walküre* (1854–6), to take one example, he specified, apart from a large number of strings and woodwind, 8 horns, 4 trumpets, 6 trombones and 5 tubas, besides 6 harps. In contrast to this, Brahms and Dvorak used orchestras little larger than that of Beethoven (the chief addition being that of the tuba), although by writing at a later date they were able to profit by a greater use of valved instruments in general, and by the more highly developed woodwind.

The latter part of the nineteenth century saw an increase in the use of percussion instruments, represented chiefly by castanets in Spanish-type pieces, by gongs, and by the tuned percussion. Descriptive music of the Romantic age often required the use of bells, a striking example being Rimsky-Korsakov's *Russian Easter Overture* (1888), where *campanelli* are specified. In his *Principles of Orchestration* (on which he was working at the time of his death in 1908) the composer suggests that this effect is best obtained by the glockenspiel

235 *A Village Choir* by Thomas Webster (1800–86), calling to mind *Under the Greenwood Tree* by Thomas Hardy. The singers are joined by clarinet, bassoon and cello. *London, Victoria and Albert Museum.*

236 Louis Antoine Jullien conducting his concert orchestra and four military bands at Covent Garden in 1846. *The Illustrated London News, 7 November 1846.*

of steel bars; for deeper-sounding bells, as also required in the overture, a tamtam is used. In the treatise Rimsky-Korsakov wrote that 'real church bells of moderate size may be considered more as theatrical properties than orchestral instruments.' From this period, too, there can be seen greater use of the xylophone and celesta, and the appearance of tubular bells.

Twentieth-century instrumentation reflects the developments described in chapter X. At the turn of the century there were vast Teutonic orchestras which reached a peak in Mahler's Eighth Symphony (1907), scored for voices, strings and

4 flutes,
2 piccolos,
4 oboes,
1 English horn,
3 clarinets,
2 E flat clarinets,
1 bass clarinet,
4 bassoons,
1 contrabassoon,
8 horns,
8 trumpets (4 offstage),
7 trombones (3 offstage),
1 bass tuba,
timpani,
1 bass drum,
cymbals,
1 gong,
1 triangle,
deep bells,
1 glockenspiel,

237 A Duo-Art Pianola piano playing with the Queen's Hall Orchestra under Sir Henry Wood in 1922 (in spite of the qualms of Stravinsky, noted above). *The Illustrated London News, 11 November 1922.*

1 celesta,
1 piano,
1 harmonium,
1 organ,
2 harps and
1 mandoline.

This was exceptional, but large scoring for traditional instruments has continued to this day in the works of such composers as Stravinsky, Shostakovitch and Messiaen. In complete contrast are such pieces for small orchestra as Stravinsky's *Histoire du Soldat* (1918), which uses only one violin, double bass, clarinet, bassoon, cornet, trombone, and eight percussion instruments played by one person. The quest for new sounds led him to plan music for *Les Noces*, for 'a mechanical piano, an electrically-driven harmonium, an ensemble of percussion instruments and two Hungarian cymbaloms', according to his *Chronicle of My Life*. Only after writing a good deal of the music did he realize that there would be difficulties in synchronizing mechanical instruments with live performers, and the idea was abandoned. The general increase in percussion instruments, largely due to importations from Africa and the East, and to the ingenuity of such masters as James Blades, has greatly augmented the sound repertoire. A *gamelan* of percussion instruments appears in Messiaen's *Turangalîla Symphony* (1948), together with a large traditional orchestra joined by a solo piano, a vibraphone and ondes Martenot. A comparatively recent scoring for small orchestra is the *Eclat* of 1965 by Boulez, for
piano
celesta
harp
glockenspiel
vibraphone
mandoline
guitar
cymbalum
tubular bells
flute
cor anglais

238 A symphony orchestra with massed choir. *London, Royal Albert Hall.*

239 A performance of Romberg's Toy Symphony at St
James's Hall, London, in 1880, with the toy instruments
played by distinguished musicians. *The Illustrated London
News, 22 May 1880.*

trumpet
trombone
viola and
violoncello.

This scoring seems to be relatively traditional when compared to Stockhausen's *Ylem*, where conventional instruments are joined by an electronic organ, electric cello, electronium, synthesizer and electric-Sax-synthesizer. Both orchestral and chamber works use the new methods of playing traditional instruments as described on pp. 183–4, indicated by signs which are frequently more reminiscent of the Highway Code than of music. It is small wonder that, at a London rehearsal of an avant-garde orchestral piece in 1968, a well-known double-bass player made the occasion memorable to all concerned by calling out to the conductor, 'Am I supposed to be playing the same thing as my neighbour?' He was not.

It is fitting to end with a subject which gives pure fun to musicians and audiences alike. Musical jokes have been played for centuries, often involving instruments such as the nightingale, cuckoo, quail and rattle which appear among the soloists in the Toy Symphony formerly attributed to Joseph Haydn, but now thought to be the combined work of Leopold Mozart and Michael Haydn. When, therefore, Antony Hopkins wrote his *Concerto for Two Tuning Forks in the*

C & A Modes for the annual 'At Home' of the Royal College of Music on 15 June 1956, he was doing so in a very worthy tradition. Meanwhile, Gerard Hoffnung, the artist and tuba-player, was entertaining thousands of people with his cartoons of musicians and their instruments, and, also in 1956, their spirit came to life around the originator in the first of several Hoffnung Concerts, held on 13 November in the Royal Festival Hall, London. Denis Brain played on a hosepipe the solo part in Leopold Mozart's Concerto for Alphorn and Strings, Malcolm Arnold's *A Grand Grand Overture* included prominent parts for 3 Hoover vacuum cleaners and a floor polisher and the distinguished actress Yvonne Arnaud was the soloist in Franz Reizenstein's *Concerto Popolare* (a brilliant combination of material from some of the best-known piano concertos), finally throwing her knitting at Norman Del Mar, the conductor, and receiving after it all a bouquet of cauliflowers. Hoffnung himself displayed his genius with his 'Stradivarius tuba . . . by Boosey and Hawkes' (as in fig. 149). His untimely death at the age of 34 caused these concerts to diminish gradually in number, but they have been recorded, and together with his books of cartoons give pleasure to musicians and music-lovers across the globe. They, and the works of other inspired musical humorists, give tonic to a world which needs to be revived.

240 *The Hoffnung Symphony Orchestra,*
by Gerard Hoffnung (1925–1959).

Bibliography

This select list includes only works in English, and the only articles included are those mentioned in the text. The following periodicals (with their abbreviations) contain the greatest number of articles on instruments:

CEKM   Corpus of Early Keyboard Music
EM   Early Music
FoMRHI   Fellowship of Makers and Restorers of Historical Instruments
GSJ   Galpin Society Journal
JAMIS   Journal of the American Musical Instrument Society
MSD   Musicological Studies and Documents

CHAPTERS I and II
Stringed Instruments, Plucked and Bowed.

Andersson, Otto: *The Bowed Harp*, London, 1930.

Armstrong, Robert Bruce: *The Irish and Highland Harps*, Shannon, 1969.

Bachmann, Werner, *The Origins of Bowing*, transl. Norma Deane, London, 1969.

Bellow, Alexander: *The Illustrated History of the Guitar*, New York, 1970.

Boyden, David D.: *The Hill Collection*, London, 1969.

Boyden, David D.: *The History of Violin Playing from its Origins to 1761*, London, 1965.

Brown, Howard Mayer: 'The Trecento Harp', *Studies in the Performance of Late Medieval Music*, ed. Stanley Boorman, Cambridge, 1983, pp. 35–73.

Cowling, Elizabeth: *The Cello*, London, 1975.

Danks, Harry: *The Viola d'amore*, Bois de Boulogne, 1976.

Dolmetsch, Nathalie: *The Viola da Gamba*, 3rd edn., London, 1975.

Ellis, Osian: *The Story of the Harp in Wales* (text in Welsh and English), University of Wales Press, 1980.

Gill, Dominic, ed.: *The Book of the Violin*, Oxford, 1984.

Gill, Donald: *Gut-strung Plucked Instruments contemporary with the Lute*, Lute Society, 1976.

Grunfeld, Frederic V.: *The Art and Times of the Guitar*, New York, 1969.

Gungi, Sumi, ed.: *Bowed Stringed-Instruments, Study of Musical Instruments* III, Tokyo, Kunitachi College of Music, 1982.

Gungi, Sumi, ed.: *Koto, Zither, Study of Musical Instruments* II, Tokyo, Kunitachi College of Music, 1981.

Gungi, Sumi, ed.: *Ud, Biwa, Lute, Study of Musical Instruments* I, Tokyo, Kunitachi College of Music, 1980.

Gungi, Sumi, ed.: *Plucked Stringed-Instruments with Neck, Study of Musical Instruments* IV, Tokyo, Kunitachi College of Music, 1984.

Gungi, Sumi, ed.: *Harp: Lyre, Study of Musical Instruments* V, Tokyo, Kunitachi College of Music, 1985.

Harwood, Ian: *A Brief History of the Lute*, Lute Society, 1975.

Hayes, Gerald, R.: *The Viols and other Bowed Instruments*, London, 1930, reprint New York, 1969.

Henley, W.: *Antonio Stradivari: His Life and Instruments*, Brighton, 1961.

Heron-Allen, Edward: *Violin-Making as it was and is*, 2nd edn., London, 1885/6.

Lindley, Mark: *Lutes, Viols & Temperaments*, Cambridge, 1984.

Lute Society Journal, The, London, 1959.

Mace, Thomas: *Musick's Monument*, London, 1676, reprint, Paris, 1958.

Mozart, Leopold: *A Treatise on the Fundamental Principles of Violin Playing (Versuch einer gründlichen Violinschule, Augsburg, 1756)*, transl. Editha Knocker, London, 1951.

Nelson, Sheila M: *The Violin and Viola*, London, 1972.

Nelson, Sheila, M.: *The Violin Family*, London, 1964.

North, Nigel: *Continuo Playing on the Lute, Archlute and Theorbo*, London, 1987.

Page, Christopher: 'Jerome of Moravia on the *Rubeba* and *Viella*', *GSJ* xxxii (1979), 77–98.

Panum, Hortense: *Stringed Instruments of the Middle Ages*, transl. Jeffrey Pulver, London, 1941.

Remnant, Mary: *English Bowed Instruments from Anglo-Saxon to Tudor Times*, Oxford, 1986.

Rensch, Roslyn: *The Harp: Its History, Technique and Repertoire*, London, 1969.

Retford, William C.: *Bows and Bow Makers*, London, 1964.

Riley, Maurice, W.: *The History of the Viola*, Ann Arbor, 1980.

Rimmer, Joan: *The Irish Harp*, Dublin, 1969.

Roberts, Ronald: *Making a simple Violin and Viola*, Newton Abbot, 1975.

Sacconi, Simone F: *The 'Secrets' of Stradivari*, transl. Andrew Dipper and Christina Rivaroli, Cremona, 1979.

Spencer, Robert: 'Chitarrone, theorbo and archlute', *EM* iv/4 (October 1976), 407–23.

Turnbull, Harvey: *The Guitar from the Renaissance to the Present Day*, London, 1974.

Tyler, James: *The Early Guitar*, London, 1980. Early Music Series 4,

Winternitz, Emanuel: *Gaudenzio Ferrari, His School, and the Early History of the Violin*, Varallo Sesia, 1967.

Winternitz, Emanuel: 'The Survival of the Kithara and the Evolution of the English Cittern: A Study in Morphology', *Musical Instruments and their Symbolism in Western Art*, London, 1967, pp. 57–65.

Woodfield, Ian: *The Early History of the Viol*, Cambridge, 1984.

CHAPTERS III and IV.
Stringed Keyboard Instruments and Organs.

Andersen, Poul-Gerhard: *Organ Building and Design*, transl. Joanne Curnutt, London, 1969.

Apel, Willi, ed.: *Keyboard Music of the Fourteenth and Fifteenth Centuries*, CEKM, 1963.

Barthold, Kenneth Van, and Buckton, David: *The Story of the Piano*, London, 1975.

Blanchard, Homer H.: *Organs of our Time*, Delaware, Ohio, 1975.

Boalch, Donald H.: *Makers of the Harpsichord and Clavichord 1440–1840*, rev. edn., Oxford, 1974.

Boeringer, James: *Organa Britannica: Organs in Great Britain 1660–1860*, Lewisburg, 1983.

Bonavia-Hunt, Rev. Noel A.: *The Church Organ*, London, 1920.

British Institute of Organ Studies Journal.

Caldwell, John.: *English Keyboard Music before the Nineteenth Century*, Oxford, 1973.

Closson, Ernest: *History of the Piano*, transl. Delano Ames, rev. Robin Golding, London, 1974.

Clutton, Cecil and Dixon, George: *The Organ: Its Tonal Structure and Registration*, London, 1950.

Clutton, Cecil, and Niland, Austin: *The British Organ*, London, 1963.

Cobbe, Alec: *A Century of Keyboard Instruments 1760–1860*, exhibition catalogue, The Fitzwilliam Museum, Cambridge, 1983.

Colt, C.F. and Miall, Antony: *The Early Piano*, London, 1981.

Douglass, Fenner: *The Language of the Classical French Organ*, Yale, 1969.

Downes, Ralph: *Baroque Tricks: Adventures with the Organ Builders*, Oxford, 1983.

Erlich, Cyril: *The Piano*, London, 1976.

Freeman, Andrew: *Father Smith*, 1926, new ed. Rowntree, John, Oxford, 1977.

Gill, Dominic, ed.: *The Book of the Piano*, Oxford, 1981.

Good, Edwin, M.: *Giraffes, Black Dragons and other Pianos*, Stanford, Calif., 1982.

Goode, Jack C.: *Pipe Organ Registration*, Nashville, 1964.

Haacke, Walter: *Organs of the World*, London, 1966.

Harding, Rosamond: *The Piano-Forte: its History traced to the Great Exhibition of 1851*, Cambridge, 1933, 2nd edn. rev., 1978.

Hipkins, A.J.: *A Description and History of the Pianoforte and of the older Keyboard Stringed Instruments*, London, 1896.

Hirt, Franz Josef: *Stringed Keyboard Instruments 1440–1880*, Boston, Mass., 1968.

Hollis, Helen Rice: *The Piano*, Newton Abbot, 1975.

Hubbard, Frank: *Three Centuries of Harpsichord Making*, Harvard, 1965.

James, Philip: *Early Keyboard Instruments*, London, 1930.

Klotz, Hans: *The Organ Handbook*, transl. Gerhard Krapf, Saint Louis, 1969.

McKinnon, James W.: 'The Tenth Century Organ at Winchester', *The Organ Yearbook V* (1974), 4–19.

Michel, N.E.: *Historical Pianos, Clavichords and Harpsichords*, Poco Rivera, Calif., [1963].

Nenpert, Hans: *The Clavichord* transl. Ann P.P. Feldberg, Kassel, 1965.

Niland, Austin: *Introduction to the Organ*, London, 1968.

Norman, Herbert and Norman, H. John: *The Organ Today*, London, 1966.

The Organ Yearbook, Buren (Gld.), 1970–.

Page, Christopher: 'The myth of the checkker', *EM* vii/4 (October 1979), 482–9.

Palmer, Susann and Samuel: *The Hurdy-Gurdy*, Newton Abbot, 1980.

Perrot, Jean: *The Organ from its Invention in the Hellenistic Period to the end of the Thirteenth Century*, transl. Norma Deane, London, 1971.

Pierce, Bob: *Pierce Piano Atlas: successor to 'The Original Michel's*, Long Beach, Calif., 1965.

Ripin, Edwin M.: 'Towards an Identification of the Chekker', *GSJ* xxviii (1975), 11–25.

Ripin, Edwin M.: *Keyboard Instruments: Studies in Keyboard Organology, 1500–1800*, New York, 1977.

Rowntree, John P. and Brennan, John F.: *The Classical Organ in Britain 1955–1974*, Oxford, vol. i, 1975; vol. ii, 1979.

Russell, Raymond: *The Harpsichord and Clavichord*, 2nd edn., rev. Howard Schott, London, 1973.

Russell, Raymond: *Victoria and Albert Museum: Catalogue of Musical Instruments, Vol. I, Keyboard Instruments*, London, 1968.

Schott, Howard: *A Catalogue of Musical Instruments: Vol. I, Keyboard Instruments*, London, 1985 (1st edn. by Raymond Russell, 1968).

Stacey, Peter and Wishart, Stevie: *Bagpipes and Hurdy-gurdies*, Oxford, 1984.

Stevens, Irwin: *Dictionary of Pipe Organ Stops*, London, 1962.

Sumner, William Leslie: *The Organ*, 3rd edn., rev., London, 1962.

Sumner, William Leslie: *The Pianoforte*, London, 1966.

Taylor, S.K.: *The Musician's Piano Atlas*, Macclesfield, 1984.

Wainwright, David: *Broadwood: By Appointment*, London, 1982.

Wainwright, David: *The Piano Makers*, London, 1975.

Walcker-Mayer, Werner: *The Roman Organ of Aquincum*, Ludwigsburg, 1972.

Wedgwood, James Ingall: *A Comprehensive Dictionary of Organ Stops*, London, 1905.

Williams, Peter: *The European Organ 1450–1850*, London, 1966.

Williams, Peter: *A New History of the Organ*, London, 1980.

Williams, Peter and Owen, Barbara: 'Organ', *The New Grove*, London, 1988.

Wilson, Michael: *The English Chamber Organ*, Oxford, 1968.

Wilson, Michael I.: *Organ Cases of Western Europe*, London, 1979.

Winternitz, Emanuel: *Keyboard Instruments in the Metropolitan Museum of Art*, New York, 1961.

Wolfenden, Samuel: *A Treatise on the Art of Pianoforte Construction*, rev. edn., Old Woking, 1977.

Yorke, James: *Keyboard Instruments at the Victoria and Albert Museum*, London, 1986.

Zuckermann, Wolfgang: *The Modern Harpsichord*, New York, 1969.

CHAPTERS V, VI and VII.
Woodwind, Brass and Free Reed Instruments.

Altenburg, Johann Ernst: *The Trumpeters' and Kettledrummers' Art* (*Trompeter und Pauker-Kunst*, Halle, 1795), transl. Edward H. Tarr, Nashville, 1974.

Baines, Anthony: *Bagpipes*, Oxford, 1960.

Baines, Anthony: *Brass Instruments: Their History and Development*, London, 1976.

Baines, Anthony: *Woodwind Instruments and their History*, 2nd edn., London, 1962.

Bate, Philip: *The Flute*, London, 1969.

Bate, Philip: *The Oboe*, 3rd edn., London, 1975.

Bate, Philip: *The Trumpet and Trombone*, London, 1966.

Bevan, Clifford: *The Tuba Family*, London, 1978.

Boydell, Barra: *The Crumhorn and other Renaissance Windcap Instruments*, (Buren, 1982).

The Brass Quarterly and *The Brass and Woodwind Quarterly*, Durham, New Hampshire, 1957– .

Brindley, Giles: 'The Logical Bassoon', *GSJ* xxi (1968), 152–61.

Brüchle, Bernhard, and Janetsky, Kurt: *A Pictorial History of the Horn*, Tutzing, 1976.

Byrne, Maurice: 'Instruments for the Goldsmiths Company', *GSJ* xxiv (1971), 63–8.

Carse, Adam: *Musical Wind Instruments*, London, 1939.

Cocks, W.A. and Bryan, J.F.: *The Northumbrian Bagpipes*, Gateshead, 1967.

Collinson, Francis: *The Bagpipe*, London, 1975.

Fitzpatrick, Horace: *The Horn and Horn-Playing . . . from 1680 to 1830*, London, 1970.

Gregory, Robin: *The Horn*, 2nd edn., London, 1969.

Gregory, Robin: *The Trombone*, London, 1973.

Gungi, Sumi, ed.: *Bagpipe, Study of Musical Instruments* VIII, Tokyo, Kunitachi College of Music, 1988.

Gungi, Sumi, ed.: *Lip Reed Instruments, Study of Musical Instruments* VI, Tokyo, Kunitachi College of Music, 1986.

Gungi, Sumi, ed.: *Reed Instruments, Study of Musical Instruments* VII, Tokyo, Kunitachi College of Music, 1987.

Hohner, M., Ltd.: *The Happy Harmonica*, New York.

Hunt, Edgar: *The Crumhorn*, London, 1975.

Hunt, Edgar: *The Recorder and its Music*, London, 1962.

Janetsky, Kurt and Brüchle, Bernhard: *The Horn*, transl. James Chater, London, 1988.

Langwill, Lyndesay, G.: *The Bassoon and Contra-Bassoon*, London, 1965.

Langwill, Lyndesay G.: *An Index of Musical Wind-Instrument Makers*, 5th edn., Edinburgh, 1977.

Menke, Werner: *History of the Trumpet of Bach and Handel*, transl. Gerald Abraham, Nashville, Tennessee, 1972.

Meylan, Raymond: *The Flute*, transl. Alfred Clayton, London, 1988.

Michel, N.E.: *Michel's Organ Atlas*, Pico Rivera, Calif., 1969.

Morley-Pegge, R.: *The French Horn*, 2nd edn., London, 1973.

Ord-Hume, Arthur W.J.G.: *Harmonium*, Newton Abbot, 1986.

Quantz, Johann Joachim: *On Playing the Flute (Versuch einer Anweisung die Flöte traversière zu spielen*, Berlin, 1752) transl. and introd. by Edward R. Reilly, London, 1966.

Rendall, F. Geoffrey: *The Clarinet*, 3rd edn., rev. Philip Bate, London, 1971.

Ridley, E.A.K.: *The Royal College of Music Museum of Instruments, Catalogue Part I: European Wind Instruments*, London, 1982.

Ridley, E.A.K.: *Wind Instruments of European Art Music*, Horniman Museum, London, 1974.

Rockstro, R.S.: *A Treatise on the Construction, History and Practice of the Flute*, transl. G.M. Rockstro, London, 1890, 1928.

Smithers, Don: *The Music and History of the Baroque Trumpet before 1721*, London, 1973.

Stacey, Peter, and Wishart, Steve: *Bagpipes and Hurdy-gurdies*, Oxford, 1984.

Toff, Nancy: *The Flute Book*, Newton Abbot, 1985.

Trowell, Brian: 'King Henry IV, Recorder-player; *GSJ* x (1957), 83–4.

Welch, Christopher: *Lectures on the Recorder*, introd. by Edgar Hunt, London, 1961.

Welch, Christopher: *The History of the Boehm Flute*, 3rd edn., London, 1896.

Young, Philip T.: *Twenty-five Hundred Historical Woodwind Instruments: An Inventory of the Major Collections*, New York, 1982.

CHAPTERS VIII, IX and X.
Percussion, Mechanical and Twentieth Century Instruments.

Blades, James: *Percussion Instruments and their History*, rev. edn., London, 1984.

Blades, James, and Montagu, Jeremy: *Early Percussion Instruments*, London, 1976.

Boston, Canon Noel, and Langwill, Lyndesay G.: *Church and Chamber Barrel Organs*. Edinburgh, 1967.

Bowers, Q. David: *Put Another Nickel In: A History of Coin-Operated Pianos and Orchestrions*, New York, 1966.

Briscoe, Desmond and Curtis-Bramwell, Roy: *The BBC Radiophonic Workshop: The First 25 Years*, London, 1983.

Buchner, Alexander: *Mechanical Musical Instruments*, transl. Iris Urwin, London, 1959.

Clark, John E.T.: *Musical Boxes*, 2nd edn., London, 1952.

Cockayne, Eric V.: *The Fair Organ – How it works*, Hyde, Cheshire, 1967.

Dorf, Richard H.: *Electronic Musical Instruments*, 3rd edn., New York, 1968.

Douglas, Alan: *Electronic Music Production*, Bath, 1973.

Douglas, Alan: *The Electronic Musical Instrument Manual*, 5th edn., London, 1968.

Foerster, Heinz von, and Beauchamp, James W.: *Music by Computers*, New York, 1969.

Givens, Larry: *Rebuilding the Player Piano*, New York, 1963.

Griffiths, Paul: *A Guide to Electronic Music*, London, 1979.

Holland, James: *Percussion*, London, 1978.

Holmes, Thomas B.: *Electronic and Experimental Music*, New York, 1985.

Hoover, Cynthia A.: *Music Machines: American Style*, Washington D.C., 1971.

Jacobowitz, Henry: *Electronic Computers Made Simple*, London, 1963.

Kettlewell, David: *The Dulcimer*, unpublished Ph. D. thesis, University of Technology, Loughborough, 1977.

La Rue, Hélène: 'The Problem of the Cymbala', *GSJ* xxxv (1982), 86–99.

Lawrie, Peter: *Electronics Explained*, London, 1980.

Ord-Hume, Arthur W.J.G.: *Barrel Organ*, London, 1978.

Ord-Hume, Arthur: *Clockwork Music*, London, 1973.

Ord-Hume, Arthur: *Player Piano*, London, 1970.

Peinkofer, Karl, and Tannigel, Fritz: *Handbook of Percussion Instruments*, transl. Kurt and Else Stone, London, 1976.

Rice, William Gordham: *Carillon Music and Singing Towers of the Old World and the New*, London, 1926.

Risatti, Howard: *New Music Vocabulary*, Urbana, 1975.

Schneider, John: *The Contemporary Guitar*, Berkeley, 1985.

Sear, Walter: *The New World of Electronic Music*, New York, 1972.

Smith Brindle, Reginald: *Contemporary Percussion*, London, 1970.

Tallis, David: *Musical Boxes*, London, 1971.

Waard, Mr R. de: *From Music Boxes to Street Organs*, transl. Wade Jenkins, New York, 1967.

Waesberghe, J. Smits van, ed.: *Cymbala (Bells in the Middle Ages)*, MSD I, Rome, 1951.

Webb, Graham: *The Disc Musical Box Handbook*, London, 1971.

CHAPTER XI.
The Use of Instruments and General Books on Instruments.

Adkins, H.E.: *Treatise on the Military Band*, 2nd rev. edn., London, 1958.

Archaeologia Musicalis, Celle, 1987– .

Baines, Anthony: *European and American Musical Instruments*, London, 1966.

Baines, Anthony, ed.: *Musical Instruments through the Ages*, Harmondsworth, 3rd edn., 1969.

Baines, Anthony: *Victoria and Albert Museum, Catalogue of Musical Instruments, Vol. II, Non-Keyboard Instruments*, London, 1968.

Berlioz, Hector: *The Memoirs of Hector Berlioz*, transl. and ed. David Cairns, London, 1969.

Berlioz, Hector: *Treatise on Instrumentation (Traité de l'Instrumentation*, Paris, 1844), rev. Richard Strauss, transl. Theodore Front, New York, 1948.

Berner, A., Van der Meer, J.H. and Thibault, G.: *Preservation and Restoration of Musical Instruments*, London, 1967.

Bessaraboff, Nicholas: *Ancient European Musical Instruments*, New York, 1941.

Bonanni, Filippo: *The Showcase of Musical Instruments (Gabinetto Armonico*, Rome 1723), ed. Frank Ll. Harrison and Joan Rimmer, New York, 1964.

Bragard, Roger, and de Hen, Ferdinand: *Musical Instruments in Art and History*, transl. Bill Hopkins, London, 1968.

Boydell, Barra: *Music and Paintings in the National Gallery of Ireland*, Dublin (National Gallery of Ireland), 1985.

The British Museum Yearbook, 4. *Music and Civilization*, ed. T.C. Mitchell, London (British Museum), 1980.

Brown, Howard Mayer: *Sixteenth-century Instrumentation: the Music for the Florentine Intermedii, Musicological Studies and Documents* xxx, Rome, 1973.

Brown, Howard Mayer, and Lascelle, Joan: *Musical Iconography*, Cambridge, Mass., 1972.

Buchner, Alexander: *Colour Encyclopedia of Musical Instruments*, transl. Simon Pellar, London, 1980.

Buchner, Alexander: *Musical Instruments through the Ages*, transl. by Iris Urwin, London, 1955.

Bullock-Davies, Constance: *Menestrellorum Multitudo*, Cardiff, 1978.

Burney, Charles: *Dr Burney's Musical Tours in Europe*, ed. Percy A. Scholes, 2 vols, London, 1959.

Carse, Adam: *The History of Orchestration*, London, 1925, New York, 1964.

Carse, Adam: *The Orchestra in the XVIIIth Century*, Cambridge, 1940.

Carse, Adam: *The Orchestra from Beethoven to Berlioz*, London, 1948.

Carter, Henry Holland: *A Dictionary of Middle English Musical Terms*, Indiana, 1961.

Clemencic, René: *Old Musical Instruments*, transl. David Hermges, London, 1968.

Cox, Angela: *Sir Henry Unton, Elizabethan Gentleman*, Cambridge, 1982.

Crane, Frederick: *Extant Medieval Musical Instruments*, Iowa, 1972.

Dart, Thurston: *The Interpretation of Music*, London, 1954.

Del Mar, Norman: *A Companion to the Orchestra*, London, 1987.

Del Mar, Norman: *Anatomy of the Orchestra*, London, 1981.

Donington, Robert: *The Instruments of Music*, 3rd edn., London, 1970.

Early Music, London, 1973– .

Fellowship of Makers and Restorers of Historical Instruments: Bulletin and Communications, London.

Ford, Charles, ed.: *Making Musical Instruments: Strings & Keyboard*, London, 1979.

Forsyth, Cecil: *Orchestration*, 2nd edn., London, 1935.

Fox, Lilla M.: *Instruments of the Orchestra*, London, 1971.

Froissart's Chronicles, ed. and transl. John Jolliffe, London, 1967.

Galpin, Canon Francis W.: *Old English Instruments of Music*, 1910; 4th edn. rev. Thurston Dart, London, 1965.

Galpin Society Journal, The, London, 1948–.

Galpin Society: *Made for Music*, Sotheby's Exhibition Catalogue, London, 1986.

Geiringer, Karl: *Instruments in the History of Western Music*, (originally *Musical Instruments: Their History from the Stone Age to the Present Day*, 1943), London, 1978.

Grove: *The New Grove Dictionary of Music and Musicians*, 6th edn., ed. Stanley Sadie, London, 1980.

Grove: *The New Grove Dictionary of Musical Instruments*, ed. Stanley Sadie, 3 vols, London, 1984.

Gungi, Sumi, ed.: *The Collection of Musical Instruments*, Kunitachi College of Music, Tokyo, 1986.

Harrison, Frank, and Rimmer, Joan: *European Musical Instruments*, London, 1964.

Hipkins, A.J. and Day, C.R.: *Catalogue of the Musical Instruments and Objects forming the Donaldson Museum* (Royal College of Music), London.

Hollis, Helen Rice: *The Musical Instruments of Joseph Haydn*, Washington DC, 1977.

Jenkins, Jean, ed.: *International Directory of Musical Instrument Collections*, International Council of Museums, Buren, 1977.

Kendall, Alan: *The World of Musical Instruments*, London, 1972.

Landon, H.C. Robbins: *Haydn Symphonies*, London, 1966.

Landon, H.C. Robbin: *The Symphonies of Joesph Haydn*, London, 1955.

Leppert, Richard D.: *Arcadia at Versailles*, Amsterdam, 1978.

Marcuse, Sibyl: *Musical Instruments: A Comprehensive Dictionary*, New York, 1964.

Marcuse, Sibyl: *A Survey of Musical Instruments*, Newton Abbot, 1975.

Mersenne, Marin: *Harmonie Universelle*, Paris, 1636 (French version of Latin edn. *Harmonicorum libri*,

Paris, 1635), transl. R.E. Chapman, The Hague, 1957.

Minor, Andrew C., and Mitchell, Bonner: *A Renaissance Entertainment*, Columbia, Missouri, 1968.

Montagu, Jeremy: *The World of Medieval and Renaissance Musical Instruments*, Newton Abbot, 1976.

Montagu, Jeremy: *The World of Baroque & Classical Musical Instruments*, Newton Abbot, 1979.

Montagu, Jeremy: *The World of Romantic & Modern Musical Instruments*, Newton Abbot, 1981.

Mozart, W.A.: *Mozart's Letters*, ed. Eric Blom, London, 1956; selected from *The Letters of Mozart and his Family*, transl. and annotated by Emily Anderson, London, 1938.

Munrow, David: *Instruments of the Middle Ages and Renaissance*, London, 1976.

Nettel, Reginald: *The Orchestra in England*, 2nd edn., London, 1956.

North, Roger: *Roger North on Music*, transcribed and ed. John Wilson, London, 1959.

Page, Christopher: *Voices & Instruments of the Middle Ages*, London, 1987.

Patey, Carole: *Musical Instruments at the Victoria and Albert Museum*, London, 1978.

Paulus Paulirinus: Howell, Stanley: 'Paulus Paulirinus of Prague on musical instruments', *JAMIS* V–VI (1979–80), 9–36.

Pepys, Samuel: *The Diary of Samuel Pepys*, transcribed and ed. Robert Latham and William Matthews, London, 1970– .

Picker, Martin: *The Chanson Albums of Marguerite of Austria*, Berkeley, 1965.

Piston, Walter: *Orchestration*, London, 1971.

Praetorius, Michael: *Syntagma Musicum II: De Organographia*, Wolfenbuttel, 1619; facsimile, Kassel, 1958.

Praetorius, Michael: *Syntagma Musicum II: De Organographia Parts I and II*, transl. and ed. David Z. Crookes, Oxford, 1986.

Pulver, Jeffrey: *A Dictionary of Old English Music and*

Musical Instruments, London, 1923.

Remnant, Mary: *Musical Instruments of the West*, London, 1978.

Rimmer, Joan: *Ancient Musical Instruments of Western Asia*, London (British Museum), 1969.

Rimsky-Korsakov, Nikolay: *Principles of Orchestration*, ed. Maximilian Steinberg, transl. Edward Agate, 1922, reprint New York, 1964.

Roberts, Ronald: *Musical Instruments Made to be Played*, 2nd edn., Leicester, 1967.

Royal Musical Association, Proceedings of the, London, 1874–?, *Journal of the ?*.

Sachs, Curt: *The History of Musical Instruments*, New York, 1940.

Selfridge-Field, Eleanor: *Venetian Instrumental Music from Gabrieli to Vivaldi*, Oxford, 1975.

Spohr, Louis: *The Musical Journeys of Louis Spohr*, transl. and ed. Henry Pleasants, Oklahoma, 1961.

Stewart, Madeau: *The Music Lover's Guide to the Instruments of the Orchestra*, London, 1980.

Terry, Charles Sanford: *Bach's Orchestra*, London, 1932.

Thibault, G., Jenkins, Jean, Bran-Ricci, Josiane: *Eighteenth Century Musical Instruments: France and Britain*, London (Victoria and Albert Museum), 1973.

Thornton, Peter: *Musical Instruments as Works of Art*, 2nd edn., London (Victoria and Albert Museum), 1982.

Tinctoris: Baines, Anthony: 'Fifteenth-century Instruments in Tinctoris's *De Inventione et Usu Musicae*', *GSJ* III (1950), 19–26.

Triumph of Maximilian I, The, transl. and ed. Stanley Appelbaum, New York, 1964.

Vinquist, Mary and Zaslaw, Neal: *Performance Practice: A Bibliography*, New York, 1971.

Winternitz, Emanuel: *Musical Instruments and their Symbolism in Western Art*, London, 1967.

Winternitz, Emanuel: *Musical Instruments of the Western World*, London, 1966.

Young, Philip T.: *The Look of Music, Rare Musical Instruments 1500–1900*, Vancouver, 1980.

Index

This list points mainly to descriptions of instruments, to their makers, to writers about them, and to occasions on which they have been played. Numbers in italics indicate pages where illustrations can be found.

MUSICAL INSTRUMENTS
AN ILLUSTRATED HISTORY FROM ANTIQUITY TO THE PRESENT

As interest continues to grow in the performance of music on the instruments for which it was originally written, many questions arise: when were particular instruments most played? What was their role? How did they develop? Dr Remnant answers these and other such questions and, with over 230 photographs, shows us what the instruments look like and how they have been depicted by western artists through the ages.

Each of the first ten chapters covers a group or 'family' of instruments: the developments of stringed, keyboard, woodwind, free reed, percussion and mechanical instruments are treated in turn. The final chapter, on the use of instruments, refers to orchestration in some detail with quotations from writers on musical instruments from Lucretius to Berlioz.

Dr Remnant places individual developments in their wider cultural and historical context and corrects the misunderstandings of the past.

The fascination of musical instruments can only be increased by reading this highly enjoyable and informative account, which will delight both scholars and amateur music-lovers.

Dr Mary Remnant is the author of two other books on musical instruments. She is well known in Europe and America as a lecture-recitalist, performing on old instruments. She also teaches at the Royal College of Music in London.